Camp Fire Yarns of the Lost Legion

T. F. Kynnersley, Esq., of Leighton, Salop, D. L., J. P.,
and late captain and S. O. Lonsdale's Horse

Camp Fire Yarns
of the Lost Legion

Reminiscences of the Maori and Zulu Wars
by a Colonial Officer

G. Hamilton-Browne
(Maori Browne)

LEONAUR

Camp Fire Yarns of the Lost Legion
Reminiscences of the Maori and Zulu Wars by a *Colonial Officer*
by G. Hamilton-Browne
(Maori Browne)

First published under the title
Camp Fire Yarns of the Lost Legion

Leonaur is an imprint of Oakpast Ltd

Copyright in this form © 2012 Oakpast Ltd

ISBN: 978-0-85706-860-6 (hardcover)
ISBN: 978-0-85706-861-3 (softcover)

http://www.leonaur.com

Publisher's Notes

Contents

PART 2

THIS SKEIN OF YARNS
IS DEDICATED TO
MY OLD FRIEND AND COMRADE IN ARMS
DURING 1877–78–79
THOMAS F. KYNNERSLEY OF LEIGHTON, CO. SALOP
D.L., J. P. AND LATE CAPT. AND STAFF OFFICER
IN LONSDALE'S HORSE
WHOSE FONDNESS FOR A GOOD STORY IS AS
KEEN NOW AS IT WAS IN THE DAYS
OF YORE WHEN IN BIVOUAC OR
CAMP WE USED TO
SPIN THEM

Preface

In introducing these yarns let me state that now I am laid up on the shelf my thoughts go back to those days and nights of the *veld* and bush, and I frequently feel I would give all the rest of the map if I could again find myself on the open lands of the frontier with a good horse between my knees and a few score of the old boys behind me. Now I hold pen instead of carbine and revolver, but why should memories of the old days pass away? Let me fancy I sit by the camp fire again, telling yarns as we used to under the dark blue skies and blazing stars of South Africa.

Let me spin you some yarns of the Lost Legion.

The Neglected Soldier

Fame is but a fleeting shadow,
Glory but an empty name;
Spite of all that I have gone through,
'Tis, I find, a losing game.

Without interest, without money,
Nothing can a soldier gain;
Though he be the sole survivor
Of a host of comrades slain:

What avail these glitt'ring honours.
Which a queen laid on my breast;
Though I've sought them from my childhood,
Would I'd fallen with the rest;

Then my heart had not been broken
Life had fled without a sigh;
Hunger presses—I am fainting—
Ought a soldier thus to die?

The Old Shekarry.

PART 1

CHAPTER 1

The Maori As I Knew Him

Camped in a London flat, sick of the turmoil, rows and worries of the big city, with its pushing, hurrying and ill-mannered crowds, can it be wondered at that I let my thoughts often wander far away to the days of my early manhood, when I passed over ten years in the dense and silent, though beautiful, bush of New Zealand, or rode across the wild, open and breezy plains of its inland plateaus? During this time I had ample opportunities for observing and studying the natives, both in war and peace: in the former especially, as I not only fought against them, but I also fought side by side with the brothers, cousins and quondam friends of the very men we were engaged against.

Queer, very queer, people they were, and, to describe them in a few words, I should pronounce them to be bundles of contradictions, whose faults made them hateful, but whose many good qualities rendered them one of the most charming race of people it has ever been my lot to meet. They have been described by numerous writers far more capable than myself, and whose pens are far more graphic than my own, but yet perhaps a few traits in their many-sided characters, that I have experienced myself, may interest you.

To begin with, let me speak of their courage, which was displayed in such a marked degree during the long wars that lasted from 1860 to 1871, for the whole of which period the Maoris were hopelessly outnumbered and, as far as armament went, were equally outclassed. Yet these brave fellows fought on and on, and even when the end came, and the shattered remnants of the so-called rebels took refuge in the King Country, the New Zealand Government, fearing to risk further war with the powerful Waikato tribes, resorted to what was called the blanket-and-sugar policy, rather than follow Te Kooti or demand his extradition from King Tawhiao, who at that time was just as independent of English rule as France was.

The first fighting took place in 1860, and soon General Sir Duncan Cameron had over 1000 Imperial troops under his command, as well as an equal number of Colonial Militia and Irregulars, and also a powerful Naval Brigade. He had also a strong force of artillery, and was well supplied with ammunition and stores of all kinds. Yet perhaps you will scarcely credit me when I tell you that never at any single moment had he more than 2000 natives in arms against him, and that he was never opposed in any single action by even 1000 men.

It must be borne in mind that Sir Duncan's force was one of the most powerful that England, up to that time, without the assistance of allies, had ever put into the field; that the men who composed it were all of them good, seasoned men, many of them being veterans of the Crimea and Mutiny; that the Militia were highly trained, most of them old soldiers, under the command of ex-Imperial officers; that the Irregulars proved themselves to be second to none in the field, and that the natives only possessed old muskets and fowling-pieces.

Now these numbers are staggering, but absolutely correct, as it is also that the above force made but small headway against this handful of savages; for although Sir Duncan forced his way into the Waikato and held a chain of forts there, yet on the west coast, especially in the districts of Taranaki and Wanganui, the settlers had to abandon their homesteads, the women and children being sent for safety to the South Island, and no man's life was safe beyond rifle range of the forts. This was the state of New Zealand in 1866, after six years of incessant war, and it can only be accounted for in the following way:—

To commence, the General and his officers were hidebound with the old traditions and maxims of the British army. They simply would not or could not adapt themselves to the exigencies or tactics of irregular warfare, nor could they be made to understand or believe that a regiment that could march in line like a brick wall might easily be worsted by a mob of savages in a New Zealand bush. Then again when attacking *pahs*: the general considered that the correct way to do so was, after a sharp bombardment, to rush the place with the bayonet.

Who could imagine for a moment that natives could hold their flimsy stockades against men who had stormed the Redan and taken Delhi at the point of the bayonet. Yet they did. Rangiriri was assaulted three times, and on each occasion, notwithstanding the splendid devotion and courage of our gallant Tommies, they were driven back

12

with great loss. Yet on the following day the 180 defenders marched out and laid down their arms. Why? For three days they had been without one drop of water. The general knew they had no water, then why did he risk the lives of his splendid men by ordering futile assaults? Rangiriri took place in November 1863, and one would have thought that the general might have learned something, by its lesson, of the ways how best to deal with a Maori *pah*; but he had neglected to do so, for in April, the following year, he invested Orakau Pah, the defenders of which exhibited gallantry seldom equalled and never surpassed in all the annals of human warfare. Let me try and give you a brief account, as I heard it some years afterwards from the mouth of one of its defenders:

Listen, Te Parione, I will tell you how I first saw white men and fought against them. It was at Orakau, in the land of the Waikato tribes, and the fight happened in this manner:

We of the Taupo tribes must pay a visit of ceremony to the chiefs and people of the Waikatos, and at the same time the Uriwera people wished to do the same. Our intention was to discuss many things with the Waikatos, and to hold a big *runanga* (deliberation) concerning the war. We journeyed there, although we knew much war was going on, and we were most anxious to hear about and see something of this war, so that we could judge for ourselves the might and fighting customs of the white men. It was necessary for us to do this, as at that time we knew but little of the white man, or the war customs of the soldiers; and as we might have to fight them later on, it was well for us to know their manners in war.

We travelled together, in two parties, as our love is not great for the Uriwera, and reached the land of the Waikatos. These could give us but a short *tangi* (reception ceremony), as the war was hot in the land and the people much engaged in fighting; but they gave us the Orakau Pah to dwell in, until such time as the *runanga* could be held. Some chiefs of the Waikatos also stayed with us in the *pah*, as hosts, and food was sent us daily, our women, some forty in number, having to fetch water from a distance, as there was none close to the *pah*.

We heard daily of the advance of the white men, and we hoped to see them, but did not go near them. It would not have been right to do so: we were on a visit of ceremony, we had no anger

13

against them, and no cause to fight with them.

One day we heard they were quite near, and our hearts were glad, as perhaps we should get our desire and gaze on them. Next day they came in sight, long columns of them, each man in his place. And it was good to look at them. They were in great numbers. We had never seen so many men at one time, and our hearts grew dark within us at their might and order. Instead of passing on their way as we expected, some of them turned to the right and some moved to our left, until we were quite surrounded; and when they were all placed they stood still and remained quiet. We were surprised and in great wonder; nor could we understand the meaning of this, until there came to us, as herald, the mouth (interpreter) of their war chief, who told us, in the name of the Great White Queen, to give up the *pah*, lay down our arms, and render ourselves prisoners to the white men. Our head chief told him that we could not do this, that we were not there to fight against the white man, but that we were Taupo and Uriwera Maoris, that we were on a visit of ceremony to the Waikatos, and that we had no anger or cause against the soldiers. But the white chief was mad, and sent the mouth again, saying we must give up the *pah* to him or he would attack us.

Our hearts were very dark with fear at the might and number of the soldiers, and we discussed the situation. How could we give up the *pah*? Had not the Waikatos lent us their *pah* to live in? And were we not responsible for the honour of it? How could we give it up? No, we must guard the *pah* with our lives, or our disgrace would resound through the land and our shame live forever. We had no wish to fight the soldiers, but we must. Now the white man is not ceremonious, for he gave us no time to dress for war, dance the war-dance, nor even to utter our war-cries; for as soon as the herald returned to his chief we saw a *taua* (war party) leave their army and come straight for the outer fence, and we had to hasten, so as to get into the trench and flanking angles.

Very great is the courage of the soldiers, but great is their folly; for this *taua* moved all in a body, close together, with a young chief walking in front of them with his sword in his hand. Soon they came near, and the young chief raised his sword and shouted. The *taua* at once rushed at us, all of them shouting loud.

Our hearts were dark with fear, for the anger of the white man was very great. Rewi (a great fighting chief of the Waikatos') had told us before to harden ourselves against the anger and shouts of the white men, and had given us orders not to fire until he gave the signal, then all to fire at one time. When the *taua* was within six fathoms of us he gave the signal, and our fire darted out from under the fence. Many of the white men fell, but the rest rushed on, some of them trying to pull down the fence with their hands, others firing through it with their guns, and some thrusting at us with their bayonets. None of them seemed to fear death, though they fell fast.

We now fired our second barrels, reloading as fast as we could, the women helping us, the men in the flanking angles also firing, so that the smoke rose in clouds, and the sky resounded with the shouting of the white men and our war-cries. All fear had fallen away from us, and we now saw that the great white chief was ceremonious, as he had only sent such a number of men as we could cope with, all his other men remaining where they had first stopped and not interfering with us. But it was otherwise with the men with whom we were fighting, as they swore at us and called us many bad names. And this was wrong, and filled us with wonder, as we had done them no evil. But perhaps it is the custom of the soldiers to do so.

The fight had lasted but a short time. I had loaded my *tupara* (double-barrelled gun) twice when a bugle called out, and the soldiers, leaving us, went back. No, they did not run away, they went slowly, looking back at us as if sorry to leave the fight and taking their wounded men with them.

We were greatly elated that we had saved the *pah*, and thought that now the white men, having no cause of war against us, and having done all that was necessary for both their own honour and ours, would pass on their way, leaving us in peace.

It was also near the time for our evening meal. The Waikato women had not, according to their custom, brought us any provisions that day, this having been delayed, we thought, on account of the fight. But as that was now over, there could be no further cause for their not coming, and if our women were to fetch water, it would be ready for the food when it presently arrived.

Our women left the *pah* for this purpose, and had been gone but a short time when they returned and told us that the soldiers would not allow them to pass, and that, on their insisting on doing so, telling the interpreter that there was no water or food in the *pah* and that they must get some, the mouth had told them that the big chief had given orders that no food or water should be carried into the *pah* and that if they passed through the soldiers they would be prevented from coming back. So they had returned.

This news filled us with wonder. Surely the white chief must be mad. Enough fighting had been done for the honour of ourselves and the soldiers. Even should he require more, how could he expect our hearts to be strong and for us to be able to fight well if he was to stop us obtaining food and water? It was folly. No man can fight as he should do when he is weak and famished. He had very many men. There had not been 300 Maoris, including women, in the pah from the beginning, and some of us had been killed and wounded; so we felt bitter towards the white chief, for our thirst with fighting, shouting and the powder smoke, was great.

Next morning we saw many more soldiers had arrived, bringing with them several big guns, and the herald again approached us. This time he told us that if we would not render up the *pah* the big guns would fire on us. He also said we should have no food or water. To this Rewi made answer: 'We will not render up the *pah* and our honour. Enough, we will fight right on forever.' And we all shouted, '*Aké, aké aké*' (Forever, forever, forever).

'Then the white chief sent word: 'Save your women, let them come out, they shall pass in safety and honour through the soldiers.'

But the women refused, and Rewi answered: 'The women will fight with us.'

No sooner had the herald left us than the big guns began to shoot, also some short, fat guns (cohorns) that threw iron balls up into the air, so that they dropped inside the *pah*. And these balls, being filled with powder, burst, inside the *pah*, with great noise, and pieces of iron flew all around, while a great number of soldiers, drawing near, began to fire at the *pah*, so that soon the whole place was filled with dust and confusion, while the air was torn with the shrieking of the pieces of iron and the whistling of bullets. We were stricken with fear, and were glad to take refuge in the underground houses of the Waikatos. And now we understood their reason for building these, and our fear soon left us, when we discovered that all this noise and trouble did us no harm. After this had gone on some time, Rewi called to us that a *taua* was getting ready to attack us, and ordered us to make ready for it. And just then the fire from the big guns ceased, so as to enable us to do so.

This was quite right, for, if they had continued to fire, we could not have left the underground houses, and then should not have had time to get into the trenches to welcome the soldiers. This made us think better of the white chief, who, we now saw, was most ceremonious, as he again only sent as many men against us as we could contend with on equal terms. And in all things, except the matter of food and water, he proved himself to be a great and wise war chief.

The *hapu* (tribe) of soldiers sent against us this time was not the same tribe as that which had attacked us previously, as they wore another number on their head-dress. And this was as it should be, for the chief had many different tribes in his army, and each of these must be given a chance of honour. But he must have been blind in his great folly, as if he wished to send all his tribes, each in its turn, against us, at the same time refusing us food and water, how could he expect us to keep our hearts strong, so as to be able to resist in a befitting manner those whose turn came later on? Then again our powder would fail. But this he had provided against, as I will tell you shortly.

Now this new *taua* acted just the same as the other had done. They all moved in a body, and when the chief, who walked in front, raised his weapon they all ran forward to try and tear down the outer fence. Some of them had also brought with them large *tomahawks* with which to cut it down, and Rewi called to us to use our second shots on these men. Shouting loudly, the *taua* charged at us, and when they reached within six fathoms of us our fire rushed to meet them. Many of them fell, and those who reached the fence failed to break in, though they did all that brave men could do. The men with the *tomahawks* were soon shot down, and the fight waxed very hot, although our war-cries were small, our thirst being very great.

Soon the bugle again called, and the white men went back slowly and in great anger, some of them shaking their hands at us and swearing loudly. But this we did not heed greatly, as we had decided, among ourselves, that this was their custom and that they did so with no intent to insult us, who had done them no wrong.

Soon the big guns began to shoot again: this time at the *pekara-nga* (outer fence), so as to try and break it down. But the fence was made of very many slender *manuka* poles, lashed firmly to many cross-pieces, these being made fast to stout posts set firmly in the ground, the lower part of the fence being just clear of the ground, so that we could fire under it from the trench that was just behind it. And behind this trench, in which we stood, were the earthworks and heavy palisading of the *pah*.

Now the outer fence being composed in this way, the shot from the big guns only broke one or at the most two sticks of the fence, and then buried themselves in the earth. This did but little harm to us, as the holes made in the fence could be easily repaired and were not nearly large enough for a soldier to pass through. The short, fat guns also began to throw their balls into the *pah*. But as long as we remained in the underground houses these did us no harm. And it was by them the white chief showed his wisdom, insomuch as he employed these balls to furnish us with powder, so as to enable us to continue fighting, as we quickly discovered that very many of these balls did not burst and from them we extracted very many charges of powder. All these big guns fired with great fury at us for some time, and then ceased, so as to give us the opportunity of getting into the trenches to receive another *taua*.

This came in the same manner as the previous ones, and went back as they did, not being able to break through the fence, and losing many men.

All the rest of that day the big guns continued to shoot at us and the soldiers to fire into the *pah*, while we suffered much from the want of food and water.

That evening the mouth came to us again with word from the chief to render the *pah* and ourselves to him.

This we again refused to do. True, we had fought enough to save the honour of the *pah*, and we should have left it before, had we been able to do so; but we were, on all sides, surrounded by soldiers, so could not escape. And if we rendered ourselves up as prisoners, we, who were, with but few exceptions, all well-born *rangitera* (gentlemen), would lose caste and become slaves. Therefore we must fight for ever, even if we should have to die from thirst. All that evening, and also at intervals during the night, the big guns fired at us; and we had to take the time between these to lick with our tongues the dew that fell from the sky, so as to try and cool our parched throats, as by now our thirst was very great.

We could get no rest that night, as the white men frequently fired these powder-filled balls into the *pah*. And we discovered another reason for their use: one being to bring us powder, the other to keep us awake, so as to be ready to resist an attack should the chief desire one to be made. We had thought, at first, they had been intended to kill and injure us, but as they had hurt no one, we now understood their proper use. And we again wondered at a chief who, being so wise in some matters, should be so foolish as to keep us without food and water, as he still had many more tribes to send to fight us.

Next morning we saw that the white men had dug, during the night, many rifle pits, and had begun to dig trenches, so as to be able to approach us closely, without our being able to fire at them. Escape we had deemed impossible before, but when the mouth came to call us to render ourselves prisoners, we again cried, as loud as our thirst allowed us: 'We fight on; *aké, aké, aké.*'

That day the big guns fired frequently, and *tauas* attacked us twice, always in the same manner as I have already told you; but the last *taua* were very full of anger, and the bugle had to call twice before they left us.

The soldiers also kept on digging their trenches, and kept on firing both from big guns and muskets.

"During the night we again tried to quench our thirst with the dew, for we were getting weak and suffering greatly; and Rewi with the rest of us chiefs consulted as to what we should do, for we saw that by the next evening the soldiers would have dug their trenches up to the outer fence and that the *pah* must fall. These were the words of Rewi, and we all agreed with them:

> O ye chiefs of Taupo and Uriwera, we have done all that brave men can do. We have saved the honour of the *pah*, we must now look to ourselves. The soldiers will enter the *pah* tomorrow, and we, through the folly of the white

chief, will be too weak from famine and thirst to resist them. It is unbecoming that we, who are gentlemen, should render ourselves prisoners; therefore only one thing remains for us to do. We must charge the enemy and try to escape by breaking through them. Perchance some of us will succeed, the remainder must die as it befits warriors to die.

He then told us his plan. 'At midday the soldiers take their meal, leaving only guards in the trenches. We will leave the *pah* quietly in a body and rush those who are behind the bank—that is, in front of the gate—and we will break through them there. They will be eating. Perchance we may find them unprepared.' To this we all agreed, each man determining to escape or die.

Next morning we saw the trenches had approached us closely, and so near were they that the soldiers were able to throw great numbers of small balls filled with powder into our trench and the *pah* itself. These balls burst on reaching us, and were thrown by the hands of the soldiers themselves, not by the big guns, though these also kept firing all the time, and we saw before night came again the *pah* must fall.

No *taua* attacked us this morning, as they wished the big guns to break down our defences, as much as possible, before they again assailed us. The sun reached its height and the firing somewhat ceased. Rewi said the time was come, and we gathered together at the gate of the *pah*, all the women being with us. Yes, it was certainly the time for the soldiers' meal, and we, who had neither eaten nor drunk for more than three days, tried to laugh when we thought how we were shortly to disturb their eating it.

Now, Parion, so that you may understand fully how these matters took place, I must tell you that about 100 fathoms from the gate of the *pah* was a bank, behind which were one of the tribes of soldiers, who bore the number 40 on their head-coverings. This bank had not been dug by them but was natural. It was not a high bank, and it sloped towards us, but was steeper on the other side and afforded the soldiers good protection from such of us as possessed rifles. There had been no trenches dug on this side of the *pah*, as the ground was hard and rocky, so there was nothing between us and this bank. When we were all ready the gate of the *pah* was removed, and we all rushed out, but without noise, and ran as fast as we could for the bank; and we had crossed more than half the distance before the soldiers seemed to notice us, as the smoke and dust lay heavy on the *pah* and around the spots from which the big guns fired. Then we were seen, and immediately many bugles gave their calls. There was much shouting, and many soldiers in the trenches jumped out and fired at us, many others running to take their allotted places.

There was much confusion. We, however, ran steadily on, turning neither to our right nor our left; nor did we return the fire. We soon came to the bank, and as we ran up the slope we could see the soldiers rising from the ground, on which they were eating, and who, when they saw us running towards them, ran to the bank, fixing their bayonets on their guns. Only a few had time to fire at us before we were on them, and with our rush we jumped from the top of the bank right over their heads. Some of them thrust bayonets at us, but as they were in confusion we broke through them, or jumped over them, without trouble, only very few of us falling here, and continued to run towards the hills that were not far off. We should have reached these, and most of us would have escaped, but all at once we were cut off and attacked by other men, not soldiers, some of them mounted (Colonial Irregulars).

These men do not have the fine appearance of soldiers, but know more about war, and are greatly to be feared; for they did not wait to get each man into his right place, but attacked us each man as he could, and being, moreover, good fighting men, they killed many of us and delayed us so much that the soldiers, having had time to regulate themselves, reached the hill almost as soon as we did. They were in great numbers and fired heavily on us as we struggled up the hills, all of us so weak that we could scarcely surmount them. The big guns also fired at us, but the horses could not follow us, and so 120 of us escaped, Rewi and myself being among these, the remainder dying as it became them.

Very many of us, however, were wounded; and I must not omit to tell you that thirty of the others who did not escape, through being wounded severely, were taken by the soldiers. These the soldiers treated with honour; nor did they make them slaves or kill them, but conveyed them carefully to big tents, where their wounds were made whole, and they were attended with much care. The women, of whom some were taken, were also treated with honour. But this was the custom of the soldiers once the fighting was finished. They bore no anger towards the Maori prisoners, but brought them much tobacco and *waipero* (rum) to show their good will and appreciation for the trouble the Maoris had taken to fight them five times. But on the medicine men learning of this good will on the part of the soldiers, they were angry, and drove them away; which I myself consider to be wrong. But perchance it is the custom of the medicine men.

And now, Te Parione, I desire your explanation on some matters; for my heart is darkened with indecision as to the reasons the great white chief had in carrying the war on against us in the manner he did. You, who are a fighting man, belonging to the tribes of soldiers, for I have been told your ancestors have all been chiefs among these tribes, may be able to clear my mind on these matters. I will place my ideas before you, then you can make my mind light.

First, why did the chief attack us? We were on a visit of ceremony, not of war. Yet he, having a big army, and the Waikatos at the time avoiding him, must find war for his men. In so much he was right, and that I understand. Again, he showed great knowledge of war, by only sending small bodies of men against us, he having so many that we should have been crushed at once had he sent them all at the same time. He also showed his great wisdom by sending us powder in the iron balls, which also kept us awake at night, so that we might be ready in case he attacked us. But as he did not attack us during the night, it was folly, as a fighting man needs rest. That he did not want to kill us we know, or he would not have made whole the wounded men.

Again, he could not have wanted the *pah* itself, to dwell in, or he would not have tried to destroy it with his big guns. And he knew we had no food or water, so must all perish from thirst, in a few days, when he could gain the *pah* without losing any men at all. He could not want our arms, as his men do not use double-barrelled guns, and if he took them from us we should have been unable to fight him, in case he saw fit to come to Taupo from the Waikato, seeking war. No, he must have wanted to let each of his tribes enjoy the honour of fighting us in their proper turn.

But then why, O Te Parione, did he forbid us food and water? How could he expect us to render full justice to his men when our great thirst even prevented us from crying our war-cries, or fighting in such a manner as would confer honour on his men whose turn came late. As it was, we could only manage to hold out long enough to fight five of his tribes: and he had many.

And now, Te Parione, the night grows old, and I have talked much. Thinking of Orakau excites my thirst and the rum bottle is empty. At daylight you go to shoot ducks, and it is needful to sleep. Think over what I have asked you, and tomorrow night, when we talk once again on war, you will be able to set my mind at rest on these matters. War is a great art, and we are never too old to acquire wisdom. Perchance that white chief had reasons that, if I understood, would exalt my name should I practise them when we fight again. Till then, my guest, rest in peace.

The above yarn is greatly epitomised, as my old host not only described most of the blows struck during the fight, but also gave me the roll-call of the Maoris, and most of their pedigrees. A Maori considers it to be a waste of words not to describe minutely every circumstance of an event, and by doing so differs from our ideas of yarn-spinning, as we consider brevity to be the soul of wit. Nor did the brave old warrior lay claim to any special merit that his band of 250 men, armed with old fowling-pieces and muskets, should have resisted the attack of over 5000 British troops, should have repulsed five desperate assaults, and for three days have braved the fire of a powerful train of artillery, while at the same time undergoing the torture of thirst.

Surely their heroic answer to the general's summons to surrender, "*Ka whawhai tonu, aké, aké, aké*" (We fight right on, forever, forever, forever), is worthy of a place among the mottoes of the proudest regiments the world has ever contained. As for their desperate and somewhat successful attempt to escape: the fact that this handful of famished men and women, in broad daylight, should charge and break through the investing lines of their enemies and, but for the intervention of the Colonial Irregulars, would have nearly all got away, is a wonderful instance of unconquerable courage.

Perhaps I may be excused for recounting one or two more instances of Maori chivalry.

During the negotiations that took place at the end of the Waikato

Rewi

war, the general asked Wirimu Thomihana, through his interpreter, how it was that the Maoris had not attempted to cut off his convoys at a place called the Hog's Back?—the said place having such natural difficulties as to render its passage almost impossible, had it been obstructed by a hostile force. Thomihana's reply was: "What a foolish question for a great war chief to ask. If we had prevented you from obtaining food, how could you have continued to fight?"

On another occasion two companies of soldiers, while on the line of march, piled their arms, sat down to rest and eat their dinners. Not far away a body of Maoris were lying *perdus*. These crept up, through the long fern, to the unsuspecting Tommies. Then, jumping to their feet, rushed through them, seizing *en route* all the rifles, belts and pouches, they disappeared with them again into the fern. The Maori chief presently informed the discomfited and helpless troops that he would not allow his men to injure them, as he considered that both themselves and their officers were far too ignorant of war to be treated as warriors, and that they might therefore return in peace to their camp, where he advised them to learn how to take care of themselves before they again came out to fight.

The 65th Regiment had been stationed very many years in New Zealand, it being supposed that their existence had been forgotten by the War Office, who had most probably lost their postal address. Some of the officers and very many of the men had married Maori women, so that the regiment was on very friendly terms with the natives. War broke out, and, naturally, the white man and Maori were on opposite sides and fought bravely against one another. This did not, however, affect their mutual esteem, for when at sunset the firing ceased numbers of Maoris used to leave their rifle pits and stroll over to their opponents' shelter trenches to exchange compliments, while the Maori women brought over plentiful supplies of pork and potatoes with which to regale their husbands, who, during the day, had been trying their best to pot their fathers and brothers.

These latter, with plenty of quiet chaff, would quietly discuss the prominent events of the past day's fighting, and the possible occurrences of the coming one, with no more animus than teams of cricketers discuss together, at dinner, the events of that day's play. At guard-mounting these friendly enemies would part, and at daylight next morning each would do his level best to put out of action his relative by marriage. This sporting relationship was kept up for some time, until, reinforcements pouring into the country, another regiment was sent to strengthen the *Haki-Hakis* (the 65th), when the Maoris, thinking that the newcomers might be enemies to the 65th, promptly left their rifle pits and, coming over to their opponents, proffered their assistance to drive away the supposed undesirable newcomers, and then continue their own fight.

I have frequently talked to Maori warriors of their old-time wars, tribe against tribe, when they have related accounts of the awful raids of Hongi, Heki, Rauparaha and others. And these stories not only teem with incidents of splendid courage, but are also blackened by the recital of as many acts of brutality, treachery and cold-blooded slaughter sufficient to satisfy Moloch himself: and relate to men who would on one occasion perform feats of heroic chivalry worthy to stand beside those of Bayard or Sir Walter Manny, while on the next day they would commit acts that would have been considered bad form in Hades even by Tilly and Cromwell. Chivalry was to disappear entirely when the natives adopted the extraordinary and debased form of nonconformist Christianity called the *Pai Marire* or *Hau Hau* faith: at which time, retaining only their courage, they relinquished every other good quality they may ever have possessed.

During the bitter and savage fighting of the later sixties, splendid actions were done by these men while attempting to carry off, from the field of battle, their wounded or dead comrades; and their determined resistance, offered up to the last, threw a halo of glory round them that even their cold-blooded murders and torturing atrocities could scarcely obliterate.

Well I think I have said enough about their courage; let me turn to the next greatest virtue possessed by man—*viz.* hospitality.

The hospitality of the Maori was unbounded. The best of everything he had was readily placed at the disposal of his guest, and even should he be so circumstanced as to have only a few potatoes between himself and starvation, these would be cheerfully surrendered for his visitor's consumption; nor was any payment expected, and if offered would have been indignantly refused; notwithstanding the fact that the recipient of the bounty might be a perfect stranger.

In those good old days, when the inmates of a *pah* or *kainga* saw a white man, of any rank or position, approaching the place, all the women, girls and children would seize mats, or anything else that came handy, and, waving these, cry as loud as they could the greetings of welcome: "*Hacre mai! Hacremai!*" (Come to us! Come to us!). And these cries would continue, and be joined in by all the inhabitants, until the stranger had entered the village. On doing so, the visitor, provided he were acquainted with strict Maori etiquette, would pay no attention to anyone, but, handing his horse over to the nearest boy, pass through the screaming, gesticulating crowd, and seat himself in front of the guest hut, usually the best *whare* in the village. Here he would be faced by all the principal men of the place, who would squat down, in a semicircle, in front of him, the women, boys, girls and men of low degree standing in rear of them, when with one accord the whole multitude would lift up their voices and weep—and when I say weep it was weeping, real weeping, and no make-believe about it.

This weeping, known as a *tangi,* was to me always a matter of wonder, as I could never understand how a Maori should be able to turn on the water-tap of his emotions at any moment he might desire to do so. I have frequently seen scores of grand old *kai tangatas* (man-eaters) squat down and, at will, cry and sob, with big tears hopping down their tattooed cheeks, as bitterly as some tender-hearted little girls would do if their favourite cat had just murdered their pet canary; and these grim old warriors, in less than a minute, would be in more urgent need of a big bandana handkerchief than a small boy with a bad attack of influenza. Old men and women would crawl out of their huts, stragglers would hurry up to join the throng, until every man, woman and child belonging to the tribe would be rocking and wailing as if their very heart-strings had been wrung with woe by the most personal disaster.

After these lamentations had lasted a few minutes, one of the principal chiefs would rise to his feet and make a short oration, somewhat in this fashion: "You have come to us, O stranger, welcome! welcome! welcome!" Then, turning to his people, he would say: "What is the use of this crying? Dry your tears. Our friend is with us, make him welcome. He is hungry, prepare food for him. He is fatigued, let him rest. Bring him water, let him drink. Our friend is with us, cease this foolish weeping. Our hearts grow light at seeing him." He would then advance to the visitor and offer his hand, in the case of a white man; but if the said stranger should be a native, of rank or family, he would squat down in front of him and rub noses. Then, placing their hands each on the other's shoulders, they would dissolve once more into tears, mussle their noses together, and for a minute or two mingle their weepings: this process having to be gone through by the stranger with every man in the village, whose rank entitled him to approach the guest.

27

The salutations having been finished, the stranger was left in peace, everyone retiring, with the exception of a chief, or some particular friend, who would remain to see to his comfort. And here at once the innate good-breeding of the Maori came to the front: insomuch as, no matter how anxious the natives were to hear the news, or the purport of the visit, the guest was never pestered with questions, not even as from whence he came, or whither he was going, and it remained entirely to his own discretion as to whether he gave them any information or not. In the meantime, girls brought him water to drink and wash with, others had swept out the *whare*, brought in fresh fern and laid down new mats for his use. Presently the sound of singing would be heard, and a group of girls, carrying small open trays made from the broad, glazed leaves of the flax plant, would, with a dancing step and a little song, approach him and place them in front of him.

These trays contained food, such as pork, eels, *enunga* (fresh-water white-bait), *kora* (the delicious fresh-water crayfish), potatoes, pigeons, and sweet potatoes, or any of them the village contained. Anyhow, the guest might be quite sure it was the very best his hosts had to offer. On their arrival the man who had been looking after him would take a morsel of food from one dish and eat it; then, rising to his feet, he would retire, at the same time wishing his guest a good appetite. Everyone else would depart with him, with the exception of one or, perhaps, two girls, who would remain on their knees beside him, to wait on him and tempt him to eat.

The evening meal being over, the chiefs would gather round their guest, and, if he should happen to be a man of any importance, long and deep would be the conversation: the subjects ranging from the health and doings of the Great White Queen and her governor, to the most trivial topics of the day. Each man in his turn would state his ideas and reasons, and was listened to with attention; while the guest's words were carefully weighed, and even, if his hearers disagreed with him, the arguments adduced to refute his statements were always expressed in a manner so polite, and in words so carefully chosen, that it was impossible for him to feel personally hurt in regard to his *amour propre*.

Of course if the visit had been premeditated the stranger would have come amply supplied with tobacco, which would be passed round, and accepted with a *bien aise* that quite disguised, or rather hid, their intense longing for it, and would be enjoyed with many a hearty grunt of satisfaction and approbation. Then the girls would *haka* (dance with songs) in the moonlight, some of them having placed glow-worms and fireflies in their hair. And the sight of flashing eyes, gleaming white teeth, flowing locks and lovely, swaying figures was sufficient to have made old Saint Anthony himself sit up; although the words of the songs that accompanied the dances, and the gestures that in part composed them, were of a nature to shock a far less austere saint, and would perhaps have even extracted a blush from an *habitué* of the old-time Jardin Mabille.

Late night would put an end to the festivities, and the stranger, all his comforts well seen to, might retire to his fern bed in peace.

It was a point of honour among the Maoris to protect their guest, as it was a point of honour, on the part of the guest, to stand by his hosts. In the yarn I spun about Orakau, I pointed out how the Taupo and Uriwera tribes refused to render up the *pah* lent to them to dwell in by the Waikatos, and that sooner than do so they fought to the bitter end. Again, in 1871, when Te Kooti, flying from us, took refuge in the King Country, and demanded the protection of the Waikatos, this was readily granted him; and the Waikato tribes, although they had no personal esteem for him, much less love or even family ties, would have gone to war with us rather than have surrendered him, had the New Zealand Government demanded him from them.

A Maori tribe considered it most unfortunate should even an accident befall a guest while dwelling in one of their villages; for if such an occurrence should happen, they ran the risk of being chaffed and held up to ridicule, by the surrounding tribes, for their inability to take care of a visitor.

Much more so was this the case during wartime. Should a white officer be detailed for duty to a native contingent, he would be looked after and his safety guarded in ways almost ludicrous and by no means congenial to himself.

This was done, because if that officer were killed or wounded, it would reflect the deepest disgrace on the tribe with whom he served; they would never hear the last of it, not only from their friends, but also from their enemies. And these would continually rate them, and charge them with the accusation that it was through their carelessness or cowardice that the misfortune had happened to the man who had been entrusted to them.

The Maori was very superstitious. He firmly believed in dreams, visions, omens of all sorts and the gift of prophecy, while the number of unlucky acts he might involuntarily commit during one day was quite

29

sufficient to account for a whole chapter of accidents on the morrow. He regarded the *tohungas* (magicians) with great respect, so long as their divinations and prophecies panned out; but there are plenty of well-authenticated cases where a warrior has wreaked his vengeance on a *tohunga* through whose false prognostications the tribe has got into a mess. Nor are incidents lacking to show that prophets, who had earned a reputation for themselves, would not rather commit suicide than allow themselves to be proved wrong in their divinations.

Let me spin you a couple of yarns to illustrate what I have just written.

It was in March 1865 that the Hau Hau apostle Kereopa, in the course of a few hours, converted the swagger flock of red-hot Christians, who, under the guidance of Bishop Williams, had earned a mighty reputation for sanctity, to the new faith of *Pai Marire*. The good bishop and his family, barely escaping with their lives from his own sheep, departed to Napier, leaving the Hau Haus in possession of his residence at Waerengahika, at which place they built a *pah* that was, in November of the same year, attacked by the Colonial forces. The Hau Haus were superior in numbers, but during the first few days the Colonials gained some trivial advantages, and on the fourth day began to sap up to the works, which they had surrounded. This day chanced to be a Saturday, and the working party were surprised by an attack, in their rear, from a body of the enemy's reinforcements seeking to enter the *pah*, which they succeeded in doing, the working party having to beat a retreat, with the loss of six men killed and five wounded. This trivial success greatly elated the natives and so bucked up one of the apostles that he at once started in and prophesied nineteen to the dozen.

Now this Johnny possessed that small amount of knowledge that is so dangerous to its owner. He had been brought up at a mission station, and accustomed to going to church, with great regularity, every Sunday. He therefore thought that all Christians acted in the same way, and that the Colonial Irregulars would be just as methodical in their religious observance as the goody-goody hangers-on at the various mission stations he was acquainted with.

Here of course he made a blooming error, for what member of the Lost Legion ever allowed preaching to interfere with fighting, or carried devotional books about with him when he had to hump his own swag.

Now this josser, thinking he knew all about the customs of the white man, considered he was quite safe in turning on his prophetic tap. So on the evening after the small success already spoken about he started in and informed his hearers that he had received a revelation, directing the Hau Haus that on the following day, which was Sunday, they were to leave the *pah* an hour before noon and advance on the white men's shelter trenches, which they would find empty, and that the majority of the latter who had not been turned into stone by the angel Gabriel would be surprised at their devotions and fall a prey, without any resistance, to the tender mercies of the Hau Haus, who, he guaranteed, were to escape, scathless, from wounds or death.

These promises seem absurd to white men, but they were implicitly believed by the Maoris, who next day acted on the strength of them.

The main position of the Colonials was in the rear of three strong thorn hedges, two of which flanked the third, and these had all been well trenched and were, of course, held, day and night, by a strong guard; in fact the men lived and slept in them. Between the centre hedge and the *pah*, a distance of less that 500 yards, stretched a smooth meadow, without a particle of cover, and the astonishment of our men was intense when, at 11 o'clock a.m., they saw some hundreds of the Hau Haus quietly leave the *pah* and advance in two wedge-shaped columns against the centre of their position. At first they thought it was a general surrender, but the war flags the enemy carried rapidly dispersed that idea; and when the two columns were well between the three hedges, and not 100 yards from any of them, the bugle sounded and a tremendous volley was poured into the misguided Maoris, who fell in heaps of dead and wounded men.

Notwithstanding the awful shock their nerves must have received from this quite unexpected slaughter, these gallant though fanatical warriors at once charged home and tried to force their way through the strong thorn fence, only to be swept away like flies. And soon the survivors had to beat a hasty retreat back to the *pah*, lashed the whole way by the heavy fire of the white men, who did not go to church.

It was during the advance that the incident I originally alluded to took place. The first volley had smashed the Hau Haus' leading column, the advance of which the apostle led in person; for, to give these prophets only their just due, they never hung back from taking the post of the greatest danger in any of the crazy enterprises that they persuaded their disciples to undertake.

Well, the first volley knocked over the prophet, who fell badly wounded, but succeeded in regaining his feet, whereupon one of the chiefs, disengaging himself from the mass of stricken and shaken men, deliberately walked up to him, drew his tomahawk and cleft his skull, then, springing forward, led his surviving followers to almost certain death. This might be called an instance of sharp and ready reckoning, but it was by no means a singular case of rough and rapid retribution; so that, taking into consideration the number of apostles who were knocked over, in a legitimate manner, fighting, and those who were *tomahawked* by furious and disappointed votaries, the trade could scarcely be called a healthy one, and it must have required a great amount of pluck on the man's part who took on himself the prophetic *rôle*. But, then, what will not some men risk for notoriety?

Now, having finished with this Johnny, let me tell you about another of a somewhat similar kidney.

The friendly tribes of the Wanganui sent a contingent to the east coast, to assist us during the Opotiki Expedition, and among them was a first-class, up-to-date prophet named Pitau. The Wanganui, at this time, were not strong in prophets, so that this man was made much of by his tribe, for although some of the young men had begun to deride prophecy, yet the old warriors still implicitly believed in the ancient cult, and regarded Pitau as a valuable adjunct to the field force.

Now it was the usual custom of the various tribes, when they went to war, to hold deep consultations with their tribal prophets, who for a consideration would advise and foretell what was going to happen, and if the war was going to prove successful or otherwise. It was so in this case. Pitau was called on to lift the veil of futurity, and, having gone through the necessary incantations, the oracle spoke as follows:—"You will be successful in all things, O Wanganui: only one man will die, and that man will be Pitau." Now this was distinctly rough on Pitau, who must either die or be declared an impostor. Anyhow, the oracle had spoken, and the war party started. The Wanganui reached Opotiki, did their duty well, and on the completion of their service were to take ship for home.

Up to this time nearly everything had panned out all right for the soothsayer, with regard to his prophecy: the Wanganui had been successful and had not lost a single man; but the oracle had distinctly stated Pitau was to die him- self, yet here he was still alive. It certainly was not his fault, for at the fight at the Kiori-kino, and also in other skirmishes, he had done his best to get killed, but seemed to bear a charmed life; yet if he returned home alive, his name and reputation as a high-toned prophet would be gone forever. The Fates, however, gave him one more chance, and he grasped it. Canoes, heavily ladened, were pushing off from the shore to the ship: he sprang into one of these, and by his extra weight swamped the canoe. The amphibious natives easily swam ashore, but so did not Pitau, for, raising his arms above his head, he allowed himself to sink down to his rest, among the eels and crabs, rather than allow his prophecy to be unfulfilled. Surely there are many names on the scroll of martyrs who have laid down their lives, to prove the truth of their convictions, less worthy of fame than that of Pitau.

And now I think I may spin you a yarn about a personal experience I had of the superstitious fears of the Maoris, although by doing so I must confess to a *mauvaise plaisanterie* I was guilty of perpetrating, and of which I am thoroughly ashamed, that created a greater emotion, among a party of highly respectable old cannibals, than any convulsion of nature would have caused.

It happened in this way: I was well aware of the great superstitious dread the Maoris had of the green lizard. These, although they exist in New Zealand, are rare birds, and during the years I was there I saw but few of them. The Maoris, however, believe that at death one of these lizards enters a man's body, and consequently look on them with horror and abhorrence. At the period I am yarning about, I was located at Ohinimutu, in the hot lake district, and had made a short visit to the town of Napier.

During my stay there, while wandering about the streets, I noticed that a speculative storekeeper had added some children's toys to his stock in trade, perhaps the very first that had ever been imported into the country, and as they attracted my attention I stopped to examine them. We are told that Old Nick is ever ready to prompt an idle man, and he must have been mighty adjacent to me that day, for on my spotting one of those old-fashioned, wooden crocodiles, painted a vivid green with bright-red spots on it, I immediately went into the shop and purchased it. The thing was constructed of small blocks of wood, sawn in such a way, and connected together with string, that when you held it in your hand it wriggled, and looked alive, while it also possessed a gaping red mouth and staring eyes. The confounded insect would not have raised a squall out of a nervous European babe of a year old; but, such as it was, I put it into my kit and, on my return up country, took it with me.

In due course of time I reached Ohinimutu, where, after a swim in the hot water and a good dinner, I retired to my private abode, a large hut built Maori fashion, but with European door and window, as I knew I should have to give audience to some dozen chiefs of the Arawa tribe, who would call on me to welcome my return and hear the news. It did not take me long to prepare for their reception, and getting the toy out of my kit, I slipped it up my left sleeve, so that it was hidden.

I then sat down in a low camp-chair and awaited my victims, who soon arrived, giving me their words of welcome as they entered, and squatting down in a semicircle in front of the fire, all of them as keen as mustard to hear the news. They were a fine-looking lot of old chaps, ten in number, and some of them almost gigantic in size. Old Hori Haupapa must have stood over seven foot high, when in his prime; and the rest were all big men. Anxious as they were to hear the news, still they were far too well-bred to ask any questions, and, as I pretended to be in very low spirits and sat speechless, heaving an occasional deep sigh, they squatted there, conversing in low whispers, with looks full of commiseration for my unhappy state.

For a few minutes we sat quiet, then I made signs to the girl who attended on us to hand round the rum and tobacco: which she did. And after each man had been served, letting go a dismal groan, I said: "Friends, I thank you for your words of welcome. My heart is very dark. I have dreamed a dream." Here I paused to let the poison work; for a dream to a Maori audience is always a safe draw, and the muttered grunts and ejaculations, passed round with nudges, showed me they were quite ripe to believe anything. So I continued: "Yes, friends, last night I dreamed a dream, and the interpretation of that dream is hidden from me." Here I paused again, and slipped the toy into my left hand, which rested on my left knee, while I held their eyes with my own, so that, in the firelit *whare*, none of them noticed my sleight of hand.

Then I continued: "I dreamed, O chiefs of the Arawa, that we all sat, as we are doing now, by this fire, when lo! out of my left hand crept a *ngaraka*" (green lizard). Here again I paused, but so did not my hearers, for old Taupua, glancing nervously at my left hand, at once spotted what he thought to be a dreaded lizard. The grim old warrior let go a howl of consternation and promptly turned a back somersault, thereby drawing the attention of all the others to the noxious reptile; and in one moment these dignified old savages, who would have faced without flinching the fire of a battery of artillery sooner than have committed a gaucherie, were trying to push and struggle through the door, with no more regard to manners or man- hood than the ordinary well-dressed Englishman displays who pushes ladies on one side while boarding a tram.

The first one to reach the door was an ancient, who did not understand the mechanism of a white man's lock, so failed to open it; and in a moment they were climbing over one another's backs, in their frantic endeavours to escape until the end of the *whare* gave way, and the big chiefs of the Arawa tribe precipitated themselves, door and all, into outer darkness, where they formed a confused heap of writhing, howling humanity. At last they struggled free, and each man made for his own hut, all fully convinced that something dreadful was going to happen and that the whole community was past praying for. Nor did the panic end here; for in a moment the tribe was roused up and, the awful news being promulgated, in two flirts of a cat's tail, every man, woman and child had cleared out of the *kainga*. Yes, those who had canoes took to them, and those who had none used their legs, and used them to some advantage, for in less time than it takes me to write it the whole of that congregation of peaceful natives had abandoned their happy homes and fled.

Well, after my first burst of laughter was over, I began to count up the cost of my stupid joke, and at once saw I was likely to have to pay dearly for my fun. To commence with, my hut would have to be rebuilt; but that was a trifle. What I had to fear was the censure of the Government, as the Defence Minister was an old Scotsman, without a particle of fun in his whole corpus, so was not likely to view the scatterment of his most pampered tribe with equanimity, and visions of reasons in writing and prosecutions danced before my eyes. It was clear that the first thing to be done was to get the natives to come back to their *kainga*; but how? I knew full well they would not suffer me to approach within a mile of any of them, and although I had some sterling friends among the fighting chiefs, yet, if I could not get speech with them, so as to explain matters to them, their good will would be of no use to me.

Fortunately, among the men dwelling at Ohinimutu was a Ngapuhi native, and I engaged him to act as messenger; but, although he was a red- hot Christian, nothing would persuade him to come near, much less touch, the wretched toy. I, however, induced this man to go over to Mokoia Island, see the principal tribal *tohunga*, and get him to come across and interview me. Fitting him out with a gallon of rum and plenty of tobacco, I despatched my Mercury and awaited his return in trepidation. On the morning of the second day he reported himself, and informed me that the *tohunga* awaited me, but that, as nothing would induce the limb of Satan to land, I must go down to the lake, and he would discourse with me from his canoe. So I had to go to the lake and *collogue* with the old sinner from the point of a jutting-out cape. After I had tried to make him understand the true state of affairs, I produced the toy; but nothing I could say would induce him to believe that it was composed of inanimate wood. No, he could see it move, swore it was alive, and sternly refused to touch it, or even come closer to me, so that he could examine it.

At last, happy thought, I suggested I should burn it. To this he consented. So, putting the unfortunate crocodile on the top of a flat stone, I collected some dry sticks and, with him watching every movement, constructed a funeral pyre, and cremated the wretched toy to ashes. Then he consented to land and came up to my hut, where he went through many incantations and gesticulations, although he avoided touching or entering it. Presently he turned to me and said: "This and all it contains must be at once burned. Have you removed anything from it?" I had not; though, expecting something of this sort to happen, I had taken every care that my servant should do so, and that absolutely nothing of value remained within it; so, like a Radical minister, I only told half the truth.

"Set it on fire," quoth he, and this I did with equanimity, as it would only give the Maoris the trouble of building me a better one, so that in a few minutes not a vestige of my late mansion remained. As everything that had been contaminated by the penny toy was now supposed to be destroyed, the old *tohunga* consented to discuss terms of peace, which consisted as follows:—first, that I should hand over, privately, to the *tohunga* himself, one gallon of rum, three pounds of tobacco and twenty-five pounds of flour, the said *tohunga* guaranteeing to at once dream a dream directing the natives to rebuild my house, with great rapidity.

Secondly, that at the general *tangi*, to be held next day, on the return of the natives, I was to provide ten gallons of rum, twenty pounds of tobacco and half-a-ton of flour, all of which was to be consumed thereat. And lastly, should I on any future occasion go to Napier, and discover any more instruments of white man's devilry, I was to bring them to him, when, with a little judicious management, we could work many miracles to our mutual advantage.

All these terms having been agreed to, Satan's representative among the Arawa departed, and the next morning all his congregation, accompanied by many of their country friends, returned, when a big *tangi* with much feasting and dancing took place; but even my very best friends looked askance at me for a long time, while for some weeks the majority of the women, girls and children would fly from me as if I had the plague.

You must not think for a moment that this avoidance was caused by ill will, or that the old chiefs bore me any malice for the shameful trick I had played them, or that I was fined the rum, flour, etc., for the evil I had done. Not a bit of it. I was mulct for my misfortune, not for my fault. In their eyes no fault had been committed. If Moses himself had returned to tell them I had played them a trick, they would not have believed him. No; had they not seen the beast come out of my hand at the very moment I was relating my dream? Trick indeed, not much. They looked on me as an awful example of misfortune, and therefore as a fit and proper personage to be politely robbed.

Yes, robbed. Had I been a Maori, not only myself but all my family would have been robbed of every single article we possessed in the world, in payment for the affliction of bad luck that had fallen on me; but as I was a white man this could not be done, so I was fined. For is not this in accordance with the ancient custom or law of *muru*, which authorises a man smitten by a sudden calamity to be plundered of all he possesses? And what greater calamity was possible to mortal man than to have an obscene lizard grow out of his hand? Therefore I was fined. As for trick, nonsense! What man dare make fun of, or render ridiculous, the dignity and majesty of the head chiefs of the Arawa tribe?

I think I may say a few more words on this extraordinary law of *muru*—a law that Europeans regarded with laughter and contempt; yet it worked very well among the natives, and should any family have met with misfortune and the law not have been put in force against them, they would have considered themselves not only slighted, but insulted. It also, among others, contained one salient good quality, as it caused all personal portable property constantly to change hands, for the family that was plundered one day would, in the ordinary course of events, rob some other family a few days afterwards, so that a canoe, blanket or any household utensil might pass through many hands and, if not worn out during its transits, might at last return to its original possessor. Yet to a white man it did seem funny that a party of natives *en route* to visit another family, and whose canoe should be capsized when landing, were not only robbed of their canoe, but that the unlucky ones would have considered themselves insulted had not their friends immediately annexed it.

I remember well that once, while on a journey to visit a *pah*, accompanied by a chief of some importance, in fact he was a native assessor—*i.e.* a sort of Maori J. P. appointed by Government—a very queer illustration of the law of *muru* cropped up.

We were to inquire into some trivial case, the defendant being the son of the chief of the place, and the utmost penalty not more than five shillings. Just as we reached the *pah* my companion, who was riding a fine, high-spirited horse, was bucked off, and while in the act of rising received a severe kick on the croup. He was picked up with much solicitude, all the natives condoling with him. The case was tried and settled, the defendant being mulct two shillings and sixpence, and next day, when about to depart, the horses being brought to the gate of the *pah*, my companion's horse was not forthcoming. At once I demanded the reasons why, and was informed it had been annexed as *muru*, for throwing and kicking my unfortunate friend, who at once acquiesced in the judgment and thanked the chief of the *pah* for his courtesy in paying him such an honour.

Again I was on a visit to a *pah* situated close to the mouth of a river, on the other side of which was another *pah*. One day my hosts started out to shoot a huge seine net, and of course the whole population turned out to assist or give advice. The noise, as everyone yelled at the top of his or her gamut, was deafening. However, two large canoes eventually got away with the net on board, and after taking a bold sweep returned to shore and landed the sea end. Immediately all hands, redoubling their yells, tailed on to the hauling ropes and pulled and howled with all their might. Just as the bag of the net came in view, a huge shark, that had been encompassed in its toils, made a bold dash, broke the net and escaped, letting out, at the same time, many large fish.

The excited and disappointed natives were just dragging the net and the still great remainder of the catch up on to the sand, when their neighbours, apprised by the yells that something unfortunate had occurred, dashed across the river in their canoes, and after a sham resistance of a few minutes swept up and carried off all the remaining fish. They might also have confiscated the net, but did not, an old chief confiding to me that the other side of the river was full of rocks, and not suitable for seine netting; moreover, the net was broken and would require repairing. Such was the law of *muru*.

Of course to yarn about New Zealand without saying anything about the custom of *tapu* would be on all fours with yarning about Rome and not mentioning the Pope. So here goes for a few remarks about the ancient but very confusing custom of *tapu*.

Anything animate or inanimate could be rendered *tapu* by the will, or even touch, of a man who was *tapu* himself. *Tapu* might also render a thing so sacred, or might render it so unclean, that to touch that thing would constitute an act of unpardonable sacrilege, or cause the toucher to be looked upon as so defiled as to be ostracised by the whole community, although the act was done innocently and in ignorance.

To break a *tapu* was looked upon, by the superstitious natives, as a direct challenge to the greatly dreaded spiritual powers, and was certain to bring swift and awful punishment.

A big chief was *tapu*, and if he went to war the essence of *tapu* became doubly distilled, so much so that he could not feed himself, nor even touch food with his hands. Nor could he even touch a cup or utensil that did not actually belong to himself, for if he did so, the article he used at once became so *tapu* that no one else could use it; consequently it became either his personal property, or had to be destroyed. This in a country where there were neither shops nor manufactories was an impossibility, so that at meal-time a chief had to eat apart, and be fed by either a girl or slave. Truly the sublime approached the ridiculous, to see a grim, tattooed old warrior squatting down, with a small girl throwing morsels of food into his mouth, or with his head thrown back, and his jaws extended to their full width, receiving a stream of water, poured down his throat, from the spout of an ancient tea-kettle.

Even an ordinary warrior, not being a slave, lost his back when on the war-path—*i.e.* his back became so *tapu* that he could carry nothing, much less provisions, on it; and this was also very inconvenient when having to march through a rough, bushed country, without waggons or pack-horses. Food could even become *tapu*, especially that which remained from the portion served out for the use of the chief, even though no part of his body had touched it; and there is a well-authenticated case, that on one occasion a slave, being on the warpath, found some food and ate it. No sooner had he done so than he was informed it was the remains of the dinner of the fighting chief. This news so horrified the poor superstitious wretch that he was at once taken ill with sharp internal pains, and died.

The Maoris always made their plantations in the bush, frequently at a considerable distance from their *kaingas*, and these, after the potatoes had been planted, would only be occasionally visited by their owners, who, to protect them, would get the chief or *tohunga* to *tapu* the plantation; and this being done, the produce would be quite safe from the depredations of others.

About the year 1870 some six brace of pheasants were turned loose in the Waikato district, and the principal chief put his *tapu* on them for seven years. These birds increased and throve in a manner truly wonderful. Not a Maori dare touch one, although long before the period of protection had expired the birds had not only spread all over the Waikato district, but also over all the adjoining ones. And they carried their protection with them, for notwithstanding the fact that they had become somewhat of a nuisance to the Arawa tribe, who were not in any way subordinate to the Waikato chief, yet they respected his *tapu*, and would have starved sooner than eaten them.

It was by making use of this *tapu* that the wonderful head of game and fish at present in New Zealand has been reared and acclimatised.

Should a chief die within his *whare*, that hut and everything it contained at once became *tapu* and was lost to use; for as soon as his body had been removed, the door was at once blocked up, and the hut with its contents allowed to moulder away, no one daring to touch, much less remove, one single article. *Tapu*, therefore, in a manner of speaking, was the antipoise of the law of *muru*, for if the enforcement of the latter rendered the portable property of an individual or tribe precarious, yet *tapu* made his title indissoluble; so the two laws or customs got on very well together, and may exist to the present day.

I cannot leave my friends the Maoris without speaking about their awful cruelty in torturing and killing their prisoners, and in the foul massacres of helpless women and children.

Yet even in this there may be something said in their favour, especially should you compare them, savages as they were, with the human monsters that every Christian European country has produced, when they would be found no more cruel or bloodthirsty.

Now I don't want to draw parallels in history, but it rather disgusts me to hear Alva, Tilly, Nana Sahib, or even Te Kooti, run down, while such a cold-blooded villain as Cromwell is extolled.

I was taught as a schoolboy to regard Tilly and Alva as the incarnations of Satan; I suppose because they made it sultry for Protestants; but it was not pointed out to me that at the very same time Alva and his Spanish troops were making it hot for Lutherans in the Netherlands, the English troops of Protestant Queen Bess were perpetrating infinitely worse brutalities on the helpless Irish, while the fiendish cruelties of Tilly's wild Croats and Pandours, at the sack of Magdeburg, were equalled, if not surpassed, at Drogheda, by Oliver Cromwell and his canting hypocritical Puritans.

I am myself an Irishman, a Protestant, a Unionist and an Imperialist, just as ready to fight for our King and Flag as ever I was during the forty years I passed on the Colonial frontiers, but I can blame none of my countrymen for the hatred they feel towards England, provided they fight like men and eschew all cowardly, underhand, secret societies; and I am convinced it will require many centuries to roll past before the recollection of the Penal Laws and the foul, savage treachery of past English rule is obliterated, while the curse of Cromwell will remain forever. Nana Sahib and Te Kooti did not, combined, kill as many helpless women and children as either Alva, Tilly or Cromwell; yet, as they killed all they could, they cannot be blamed for that, and I have no doubt that on their arrival in Hades they were assigned just as honourable entertainment and particular attentions as the aristocratic fiend, the priestly murderer or the Puritan cut-throat.

It must also be remembered that the atrocities committed by Te Kooti and his fanatical followers might be blamed upon the fiendish faith they had adopted and had never been practised by the Maoris during the previous six years of the war, also that they were more or less fighting in defence of their country against invaders. Again, Te Kooti had been the victim of gross injustice, at the hands of the Colonial Government, insomuch as he had been transported without trial, and that the evidence against him was not only insufficient, but was also of such a nature that the law officers of the Crown could find no excuse even to bring him to a trial, so that many of his brutalities were prompted by a desire for *utu*, a custom universally practised by the Maoris.

Please don't think I have written the above for the purpose of deifying England's enemy, or to slander my own countrymen like a Radical Little Englander, for I would have, at any time, blown the roof off Te Kooti's head, or that of one of his followers, with as little compunction as I have since shot a mangy jackal; but I have written it simply to show that, if savage New Zealand produced one fiend, in the shape

41

of Te Kooti, Christian England produced a worse one in the shape of that sanctimonious hypocrite, Oliver Cromwell, and that therefore we should not endanger our own glass by throwing stones.

I alluded just now to the custom of *utu*, which means payment or revenge, and is very similar to the law of the Jews, that laid down the maxim of an eye for an eye and a tooth for a tooth—an axiom which the Maoris believe in thoroughly.

It was the practice of this custom that led to many of the sanguinary combats and massacres that took place between the armed traders and the natives during the first half of the past century. These traders visited New Zealand and exchanged muskets, powder, ironware, etc., for flax, whale oil, curios and men's heads. They were a hard-fisted, lawless crowd, who, in their brigs or schooners, well armed with musket, pike and carronade, would anchor in one of the splendid natural harbours and begin their traffic with the haughty, warlike savages.

Business carried on between such men as these often brought about a row, which a musket shot or a slash from cutlass or tomahawk would not improve, and the ship would then sail away, after most likely the killing or wounding of some natives. The remembrance of the blood spilt would be treasured by the Maoris, and the next trader who visited that place would have to pay for the evil deeds of the previous visitor. Now the Maori looked on all white men as belonging to the same tribe, and the custom of *utu* allowed any man injured by an individual to wreak his vengeance upon any member of the said individual's tribe, provided his particular enemy were absent. In this he was backed up by all the members of his own tribe, especially if blood had been drawn; for tribal blood must be paid for with blood, and no Sicilian clan ever carried out a vendetta more thoroughly than a Maori *hapu*. This being so, the Maoris eagerly looked for the next vessel, to take their blood payment for the blood spilt.

Knowing full well that their canoes and spears were no match for the well-armed ship, they would bide their time and have recourse to treachery. The white men would be received with apparent good will, and, if foolish enough, might be lulled into a mistaken sense of security. This being done, the majority of the crew would be enticed ashore, where, taken off their guard, or separated, they would be attacked, killed and eaten, while the ship, weakened by the loss of so many men, was sometimes boarded and captured, the natives thereby obtaining *utu* for the original injury done them.

Maoris were very punctilious about the honour of their tribes and ancestors, this being carried to an extent almost ludicrous. *Par exemple*, a year or two before I left New Zealand an old woman belonging to one tribe was planting potatoes, and as she shoved each tuber into the ground she called it by the name of one of the principal living chiefs or dead heroes of an adjoining tribe. This came to the ears of the said tribe, who immediately prepared for war, despatching an ultimatum that, unless the plantation and all the spuds it contained were at once destroyed, they would attack their insulting neighbours. The *casus belli* must seem very absurd to a white man; but it was different to the offended tribe, as when, in the course of events, the murphies became ready for the pot, the scandalous old dame would be able to declare that she was not only devouring their living chiefs, but that, vampire-like, she was feeding upon their defunct ones.

I mentioned that the Maoris performed many splendid acts of courage in getting away their wounded and even their dead. This was done not only for love or comradeship, but to prevent the enemy from using their flesh in lieu of butcher's meat, and also to save their bones being turned into useful and ornamental articles by their opponents.

For instance, let us suppose that during some ancient war, the Waikato tribe fighting against the Taranaki, the former should have killed and captured the body of a great war chief whom we will call Te Rawa. The flesh of the dead man, in the first place, would be eaten—a great indignity—but that would not be the end of him, for the bones would be preserved, and turned into fish-hooks, flutes and ornaments, the teeth strung nicely on flax, making a necklace; and it was not pleasant for the victim's descendants to hear that their revered though unfortunate ancestor was still furnishing food and bijouterie for the offspring of his slayer.

Now all the aforementioned useful articles were called by the name of the man they had, in the first place, belonged to—in this case Te Rawa. The owner of the fish-hook could boast that he was still eating Te Rawa, as he would call all the fish caught by that special hook Te Rawa. Then, pointing to the necklace, he might brag he was wearing Te Rawa, and when inclined for music he would tootle on his flute and proudly declare he was playing Te Rawa; so that the unfortunate descendants of the poor old defunct, whenever they heard of this, would have to blush under their tattooed skins at the very name of their much-deplored ancestor.

It was therefore a most sacred duty to rescue a dead or wounded comrade from the enemy, even when fighting against the white men;

for although the natives well knew that we did not use their defunct relatives for rations, nor turn them into musical instruments, yet it had become so strong a custom among themselves to guard against such a possible catastrophe, that they still practised it although unnecessarily.

I must revert once more to the custom of *utu* so as to point out the fair-mindedness of the natives should this law be used against themselves. Let me give you just one instance.

The circumstance took place after the capture of Ngatapa. Some 130 Hau Haus had been taken prisoners, these being shot out of hand and their bodies thrown over a precipice; but six or eight of them remained alive, in our hands, as it was not certain they had participated in the Poverty Bay massacre. They were confined in a hut awaiting trial and, as all the murdered people were dead, it was a moot point whether these fellows would not get off for want of evidence. One of the men, however, whose relations had been murdered, determined that they should not slip through the clumsy fingers of the law, as alas so many of the blood-stained villains had succeeded in doing. He volunteered to act as one of the guard round the hut and, borrowing another revolver from a mate, he took the first opportunity to enter the hut and deliberately blew out the brains of all the inmates.

This act of summary justice was fully approved of by the Maoris, as it bore out the custom of *utu*; for if the defunct Hau Haus had not murdered the man's family themselves, yet their tribes had done so; and they considered it a square deal, as blood had been paid for by blood.

I could yarn on about these queer people for hours and tell you of plenty of other quaint customs, such as their wakes, marriages, etc., also about their industry and other qualities, good and bad, for, faith! they have them mixed like all other people. But if you have followed and appreciated my first attempt it will encourage me to write more of my humble experiences on the frontiers of the Empire with the old Lost Legion I love so well.

CHAPTER 2

How Matene Failed to Convert the Lower Wanganui

It was in April 1864 that Te Ua, the crazy founder of the Pai Marire faith, despatched his apostle and prophet, Matene Rangitanira, to convert the tribes of the Wanganui River to the new religion.

Now these tribes were divided into two sections, who, although closely connected by blood, lived under separate chiefs, and notwithstanding the fact that they were allied for mutual support against outsiders still, like many European families, harboured jealousies among themselves. There was also this difference between them: the Lower River tribes had from the first always been friendly disposed towards the settlers, or at all events had tolerated them, while the Upper River natives detested the white man, although the latter had in no way encroached on them, nor had they ever had much to do with them, as their country was at a considerable distance from the English settlements, the only means of communication being the river.

The Upper River natives were also, at this time, greatly enraged against the white man and desirous of *utu* (revenge), on account of the death of one of their principal chiefs, who had been killed the previous year, together with thirty-six of his men, at the storming of Kotikara. Matene, who was a member of the Wanganui tribes, arrived in April 1864, accompanied by a party of Taranaki fanatics, at Pipiriki, an important native village situated on the upper waters of the Wanganui River, and began his mission.

At this place Mr Booth, the resident magistrate for the district, dwelt, and although at the moment he was absent in the township of Wanganui his wife and family, together with his brother and his family, were there. Mr Booth was a most popular official with the Maoris, and it is quite possible that, had he been at his post, he might have been able to put a stop to the apostle's preaching before it became too late; but unfortunately he was absent on duty and was much delayed during his return journey by the paucity of water in the river, so that it was the end of the month before he reached Pipiriki, and the evil teaching had taken a firm hold on the natives.

Matene made such good use of Mr Booth's absence that in a few days he had converted the great majority of the Upper River natives and had erected a *Niu* (Hau Hau worship pole), on which Captain Lloyd's head was suspended, and the tribe's men and women, mad with fanaticism, danced furiously round it. During Mr Booth's slow progress up the river the reports he received at every village he passed grew worse and worse, while at Hiruharama the chiefs begged him not to go on, as they warned him that the people farther up had joined the Hau Haus and were all stark raving mad. Mr Booth, however, was grit right through; his brother and their families were in direful danger and he considered it to be his duty, both as a relation and also as an official, to risk everything in trying to save them. He therefore pushed on, trusting to his great influence and friendship with the principal chiefs and tribes to pull him through, so as to enable him to save his brother and their respective families.

On his reaching the landing-place at Pipiriki he immediately saw that whatever influence and friendship he may have, at one time, held over the people was a thing of the past, as, instead of the shouts and songs of welcome by the women, and the gladful rush of young war-riors to haul his canoe up the bank so that he could land dry-shod, all the population lined the high river bank, making hideous grimaces at him and howling like a lot of wild beasts.

Giving up all hope and expecting immediate death, Mr Booth sat quietly in his canoe waiting to receive it with the calm courage of a British pioneer, when suddenly a young but important chief, Hori Patene by name, forced his way through the crowd of yelling savages and, jumping into the canoe, started to *tangi* (shed tears of welcome) and rubbed noses with him. When this ceremony was over Hori per-suaded Mr Booth to go home, and although he fully expected to be cut to pieces every yard of the road, still accompanied and protected by the gallant Hori, he succeeded in reaching his house, where he found his wife and children more than half dead with horror and fear, expecting to be tortured and brutally murdered every minute. No sooner had Mr Booth reached his house than Hori started off and crossed the river, returning with Mr Booth's brother and his family, so that all the whites might be together, under his (Hori's) protection, or, if the worst came to the worst, they could all die in company.

It was now sunset and the Hau Haus began their devotions, and, as the *Niu* had been erected in front of Mr Booth's house, the unfortunate inmates could not help seeing the awful *cantrips* nor hearing the foul incantations. Huge fires were lit, and by their light hundreds of men and women, in parties of about fifty at a time, danced round the pole on which hung poor Captain Lloyd's head. Starting slowly and with low-pitched but deep voices they began to chant the mystic words, Hau Hau Pai Marire, while circling round the ring; but gradually, as the spirit got hold of them, they put on the pace until, like a mob of drunken demoniacs, they leaped, stamped and cavorted round the *Niu* with foul, indecent gestures, grimaces and contortions of body, far beyond the conception of an ordinary human being, while the mystic words were howled out at the top of their *gamuts*, so that they resembled a hideous phantasmagoria such as might be seen by a lunatic suffering from a bad dose of d. t.

Hideous and disgusting as the contortions of the men were, those of the women were worse; for no sooner had the spirit entered into them than in their mad gyrations they leaped at the suspended head, trying, with their teeth, to bite and worry the smoke-dried flesh and hair of the unfortunate officer; and this they continued to do until at length, foaming at the mouth and worn out with their crazy frenzy, they either staggered from the ring or fell in convulsions on the ground, to be dragged away by the next batch of worshippers who were anxiously awaiting their turn. And this awful pandemonium went on all through the night. Just think, my home-staying countrymen and women, who sleep in peace under the guardianship of our splendid police, what must have been the feelings of those English ladies and men who, with their helpless children, had to witness such scenes, knowing and fully expecting, as they did, that at any moment they might be dragged out and, after they had all been subjected to prolonged torture, should then be brutally murdered, with every barbarity and indignity that fiends could invent or devils could inflict.

During the night a council was held and Mr Booth could hear the Taranaki men who had accompanied Matene urging the Wanganui to torture and kill himself and family. Nor did the latter seem to want such urging, as of all his whilom friends only Hori and one other man spoke on his behalf, contesting right manfully that the honour of the

GATEWAY TO MAORI *PAH*

Upper River tribes would be forever disgraced should the white people not be allowed to depart in safety, as they were tribal guests. For two more days and another night the unfortunate whites were kept in suspense, Hori and a few other young chiefs, whom he had persuaded to join him, standing between the would-be murderers and their prey. And these noble young savages eventually saved them.

It was near sunset on the last of these days, and after a very stormy meeting had been held, that Hori rushed into Mr Booth's house, saying: "At last they have consented to let you go. Come at once; leave all your property to me; for they may change their minds any moment." Immediately they jumped up and followed him down to the canoe landing-place. *En route* they had to pass through a swarm of armed Hau Haus who had lined the high river bank, and while doing so Mr Booth heard some of them say: "Wait till they get into the canoe and then we will fire a volley so as to shoot them down in a heap." Hori over heard the same remarks and said to Mr Booth: "Take no notice of them. Go slowly until you are out of sight; I and my friends will keep in the line of fire between you and the Hau Haus." This the gallant young fellow did, and, as the murderous brutes dare not run the risk of killing a Wanganui chief, Mr Booth and his party paddled out of shot and reached the township of Wanganui safely the following night.

The above yarn is a true though short narrative of one of the numerous attempts made by chivalrous Maoris to protect helpless white men from the blind, ferocious fanaticism of Te Ua's prophets. Alas! it was one of the very few successful ones, though many brave natives lost their lives and suffered torture rather than give information to the Hau Haus as to the whereabouts of white fugitives. Surely their names and actions should be remembered.

Immediately after Mr Booth's escape Matene and the Taranaki Hau Haus persuaded the tribes of the Upper Wanganui to attack, with the intention of utterly destroying, the white settlers and thriving township of Wanganui, situated close to the mouth of the river, and at once all hands turned to, to prepare their war canoes for that purpose. Before, however, starting on this expedition, they sent ambassadors to their relations, the Lower River natives, so as to inform them of their purpose, and ask for their co-operation; announcing at the same time that, should their relations not care to join in and make a family party of the expedition, they (the Upper River natives) would still carry out their programme—*viz.* descend the river and wipe out every white man, woman and child in the district!

49

These emissaries, arriving at Hiruharama, a village that may be called the frontier post of the river tribes, delivered their cheeky message, which to the recipients was intolerable, as the Lower River tribes claimed the right-of-way on the river to the westward of Hiruharama, and although it had been frequently attempted in times past, no war party had ever, up to date, succeeded in forcing a passage, and none ever should succeed, so long as a Lower River native warrior could handle musket or swing tomahawk. This being the well-known determination of the Lower River tribes, the chiefs at Hiruharama returned an evasive answer to the Hau Haus, at the same time despatching a fast canoe downstream, so as to warn all their friends of the threatened eruption and give the tip to the white men of their imminent danger.

Then, not being in sufficient strength to withstand the brunt of the encounter, the village was immediately abandoned, all the inhabitants retiring downstream, collecting *en route* the people belonging to the *pahs* Kanaeroa and Tawhitinui; but on reaching Ranana they halted, being joined at that place by the bulk of the warriors of the Lower River. Close to Ranana was the island of Moutoa, a classic battleground, every square yard of which had been drenched with blood, shed in old-time wars, and on this island they determined, should their relations attempt to carry out their threats and try to force their way down the river, to resist them to the last gasp. In the meantime the Hau Haus, uncertain as to what sort of reception they would receive, were cautiously descending the river, and as they found every village deserted they halted at and occupied Tawhitinui, which was situated some two miles above Ranana and on the other bank, and from this place opened negotiations with their relations.

The last few days had been passed by the white population in consternation almost amounting to despair. The outlying farmers and settlers, abandoning homes, stock and everything they owned, rushed into town, where each man anxiously asked his friends: "Can we trust the Lower River natives?" "Will they become converted and join the Hau Haus?" "If so, what then?" True, they possessed one great factor in their favour, and that was the firm and undeviating friendship of old Hori Kingi Te Anaua (the paramount chief of the Lower Waikato), whose name should be remembered and treasured by every white man, woman and child on the west coast of New Zealand. For when the first settlers landed at Wanganui, Hori, then the most renowned warrior on the coast, had taken their leader by the hand, and declared himself to be the friend and protector of the white man, and this promise the pagan cannibal warrior carried out both in letter and spirit till the day of his death. But then, alas! Hori by this time was a very old man, and although the glamour of his great deeds enveloped the aged chief like a halo, and his people regarded him as a being something more than human; still, taking into consideration the astonishing way the crazy Pai Marire faith had been accepted by the Upper River natives as well as by many other tribes, it was very doubtful whether old Hori would be able to restrain them at such a crisis.

Moreover, all the Lower Wanganui natives were strong supporters of the Maori King movement, and many of their important sub-chiefs, especially Mete Kingi Te Anaua, a chief only second to Hori in influence, hated the white men; so that the settlers may well be pardoned for their consternation; as, in case the Lower River natives saw fit to join their relations and become Hau Haus, even should they (the settlers) successfully repulse the combined native attack, and save their own lives, still the township and all the outlying farms must go up in smoke. They therefore made what preparations they could for defence and anxiously waited the termination of the native *runanga* (meeting). As I have previously stated, the Lower River tribes had massed at Ranana, the Hau Haus occupying the adjacent *pah* Tawhitinui, and on 13th May 1864 the prophet Matene, with a numerous deputation of his newly made converts, paddled over to Ranana to open negotiations.

Now it is quite possible, nay, even probable, that had Matene opened the proceedings of the *runanga* with prayer and incantations, as does the British House of Parliament, he would have succeeded in converting the opposition party and so have gained his nefarious ends; but this he did not do, as no sooner had the deputation been announced than Matene issued this insolent ultimatum—*viz.* that they (the Hau Haus) were determined to descend the river, peacefully if allowed to do so, but otherwise would win through by force. Whoop, hullabaloo, that ultimatum, short as it was, upset the fat into the fire and brought Haimona, chief of the Ngatipa-Moana and a mighty fighting man before the Lord, on to his feet, who replied:

Och it's force the river ye'll be after, is it? Well, divil a drop of it ye'll mix wid yer whisky beyand the island of Moutoa; mind yez that, ye black-advised, audacious Hau Haus; but av it's a fight ye want, sure there's that same island Moutoa, that's

51

moighty convanient, and maybe ye'll not want to go furder whin we've finished wid ye; so come on now, M'Matene, Esq., an trid on the tail of me mat, ye ruddy heretic, or get back to the ould Te Ua, an' may the cuss of Cromel rest on him and his Pai Marire monkey tricks.

Now, as I am trying to be a truthful narrator, I am bound to confess that the above is not a verbatim report of the oration spoken by Haimona, although the sentiments expressed in it are exactly similar and both contained a direct challenge; which challenge was immediately accepted, and as there was nothing further to squabble about, both parties went into committee to amicably discuss the coming fight, settle the details and sign the articles, which were as follows:—

1. That a fight should take place the following day on the island of Moutoa.

2. That the freedom of the right of road on the river should be the stake.

3. Seeing that the combatants were closely connected by blood relationship as well as by alliance, and that it would be bad policy to weaken the fighting strength of the combined Wanganui tribes by indiscriminate slaughter, it was therefore agreed that only 100 men a side should take part in the combat.

4. That as the Lower River natives were the owners of the island, they should land on the lower end before daylight. That the Hau Haus should land at the top end at daylight and that their disembarkation should be unopposed.

5. That both sides bound themselves to refrain from all ambuscades, tricks or trickery, but were to meet and fairly fight it out to the bitter end.

Next morning at grey dawn 100 picked men, of the Lower River tribes, were ferried over to Moutoa, landed and arranged themselves in order of battle, divided into two companies of equal strength, and each company was told off into three subdivisions, these being led by renowned warriors. The leading company or van was commanded by Tamehana Te Aewa, who was also C.O. of the whole outfit, who had under him Hemi Napi as leader of the right subdivision, Riwai Tawhitorangi leader of the centre and Kereti of the left. The supporting company was commanded by Haimona, but, through an error in tactics, it had been located 200 yards in rear of the van, a distance far too great for men armed with double-barrelled guns to render effective aid; and this error nearly caused disaster.

To the tick of time the Hau Haus disembarked at the top end of the island but, alas! their pristine chivalry had been already tainted by their infernal religion, as they landed 130 men instead of the stipulated number, which was not cricket. They had also a powerful moral factor in their favour—*viz.* they (the Hau Haus) believed themselves to be invulnerable, while most of their opponents more than half believed the same thing, so that, notwithstanding their splendid courage and determination, very many of the latter considered themselves to be hopelessly handicapped in having to fight against men who were aided by angels. This nervousness must have increased as Tamehana led the leading company on to the attack, for when within thirty yards of the Hau Haus the centre and left subdivisions fired a volley, of which every bullet flew wide, not one single Hau Hau being hurt; of course this vile shooting had the effect of confirming the fears of the Lower River natives and exhilarating their opponents.

The latter made haste to return the volley, and just as they did so a Roman Catholic lay brother rushed in between the combatants, exhorting them to terminate this fratricidal strife. Poor devil, he met with the end that many men who interfere with family jars do meet with, as the volley finished him off before he could finish his first argument; and it has often been a matter of speculation to me as to whether he was a martyr or only an interfering busybody. This same volley also was a most disastrous one for the Lower River natives: Riwai and Kereti with many of their men fell dead, while the survivors of their own subdivisions, disheartened by the loss of their leaders, and now fully convinced of the invulnerability of the Hau Haus, broke their ranks and fell back in disorder, Hemi Nape and his men, however, refused to fly and in a few moments proved that at all events some of the Hau Haus were far from being immortal, much less invulnerable.

Fine fighters Hemi Nape and his boys, were and well they bore themselves, but alas! how could they, less than twenty in number, withstand such overwhelming odds?—so that though they fought like fiends incarnate still they were driven back and must have been quickly wiped out. Help, however, was at hand, for suddenly old Tamehana Te Aewa, with the roar of a wild bull, threw himself into the vortex of the combat and, begorra! he made things lively. You see, when the centre and left subdivisions gave way he tried to rally them, but failing to do so he returned alone to the fight, so as to throw in his lot with the lads who scorned to fly. Just at the moment he arrived Hemi had ordered his men to take cover, but that did not suit Tamehana, who charged the Hau Haus like a whirlwind and killed two of them with a clean right and left; then, throwing away his empty gun, he picked up a spear dropped by one of the dead men and drove it through a third one's body, grabbing, as the dying man fell, his gun and *tomahawk*.

The gun was unfortunately not loaded, but he made use of it by braining a fourth man with the butt and then sank the blade of the tomahawk so deep into a fifth man's skull that as he tried to wrench it out the tough handle went to splinters. Immediately he seized his last victim's gun and was about to use it when a bullet struck him in the arm, and he had just time to shoot the man who had wounded him when another smashed his right knee to pieces and put a termination to his day's sport. When he fell the Hau Haus made a rush to finish him off, which rush was met by a counter-charge of Hemi Nape's men, who, although they were all wounded, determined to die rather than allow old Tamehana to be killed or captured. Led by Marino, Hemi's son, for Hemi himself had been shot dead a moment before, they threw themselves on the Hau Haus and made such a determined stand that it gave time to Haimona with his supporting company to come into action.

This grim old warrior had been originally posted too far in rear of the van and had lost some time in rallying the fugitives, whom he tongue-lashed out of their cowardly nervousness, his endeavours being helped by the scornful yells and entreaties of the men and women spectators, who, mad with excitement, watched the apparently lost battle from the bank of the river. Then promptly adding the whilom runaways to his own party, he rapidly advanced to make his effort. There was no fear now of the late fugitives turning tail again, for nigh crazy with shame and contrition, they would far sooner face a thousand deaths than be branded as cowards through the length and breadth of New Zealand.

Deflecting his advance to the right, he cleared the expiring struggle in which the remnant of Hemi's men were still dying hard, and then by a quick change of front to the left he outflanked the Hau Haus and at close quarters poured in two death-dealing volleys that decimated the fanatics. Then without a moment's delay "out *tomahawks*" was the order and, led by Haimona himself, the newcomers rushed madly into the fray. Immediately the aspect of the combat changed. Up to this time the Hau Haus had had much the best of it, but now fickle

54

Fortune turned her back upon them and old Tamehana's *bearsark* rush, together with the glorious stand made by Hemi Nape's men, were to reap their reward; as from the moment Haimona's party took a hand in the game the Upper River natives had to fight, not for conquest, but for their lives. The volleys they had received had killed several important chiefs and many men, while the furious charge of Haimona's party on their left flank all but routed them; still they were Maori warriors, as brave as any men on earth, and although broken and confused they turned to meet the attack with the greatest courage.

Now began the last phase of a fight that Homer himself would have loved to sing about. Howling for blood, Haimona's men rushed into hand-to-hand combat. Both sides had discarded their guns, both sides ceased from yelling as they came chest to chest, but the tomahawks gave out a sharp click, as they clashed against one another in the air, that provided the alto part to the sickening scrunch of the inflicting wound, the guttural grunt of the wounder and the sobbing groan of the wounded. Faith! it was a fine fight.

The impetuosity of the desperate charge bore the Hau Haus backwards, and in spite of their furious efforts they were forced to continue the retrograde movement, for the Lower River Maoris, fighting as they were with their tribesmen and women looking on, outdid their best, while the men who had previously fled, madly anxious to obliterate their shame, and who, careless of wounds and death, only strove to kill, fought like demons. The Hau Haus were therefore steadily driven back, and as the bloody tussle continued they at last reached the shore of the island, when, unable to make a stand, or retire farther, those that remained on their feet were forced to plunge into the rapid current and attempt to escape by swimming. Of these but few reached the opposite bank, and of those who were lucky enough to do so twenty were captured by Mete Kingi, who, with 350 Lower River warriors, had watched the fight.

The end of the prophet Matene brought the whole show to a tragical finale. He had fought bravely through the fight; for, as it is only right to give the devil his due, I may here state that all of Te Ua's prophets were game to lead any cracked-brained exploit they might have persuaded their misguided disciples to undertake, and consequently vacancies frequently occurred in the apostolic ranks. Well, Matene was still alive when the remnant of his men were forced into the river, so he had to frog it with them, and was swimming away for all he was worth when the eagle eye of Haimona spotted him. The chief turned to his *aide-de-camp*, Te Moro, and handed him his bone mere (a short battle-axe made out of whalebone and greatly used by the natives before the introduction of steel- bladed tomahawks), at the same time pointing out the fugitive and remarking: "There is your fish." In plunged Te Moro, who, swimming rapidly, overtook his prey and grabbed him just as he reached the bank. In vain the prophet tried to save himself by his incantations: "*Hau Hau, Pai Marire. Hau*—" He gasped the remainder of his discourse, being interrupted by a smashing cut from the mere, and Te Moro swam back, towing the dead body, which he threw down at Haimona's feet.

The fight being over, it was now necessary to count the cost. Out of the 130 Hau Haus who had landed 70 lay dead, 20 badly wounded and 20 were prisoners, all the balance, with the exception of one who was known to have made his escape, being probably more or less disabled, were drowned. The loss of the Lower River natives was 16 killed and 50 badly wounded; so that it may be called a very good fight indeed, second only to that remarkable combat between the two Kilkenny tom cats—but then they were Irish, you know.

The result of this family fall-out effectually saved the white settlers, as, in the first place, it put a limit to the spread of the Pai Marire religion on the Wanganui River and prevented the Lower River natives from casting in their lot with the Hau Haus, which, probably, they would have done had Matene approached them in a conciliatory manner instead of rubbing them up the wrong way, by threatening to force the right-of-way on the river. The township was saved, as were also the outlying farms and much stock, and the settlers showed their appreciation of the Lower River natives' gallant conduct by attending *en masse* the obsequies of the chiefs and warriors killed in the fight. This side show, as one may call it, to the general war that was then raging all over the country was kept up in a desultory sort of way and ended in so quaint a manner that I think I may be pardoned for relating the facts.

After the gentle passage-at-arms on Moutoa, the discomfited, but still bigoted, Upper River natives retired to their own country, halting when they reached Ohotahi, a *pah* situated higher up the river but close to Hiruharama. Here they fortified themselves, being allowed ample time to do so by their chivalrous opponents, as it would have been bad form and quite foreign to Maori war etiquette for one enemy to attack another until the defenders had made everything ready for their assailants' reception. It was therefore not until February 1865 that a strong party of the Lower River Maoris, under the command of Honi Hipango, advanced up the river and commenced the siege. At the first Honi gained some advantages, and a few men were killed on either side, though much time was lost in ceremonious sparring; but at last they really got to work, and Honi was preparing to rush the place when he was mortally wounded.

His death enraged his men, and the final charge was moving forward when a woman came out of the gate, waving a white flag; she was quickly recognised as being the wife of Pehi Turoa, who in reality was the great ancestral chief of both sections of the Wanganui tribe. The appearance of this aristocratic old dame at once caused an immediate cessation of hostilities, the firing ceased, and both sides, quitting their shelter trenches, met together, squatted down and commenced an elaborate *tangi* (ceremonious weeping), in which they mutually bewailed the killed on both sides; for the reader must remember that both factions were closely connected by blood.

The Lower River natives were now on the horns of a dilemma; eighty Hau Haus were at their mercy, among them being Pehi Turoa himself, and these unfortunates should, by all the rules of the game, be at once immolated as *utu* for the death of Honi Hipango, Esq. But it was impossible for them to slaughter, in cold blood, their own relations; neither could they make their own kinsmen prisoners, especially old Pehi, for that would smother themselves with dishonour, as it would degrade their own great hereditary chief and a number of their own blood relations to the status of slavery, which would entail shameful ignominy on the whole of the Wanganui tribe. What then should be done with Pehi and his party? It was a very hard nut to crack, and all hands went into committee to solve the problem, which was at last done in this way, Pehi himself being the fount of wisdom from which the adopted suggestion emanated:

The old chief propounded that whereas, for reasons stated above, it was inexpedient that himself and party should be knocked on the head, or degraded to slaves, the only other course open was to let them go; and that, as it was unseemly for warriors to promenade around the country unarmed, it would be necessary for them to take their weapons with them. And to this suggestion both parties gave a cordial assent.

A treaty was therefore made in which both factions resolved that they would allow no religious rancour to disunite again the Wanganui tribe, and that although each party retained the right to fight on the side of either white man or Hau Hau, yet that said fighting must be enjoyed outside their own country: and this compact was honourably kept to the end of the war. Up till 1869 the Upper River natives as a whole sat tight, then joined us so as to exact *utu* on Te Kooti for the murder of one of Turoa's relations. The Lower River natives became our most staunch allies, for being men of discernment they quickly tumbled to the fact that it was far more humorous and better sport to fight their old-time enemies, the Taranaki Hau Haus, and draw pay and rations while enjoying their favourite "divarsion," than to stay at home, or, like their misguided relatives, dance round a pole and howl, "*Hau Hau, Pai Marire.*"

I think before I terminate this yarn I may tell you about a rather quaint incident that happened during the siege of Ohotaki, and as it portrays an idiosyncrasy or trait in Maori character you will pardon my doing so.

Well, one night a party of Lower River natives attempted to surprise an outlying detached post they knew to be weakly held. They crawled up to the place, and were about to rush it when a woman's voice called out: "Take care what you do; Te Miere and Te Mokena are here"—these being the names of two aged men at that time quite past fighting, but who, in their prime, had been mighty warriors of great and bloody renown. At once the storming party retired, for to have captured a place the garrison of which contained two such notable veterans would have injured the prestige of both parties in the eyes of the fighting population throughout New Zealand.

CHAPTER 3

How a Scout Won the New Zealand Cross

Up to the year 1879 the Victoria Cross was not to be won by any officer or man of H.M. Colonial Forces, although one civilian (Cavanagh) had received it during the Indian Mutiny, yet in New Zealand the greatest honour to be won by a Britisher was denied to all but those actually serving in H.M. regular army or navy. This being so, the New Zealand Government obtained royal sanction to issue a similar cross, only manufactured out of gold and silver instead of bronze, to be won by the Colonial troops, and this decoration is designated the New Zealand Cross.

The yarn I am now going to spin you is how Trooper George Hill won his while employed as a scout on the east coast.

In March 1869 the great hardships, the bitter weather, the large number of wounded and, above all, the cowardice of our allies, the Arawa tribe, by far the most pampered by Government, and the only New Zealand tribe that can be called cowards, necessitated the Colonial Field Force falling back from the high plateau of Taupo to Fort Galatea to recuperate and refit. This gave Te Kooti leisure to look around for more devilments, and he determined to strike another blow at the settlements on the east coast. Calling a meeting of the Hau Hau tribes at Ruatahuna, he proposed to attack the friendly natives and the white settlers at Mohaka or Te Wairoa.

The former place was chosen and Te Kooti, with 100 bloodthirsty fiends, started to carry out the raid. Crossing the Huiarau ranges they came to the Waikare Moana Lake. Here one of those chance occurrences happened that enabled the astute Te Kooti to keep his hold over the superstitious natives. On reaching the lake he issued orders that no man was to cross over before he did so himself This order was disobeyed, for a canoe full of warriors at once started. The lake, a very large one and, like all others, surrounded by high mountains, is subject to being swept by sudden and heavy squalls. One of these overtook the disobedient warriors, capsized their canoe and although all managed to get ashore, yet one died from exhaustion, the remainder losing all their arms, food, etc.

Te Kooti took advantage of this disaster and made capital out of it. He informed his men that the order he had promulgated had been issued direct from God, and that the disobedient warriors had been punished for non-compliance with it. Then, seeing the weather was propitious, he entered a canoe and crossed in safety, his men following without further misadventure. Te Kooti by doing so gained much credit in the prophet line and stricter obedience from his superstitious followers. The lake being crossed, they pushed on without delay to the Upper Mohaka, surprised before daylight the Arakaihi village, and butchered every soul in it, man, woman and child, with the tomahawk, so as not to alarm some settlers on the other side of the river. When daylight came they crossed the river and murdered with the greatest brutality two white men with their wives and three little children, as also they did another white settler who was unfortunate enough to fall into their hands alive.

Not satisfied with his morning's successful battue, Te Kooti and his gang, now increased to 200 men, hurried on to the Lower Mohaka, which consisted of two friendly *pahs*, with a sprinkling of white settlers, a public-house, store, etc. They arrived there early in the day and at once attacked the smallest *pah*, known as the Huke Pah. The Mohaka friendlies had received news of Te Kooti's rapid approach and had sent messengers to warn the troops stationed at Te Wairoa, only nineteen miles away, and the authorities at Napier fifty miles distant (of this more anon).

Nearly all the Mohaka warriors were absent, and the garrison of the Huke Pah consisted of six men and a large number of women and children. One of the defenders, however, named Heta, was a grand specimen of a Maori warrior, and under his influence they kept the Hau Haus at bay all that day and night, and might have held out, had not Te Kooti resorted to stratagem and by a foul piece of treachery succeeded in entering the works early the following morning, when he caused every living being, regardless of sex and age, to be massacred in cold blood.

He then turned his attention to the other *pah*, Hiruharama, which was garrisoned by only ten men, but also contained many women and children. Here he again tried treachery, but this time failed, as the defenders had seen what had happened at Huke and were determined to die fighting. He therefore had to commence to sap up to the palisades, which were old and rotten, but the nature of the ground, very hard limestone, delayed him.

It was now that Trooper George Hill chipped in and took a hand.

Te Kooti's lightning raid had been well conceived and brilliantly carried out, but luck was decidedly in his favour, as unfortunately it so chanced that the officers in charge of the safety of Hawke's Bay district were on the whole a very poor lot, as far as efficiency went. Many of the regular Colonial officers had been killed or rendered *hors de combat* during the previous twelve months, the remainder were with the Field Forces at the front, so that the duty of guarding the settlements was left in the hands of the militia or volunteer officers, and these were quite unfit to cope with Te Kooti.

They had plenty of good men, both friendly natives and volunteers, with a sufficiency of Armed Constabulary (the Colonial Regulars) to give them backbone, but the officers (unfortunately) considered discretion to be the better part of valour and mistook timidity for prudence, so much so that they missed their chance and covered themselves with something like disgrace. At Te Wairoa the O.C. had at his disposal 50 mounted men, 25 of whom were Armed Constabulary, splendidly trained and mounted, the other 25 armed settlers, all good men. He also had 200 friendly natives, and the whole of these men were simply spoiling for a fight.

With one half of them he could have saved the Huke Pah, and cut up the Hau Haus, very many of whom had sacked the public-house and were lying about dead drunk; but he did nothing, for on receipt of the news, which was quickly confirmed, and although he was quite aware of the weakness of the *pah's* garrison, he asserted he still had doubts as to the truth of his information and only despatched Trooper George Hill, of the Armed Constabulary, to see if Te Kooti was really playing high jinks at the Mohaka.

Trooper Hill left Te Wairoa, on horseback, and rode in the direction of the Mohaka. About halfway he met two mounted settlers, Lamplough and Burton, who, having heard of Te Kooti's advent, were doing a scout on their own; these men at once offered to accompany him, and did so. On reaching the vicinity of the Mohaka they dismounted, tied up their horses and crept up a ridge from which they could observe the place. From this point of vantage they could see the Huke Pah, with the flag still flying, and also the puffs of smoke from the rifle pits of the enemy, so that they were fairly able to judge the number of the attackers and locate the positions they occupied.

As there could now be no longer any doubt that Te Kooti and his gang were on the warpath. Trooper Hill, leaving the two settlers, both of them good men, on the ridge to observe the enemy, mounted his horse and returned towards the camp as fast as he could get his horse to go. Unfortunately his horse knocked up, but just then he met three of his comrades, who had been sent out to look for him. Despatching one of them to Te Wairoa with his report. Hill and the other two men, Tew and Mitchell, returned to Mohaka. Here they tied up their horses and joined the settlers on the ridge, so as to keep the enemy under observation and be able to supply the O.C. of the relieving force with information.

Of course the A.C. troopers never doubted that a relieving force would be sent at once, probably wondered why there was not one on the job already; but they were not accustomed to militia officers. Their own officers had no use for timidity, and regarded prudence and discretion as very good horses only to be trotted out at long intervals; anyhow, not one of the men on the ridge would have believed an angel, had he informed them that no relieving party would be sent at all.

The five men remained on the ridge till after dark, and then descended to the flat where they had tied up their horses. They had, however, been guilty of an act of folly, insomuch that they had not left one of their number in charge of their mounts, for on reaching the place where they had left them tied up they found one of them had broken his tether rope and had levanted. As it was necessary to find the brute, Hill and Tew started away on foot to do so, each man taking his own line of search. The other men, instead of remaining quiet, waited a few minutes, then mounted their horses and rode over the flat to assist in the hunt. While doing so, in the pitch darkness, they stumbled over Tew and foolishly challenged him in Maori. He promptly answered with a carbine shot that killed Lamplough's horse.

Burton, fancying Tew to be a Hau Hau, returned the fire, his horse at once bucking him off and galloping away. The third man. Trooper Mitchell, hearing the firing and the galloping of the horses, thought they were attacked by the enemy, so, shouting to Hill to run, he rode as hard as he could in the direction he fancied his comrade had taken, in order to assist him. He had not gone far when his horse turned turtle over a flax bush, fell with him, getting away and galloping off. All of the five men were now dismounted, each man thinking he was surrounded by Hau Haus, so they all bolted for an adjacent flax swamp and hid in the water all the remainder of the night—a just punishment for their carelessness and folly. Daylight revealed the fiasco, and as they were dismounted they took cover and waited for the relief party that did not come.

Towards midday 100 Maoris turned up under the command of a grand old fighting chief, Ihaka Whanga, but less than 30 of them were to be relied on, the rest semi Hau Haus, as much to be feared as trusted.

At once the ridge was lined and Hill saw that the Huke Pah had fallen, but that the Hiruharama Pah still held out though closely invested. The garrison, seeing friends on the ridge, shouted to them for assistance, as there were not enough men to hold the place should it be rushed. Among Ihaka Whanga's party were twenty-five Mohaka men, and these were the boys ready and willing to grasp at any plan, no matter how desperate, to relieve their relations and save the honour of their *pah*. George Hill was the man for the emergency. He explained the only plan was to cut their way through the besiegers. He was game to lead, were the twenty-five game to follow? Of course they were. So, without any thought of prudence, discretion, or even modesty, Hill whipped off his boots, tunic, and riding breeches, so as to be able to run the better, and the gallant twenty-six, shouting their war-cry, charged the Hau Hau rifle pits.

Yes, they charged and charged home, for they broke their way, by sheer pluck and hard hitting, right through the ranks of the enemy (Hill killing his man *en route*) and reached the gate of the *pah*, which they entered, only two of them being wounded during the rush.

The men left on the ridge opened fire on the Hau Hau rifle pits, until Te Kooti sent a party to take them in the rear, when the untrustworthy natives all bolted, the four white men retired, and only old Ihaka with two of his men were left. These three splendid warriors held the position to the last gasp, then Ihaka gave the word to scatter and try to get away. The two men were caught and killed, but the old veteran managed to elude his pursuers and reach Te Wairoa in safety, where he gave the O.C. his opinion of his conduct.

On Hill entering the *pah* he found it to be manned by small boys

A Maori girl

and girls, standing on mounds of earth and stones to enable them to fire over the parapet, and that even with his twenty-five men he had not nearly enough hands to man the works. He at once went to the point of the greatest danger, a bastion, and could hear the Hau Haus sapping through the hard ground. He quickly noticed that the palisades were rotten, so much so that if the enemy could sap near enough to throw a pole, attached to a long rope, over the fence, a strong pull on the rope would cause such a breach that a storming party could at once enter, when numbers must gain the day. Fortunately there was in the *pah* a number of oxen chains; the ends of these he made fast to the big corner posts of the work, and passed the chains outside the weak palisades, so rendering that style of attack abortive.

In the bastion with him he had only two men, two small boys and three little girls, supplemented occasionally by the Maori clergyman, who, between long prayers for the safety of his flock, hurled all the vituperations and cuss words to be found in the sacred writings at the heads of Te Kooti and his followers.

Hill, when he entered the *pah*, was famished for want of food; he naturally asked for some, and was furnished with a cup of tea, one biscuit and one apple. Surprised at such meagre fare, tendered by the most hospitable people on earth, he asked for more and then ascertained that the food he had just eaten was the very last particles of provisions the place contained. But the garrison swore that before they surrendered they would eat their own children rather than let them fall into the hands of Te Kooti.

All the remainder of that day and the ensuing night heavy firing was kept up, the Hau Haus attempting to tear down the palisades; but they were, thanks to Hill's dodge with the oxen chains, unable to gain an entrance, although the defenders had frequently to rush from side to side of the works to oppose them. At daylight next morning it was discovered the enemy had constructed a line of rifle pits, close to the front face of the *pah*, on which were hoisted flags, and at sunrise, with much bugling, volley after volley was poured into the defenders' works.

Hill mustered his scanty and tired garrison to repel the expected rush, and lay quiet, having directed his men to reserve their fire till the rush was made.

After some considerable time had passed the flags were suddenly withdrawn, the bugling and volleys ceased, and a dead silence ensued. The defenders, on the *qui vive* for some fresh devilry, sat tight, until one of them, unable to stand the suspense any longer, crept out and crawled to the edge of the cliff to reconnoitre. He reached the edge, took one glance, and was on his feet in a second, letting out a wild whoop of triumph. Out tumbled man, woman and child; they lined the edge of the cliff, and with one accord broke into a wild war-dance (the parson leading), for still close, but in full retreat, they saw Te Kooti and his baffled gang of murderers. Oh, but it was a glorious triumph, and must be celebrated with befitting honours, that the great false prophet with his much-feared, blood-smeared warriors had to turn their backs on a nearly defenceless *pah*, whose garrison consisted chiefly of women and children.

Trooper George Hill, however, had his duty to perform; he had no time for feasts nor triumphs, for although the Maoris begged him to remain, assuring him the roads would be ambuscaded, he caught one of Te Kooti's knocked-up horses and started along the Napier Road, so as to convey the intelligence that the Hau Haus had retreated. Twelve miles along the track he met with the advance guard of the re-lieving column, who had taken three days to do a journey that should have been completed in eight hours. The men, mad with the procrastination and incompetency of their officers, were nearly in a state of mutiny, but it was of no avail; for although Trooper Hill reported Te Kooti had retreated, and offered to guide the mounted men on his track, and at all events regain the plunder, nothing was done, and the Hau Haus were allowed to retire in peace.

There is no need for me to say any more about the officers, plenty was said about them at the time they were incapable; let them rip.

Trooper Hill, however, did not think he had yet finished his work, for as soon as he had snatched a bite of food he volunteered to go out and scout for some of the unfortunate white women and children who were known to be fugitives or hidden in the wild bush and fern ranges. This he did, and succeeded in finding, relieving and bringing into safety several of the wretched, starving creatures, who otherwise must have died from privations.

Trooper George Hill received the New Zealand Cross, and I for one say he richly deserved it, not only for the courage he displayed in action, but also his gallant conduct saved the honour and repute of the white man amongst the friendly Maoris who were disgusted by the unfortunate behaviour of the officers.

CHAPTER 4

A Hau Hau Martyr

Let me spin you a yarn of how a Maori was so imbued with fanaticism that he faced in cold blood extinction for the same.

Many of the Hau Haus, bloodthirsty, cruel fanatics as they were, whom the Colonial forces ruthlessly knocked on the head during the latter half of the New Zealand wars, are just as much entitled to be enrolled in the army of martyrs as are the early Christians or any other poor devils who have perished by fire or sword for believing and sticking to their faith.

Again, there are many instances of Hau Haus who were so strong in their convictions that they of their own free will deliberately offered themselves up to undergo the fiery ordeal by leaving their harbours of safety and, unarmed, trusting alone to spiritual aid, faced certain death; and I have never read of any persecuted communities doing the same.

When in 1865 the Pai Marire religion was promulgated by a demented Maori named Te Ua, the two principal promises held out to induce the Maoris to join the new religion were: first, that they should be rendered invulnerable in action; and, secondly, that they should be granted the gift of tongues. They were also promised the assistance of legions of angels, and that those white soldiers who were not turned into stone should with the rest of the settlers be driven into the sea, after which the natives should be given the knowledge of all the European arts and sciences. Please note he made no promise about a future state, nor, like Mahomet, did he invent any gorgeous paradise, thronged with pretty girls, where free drinks would be served out *ad libitum*.

Now these were queer promises to captivate a Maori warrior, as after the first excitement there was but little in them to induce him to abandon Christianity and cling to Hau Hauism, Let us take them *seriatim*, remembering at the same time that the Maori is an astute reasoner. First of all the promise of invulnerability. Well, that would be all right so long as they only had to fight against the white man, but the *pakeha* was to be driven out, and what would follow then? War was the Maori's greatest pleasure, and each tribe hated his neighbour quite as much as he hated the white man. Yet his neighbour was to become just as invulnerable as he was to be himself.

Where, therefore, would be the fun if he could not kill his enemy, eat him, nor turn his bones into useful and ornamental articles? Bah! the zest of war would be gone. Then again the second promise. What on earth use could the gift of tongues be to a man when there was not to be a single foreigner left in the country with whom to *collogue?* As for the other promises, they were not worth a row of pins, for if the warriors became invulnerable they wanted no further angelic aid; and as far as acquiring the arts and sciences went, so long as they could learn how to make rum and grow tobacco, all the rest could go swing, they being willing to live as their fathers had lived before them.

Now I am sure that if the natives had only reasoned as I have just done they would not have thrown off their Christianity in such a hurry and become stark raving Hau Haus; but they seem on this occasion to have lost their wits altogether, for, carried away by the crazy incantations of Te Ua's apostles, they not only embraced the new faith, but believed in the truth of it, so much so that there are plenty of instances of their laying down their lives for it—and no man can do more.

Another wonderful thing- is that even after four years' continuous fighting, during which period the angel had not only failed to bear a hand, but had not even rendered one man invulnerable, as apostle, priest and warrior had been put out of mess by the white man's bullet, still they were strong in their faith, and there are plenty of instances of Hau Haus, believing in the promise of the angel, offering their bodies as a target so as to prove the truth of their religion. And now for the yarn.

The scene is a Maori *kainga* on the east coast of New Zealand, date 1869, time of day about 9 a.m. The village, composed of some twenty huts, stands in a clearing surrounded by dense bush, and in the foreground stands the *Niu*, the sacred pole round which the fanatics perform their mad dances and mystic incantations. I said it was a Maori *kainga*; so it had been, though the only Maoris at present inside it are perhaps a score, and these lie about very dead indeed. The remainder of its whilom inhabitants have fled away into the depths of the bush and are safe from the pursuit of the strong party of Colonial Irregulars, who, having, after a long, wearying night's march, surprised and rushed the place at daybreak, are now in occupation of it. These men, having eaten their frugal meal, and worn out by their overnight's march, with the exception of the guard lie around booted and belted and with their carbines by their sides, trying to get what sleep they can, as at any moment they may again be called upon for active service.

On the low fence surrounding the *Niu* ring, which is about thirty feet in diameter, the ground within the magic circle being trampled as hard and smooth as stone pavement by the feet of its former worshippers, lounge some half-dozen officers smoking and dozing. The day is a fine one, the sun shines hot, the white men rest, the Hau Haus, far away in the recesses of the bush, bind up their wounds and talk of *utu* (revenge). No, not all of them, for the undergrowth parts and out into the clearing strides a big, stark-naked Maori, who, without paying the slightest attention to any of the astonished and by now wide-awake men, passes through them and, without apparently seeing the group of officers, enters the *Niu* ring, where, after saluting the pole, he prances slowly round it, chanting in a minor key the words: "*Hau Hau, Pai Marire*" (Wind, wind, good, peaceful), over and over again.

Gradually he gets up steam and, paying no attention to the throng of armed enemies who now surround the mystic circle, he cavorts higher and faster, while his monotonous chant is raised to the full gamut of his deep, bass voice. Presently he foams at the mouth, his features become distorted, sweat pours through his skin like water, on his hands held rigid his fingers quiver, while with leaps and bounds his stamping feet beat time to the chant of "*Hau Hau, Pai Marire*."

How long this exhibition would have continued the Lord only knows, for it was brought to a sudden termination by a big Scotch Presbyterian sergeant, who, being as bigoted as they make them, could not tolerate the ritual of a foreign denomination, so he stepped out of the crowd of men and, as the fanatic devotee pranced past him, he with a leg as brawny as that of a Highland stot let fly a kick, at the same time exclaiming: "Hae done, ye pagan, wi yer satanic *cantrips*." Out flew the No. 12 boot, which, catching the unfortunate bounder fair and square on the crupper bone, launched him through space till, the momentum being expended, he landed on his nose at the Colonel's feet.

"Get up," quoth the O.C. in Maori, at the same time giving the officious non-com. a look that made the ower-guid mon wilt. "Now, what made you come here?"

The colonel spoke the language like a native, and what he did not know about Hau Haus was not worth learning, so he was not in the least bit surprised when the somewhat blown native staggered to his feet and answered him in perfect English: "I came here among you to turn you all into stone, and should have done so had not that man, whose head is fit to be boiled, interrupted me."

"Ah," replied the O.C, "I know you; you assisted Nama to torture women and children at Poverty Bay."

"I did," triumphantly exclaimed the fanatic, "Sweet is the blood of women and children." (Note this fellow had been mission bred and educated, in fact had acted as a lay Bible reader.)

"Ah, is it," growled the colonel. "Sergeant O'Halloran, detail four men, take this fellow to that tree and do your duty."

The sergeant saluted smartly, quickly told off four men, advanced to his prisoner, whose arm he grasped with a shoulder-of-mutton fist, at the same time exclaiming: "Come along wid me, ye bloody-minded Fenian."

A few steps took them to the huge tortara-tree that had been pointed out, against the trunk of which the sergeant, drawing his revolver, placed the Hau Hau. "And now," said he, "a Christian ye were wance, and a bloody pagan ye are now, bad luck to the likes of ye, but ave ye wist to recant and make yer sowl, sure it's foive minutes I'll give ye to make it.—Fall in, boys, tin yards forninst us."

Now no good soldier man, be he regular or irregular, likes to make one of a firing party, told off to shoot a man in cold blood, law or no law, and it is usual in such cases to detail the worst characters in a regiment to perform that obnoxious duty; but when it comes to letting daylight into a fiend who brags of having tortured helpless women and children, then no frontiersman jibs at making one of a party to do so. Therefore, no matter how distasteful the job might be to any of the four men told off on this special occasion, they fell in with great alacrity and brought their carbines to the shoulder like one man.

"Hurry up, ye spalpeen, and make yer sowl," quoth the sergeant.

"You can't shoot me," replied the fanatic, "the great Gabriel and all his angels protect me; you can't kill me,"

"Nabocklish" (maybe not), answered the imperturbable non-com., "but by the holy poker we'll have a darned good try. Will yez call on the blessed saints or not, ye contumacious blaggard?"

"*Hau Hau, Pai Marire,*" shouted the fanatic, raising his arms, stretching them to the full extent and turning the hands, palms outwards, towards the firing party.

"Ah, thin ye won't," growled the now somewhat enraged noncom.; "thin go to hell yer own way. Ready!"

"*Hau Hau, Pai Marire,*" yelled the fanatic.

"Present! "ordered the Sergeant.

"*Hau Hau, Pai Marire,*" triumphantly shrieked the Maori.

"Fire!"

"*Hau Hau*" *bang* came all together, and the misguided fanatic, smote full in the chest by four Sneider bullets, collapsed and fell on his face as dead as Julius Caesar.

Now was that Hau Hau, blood-stained brute as he undoubtedly was, a martyr or only a bally fool? Remember, he had only a few hours previously escaped from out of a sharp fight in which many of his co-religionists had been killed, and after winning through to safety himself he is so strong in his faith that he voluntarily returns alone and unarmed to justify the truth of his conviction, although he well knows he is facing certain death providing he be wrong in his belief.

You may call him which or what you please, but I maintain that he is just as much to be enrolled in the army of martyrs as any of the poor devils who were stretched on red-hot gridirons, or were put to death in other unpleasant ways, for testifying to what they believed to be the truth.

CHAPTER 5

A Brush With Bushrangers
(Told by the Old Identity)

In Australia, during the early seventies, bush- rangers were still to the fore, who with cattle-thieves and hostile blacks made the squatters on the back blocks keep their eyes skinned, and the banker in the bush townships cash a cheque with one hand, while he kept the other on his revolver.

True the mounted police were very good, none better, but, like the British army, there were not enough of them, and the amount of work in covering, protecting and patrolling such enormous areas of country was far beyond what their limited number could properly do. Indeed, there are plenty of well-known cases where the bushrangers have overcome the police, handcuffed them in their own station, then stuck up the bank and, after raiding the town, started off on the best horses in the place and disappeared into the bush, not to be heard of again until they bailed up a coach, or stuck up some station, perhaps 150 miles away. Well, to get on with my yarn.

Some six and thirty years ago I was on leave in Australia, and was putting in some of it as a guest on a large cattle run and sheep station owned by two old friends of mine who had already become wealthy men, and who owned an enormous number of cattle and sheep.

The house, like most of its sort at that time in Australia, was built of split slabs of wood, with a shingle roof. It contained four good-sized rooms and a very wide hall running right through it, which was used as a dining-room and lounge.

The kitchen and offices were close to, in rear of the house, and the men's quarters, stables, store and outhouses were nearby. The whole block of buildings stood in the open, and was surrounded by wire-fenced paddocks, so that no one could approach within a long distance of the house on any side without being seen. My friends' home staff at that time consisted of six white men, all good and to be relied upon, also two China boy-cooks, and a few aborigines (black fellows) who were used as trackers and stock-riders. All of these men were well armed, so that with our three selves we made a garrison quite able to beat off any attack of bushrangers or blacks,

I had come up from Brisbane with one of the partners to join in mustering semi-wild cattle, cutting them off from the bush by moon-light and driving them into a mob of tame cattle driven along for the purpose, and then forcing them into a run that led to the stockyards, where they would be drafted and disposed of. There is no more ex-citing work in the world for a good horseman who is well mounted, can use a stock whip, and who puts no excessive value on his neck or bones.

The cutting-out was to begin next week, and some of the best of my friends' numerous and splendid stud of horses had been brought in from the paddocks and fed up on hard food, so as to get them into good fettle and wind for the work.

At Brisbane and all the way up by Cob & Co.'s coach we had heard plenty of shaves about bushrangers, especially of one gang led by a scoundrel called Ginger, who, having been hunted over the border from New South Wales, was making things lively in Queensland; as if that colony had not sufficient blackguards of her own growth to look after. These shaves were confirmed at the small bush township, where we left the coach, by the solitary trooper in charge there, who informed my companion that the sergeant and other troopers were away on patrol after this bounder.

There was no telegraphic communication in those days, and all the information we could get was that Ginger's gang consisted of four, or it might be eight, men. So our traps having been placed in a light cart that had been sent for them, we mounted two slashing horses and rode the forty miles to the station, my friend hearing the news from his head stock-rider, named Blake, who had brought over the horses. This man, a splendid stamp of a Sidney-side Colonial, was convinced we should hear more of Mr Ginger, but feared we should be disap-pointed in our muster, as our neighbours, having to look after their own homes, would not come in for it.

Well, we reached the station, and I put in two days very content-edly indeed, picking and trying my horses, selecting a stock-whip and kit, and amusing myself generally, so much so that on the evening of the second day, after a good dinner, when we were sitting smoking under the verandah, I bothered my head not at all about Ginger. Presently one of my friends looked up and said: "Hallo, here's someone coming, and in no end of a hurry too." We looked and saw the township trooper riding as fast as he could get his horse to travel towards us. He reached us and dismounted, giving his pumped-out horse to one of the blacks who had come for it, and took and drank thankfully the proffered drink, then said: "Mr—Ginger is in the district, and I have been riding since yesterday morning giving the squatters notice to be on the *qui vive*. I left your station to the last, as the inspector knows you are well armed and your men are to be relied on."

"Come and have something to eat first and tell your yarn afterwards," quoth my host, and we adjourned to the hall, where, after the trooper had eaten with the appetite of a half-starved dingo, he informed us that Ginger had reached the district, sticking up stations on his way, and that the inspector with fifteen men were on his track. He had evidently intended to stick up the township, but the arrival of the police had prevented this, so he disappeared, and the inspector thought he would make the attempt to break south again. He therefore requested my friend for the loan of as many men and horses as he could spare, so as to accompany the trooper and stop a gap called the divide, through which the scoundrels might try to break, and where he promised to meet them, during the next twenty-four hours, but at the same time warned them not to leave their station short- handed, as it was quite possible Ginger, close pressed, might try to stick them up so as to steal fresh horses and food.

Blake was sent for, a short council of war was held and his proposal that himself, two of the white men and two black trackers should accompany the trooper was decided on. "And perhaps," said he, "the captain here would like to come with us; fighting is in his line, and, my word! if we corner Ginger we shall have some."

Now Ginger was no business of mine, unless he attacked me; but, being an Irishman, I could not let the chance of a fight pass, and although my friends tried to dissuade me, I determined to go.

We were to start at midnight, so we who were to go lay down to get what rest we could, leaving the others to get the horses ready for us. At midnight we were roused up, and after swallowing a mug of tea and some food, a hurried glance over my horse and kit, to see that my water-bag was well filled and properly slung to the D's of my saddle, we started.

We were all superbly mounted and well armed, each man carrying two revolvers; I would sooner have carried a carbine, but I was dissuaded, and we had cause to regret it. The fight might have finished much sooner had I done as I judged best; but I was in what was to me a foreign country and, having no official status, gave in to the others. So we started, the blacks leading; and they did lead us. No sooner were we clear of the paddock fences than we broke into a canter, and made for a dense line of bushes about five miles off, and just as we reached it the moon went down. I expected to see the blacks pull up and walk their horses, but not a bit of it.

On they went at the same pace. The bush was some miles through, but no crow could have crossed it in a straighter line than they did. On reaching the open ground on the other side we halted and dismounted, for a short time, so as to give our steeds a blow. It was now pitch dark, with not even the glimmer of a star, yet no sooner had we mounted than we broke into a canter again, and rode through open park-like country and bush till the east began to lighten, when we pulled up at a small water-hole.

This was the spot our guides had aimed for, and it was at least twenty miles from our starting-point, so it will give you some idea of the marvellous abilities of these creatures. To be able to ride twenty miles at a sharp pace, through trackless country, on a dark night, and exactly strike the spot they aimed for, was to me wonderful. It may not strike you so, but try it.

We off-saddled, rubbed down, watered and fed our horses out of their nose-bags, then ate some cold mutton and damper, and dozed for a couple of hours, leaving the blacks to keep watch over us and our horses. Saddling up again we rode through clumps of bush and up gently rising ground towards a range of heavily bushed mountains, some ten miles off, through which ran the divide, or pass, we were to guard. We halted when we reached the foot of the range, and took cover in a small clump of bush, off-saddled and sent one black on foot to scout the pass and find by the spoor if anyone had crossed it during the last twenty-four hours.

Of course, being an utter stranger in the land, I knew nothing of the lay of the country, nor even where the pass was; but a rather acrid discussion took place between the stock-riders, who declared we were badly posted, and the trooper, who asserted we were not. Unable to give an opinion either way, I was lying down with my head on my saddle when we were roused by some shots. I jumped to my feet just in time to see our scout burst out of a clump of bush and run like a hare towards us, closely followed by four mounted men firing at him.

They were about 500 yards off, and had I had my carbine I could easily have covered the black, and perhaps have ended the job there and then; but my carbine was like the Dutchman's anchor, left at home, so there was nothing to do but throw our saddles on and try to save him. Quick and smart as we were, we were too late to save poor Tarpot, who was ridden down and riddled. As each of us got into his saddle he charged, and the bushrangers, seeing us coming, turned and galloped back to the bush from which they had issued. I was the fourth to mount, and as I galloped out of the bush I saw the three men in front of me riding in file as hard as they could gallop, with as much as from twenty to thirty yards between them.

This was rot; as, if the bushrangers made a stand on reaching their bush, as they were certain to do, they would simply shoot us down from behind cover, one after the other. I therefore shouted to the leading men to rein in and let us get into line; but their blood was up, and on they went. I pulled out to their left, and Blake and the remaining black pulled out to my left. We were therefore in extended line, some fifty yards to the left rear of the last man of the leading three who were in file. The distance was short, and as we were all riding like fiends we soon crossed the open ground between the two clumps of bush.

The trooper, who was the leading man, was within thirty yards of entering it when I saw him throw up his hands and fall headlong from his horse. In a second No. 2 had done the same, and a moment later No. 3 went down, horse and man. Myself and the other two, riding wide of the line of fire, escaped and, although several shots were fired at us, gained the bush unhurt. Then, being on equal terms with the bushrangers, we wheeled our horses to the right and rode at them.

Just at this moment I heard shouts and shots going on close to, at the other side of the bush, but had no time to inquire if it were friends or foes. I spotted a horse's head coming round a tree-trunk, and was ready for the rider. He appeared, and saw me; but I had him already covered, and had the pleasure of seeing him lurch out of his saddle and come a heavy crumpler. My mates were alongside of me, and we were just going after another bounder, whose horse's hindquarters were disappearing, when an officer and three troopers broke out on us, and called on us to bail up. In less than a minute we explained who we were, and I was just starting off after the fugitives when the officer called on me to halt, and in a rather haughty manner informed me that he was in command of the party, and that he intended to halt until he had collected his scattered men, some of whom were wounded. As he only stated the truth, I was not such a fool as to feel offended with him, so I went with Blake to see if anything could be done for our fallen mates.

The trooper and the first stockman were both dead, the third man was unwounded, but his horse had been killed, and he had been knocked stiff and silly by the heavy fall. However, after some water and a stiff nip he was soon all right, and swearing he would make the blank-blank-blankety-blank bounders who had killed his pet stock horse and his mate sit up.

We quickly caught the loose horses and were soon joined by the officer and his troopers, who were a very fine, smart-looking crowd, but, to my mind, far too big and too heavy for this sort of game. They had two of their number badly wounded, but had wounded and captured three bushrangers, so that, with the one I had put out of mess. Ginger could now have only three men with him. The officer, therefore, determined to follow their spoor with our party and four of his own men. Messengers were despatched to other patrols and to the nearest station to obtain a conveyance for the wounded men, and we started under the guidance of Jampot, our remaining black.

"Do you think he will be able to track them?" I asked Blake.

"My word," he replied, "Jampot has now a blood feud against Ginger, and will follow him to the death. Ginger may turn and twist how he likes, but unless he can grow wings, or kill Jampot, Jampot will kill him."

I had seen plenty of tracking in my time—I even had the cheek to fancy myself a bit at it—and had seen good work done both by white men and Maoris. I had even seen a tame black fellow after stray cattle; but I was now to see a real warrior black, with a blood feud, at the game. I expected a great deal, and I was not disappointed—in fact I saw more than I had ever imagined to be possible. Well, we were ready to start.

Jampot had made use of the time in transmogrifying himself into a fiend, and he certainly looked a hideous nightmare in his war paint. Jumping on his horse, he rode to the end of the bush, circled once or twice to take note of the different spoors, then broke into a canter and rode nearly due south.

Mile after mile he kept on, over all sorts of ground, through bush and over hard land, never pausing for an instant.

"Do you mean to tell me that that black fellow can see spoor going at this pace and over such ground as we are now on?" said I to Blake.

He only nodded his head and muttered: "My word! "This is a great Australian expression, and will signify almost anything.

We came to a creek, and Jampot was off his horse in a second and was examining the rocks round the water-holes. All at once he held up his hand; Blake and myself went carefully to him.

Blake and he talked gibberish for a minute, then, turning to me, the former said: "Jampot tells me one of them is badly hit and can't go far."

"How on earth does he know that?"

"He has seen blood on the trail and can tell by the tracks on these rocks."

"Tracks? "I said. "Where are they? "

He spoke to Jampot, who immediately put his finger on several places on the rocks.

I examined the spots closely, but could see nothing, not even when I used a prospecting-glass I had in my pocket. Yet this marvellous savage could distinguish spoor with his naked eye, and had spotted blood-marks on the trail while going at a smart canter in blazing sunshine, where I could only now and then just barely see hoof-marks. Jampot was now very keen to go on, so after we had given our horses a blow and a few go-downs of water it was a case of mount and canter.

Away we went, Jampot leading; but now he went slower, and occasionally swerved from his line, bending down and regarding the ground intently. We had only gone a couple of miles or so when he turned in his saddle and, with a grin on his face a fiend would have envied, pointed at a small clump of bushes to his right front, and made directly for them.

Drawing our revolvers, we followed, to find him dismounted, bending over the body of a dead man.

He was a fine-looking, clean-built young fellow, and seemed far too good for the game he had been playing. But there was no time for moralising; so, preventing Jampot from mutilating the remains, we again mounted, broke into a canter, and went on.

The weight they carried had now begun to tell on the troopers' horses, and they showed signs of having had enough of it: and presently we came to a dead horse. He had been wantonly shot, and it made my blood boil to see the poor brute lie there.

We were now approaching a long bare line of hills, and suddenly

Jampot let a yell out of him and pointed at them. I unslung my field-glasses, and could see three men, dismounted, leading their horses, nearly at the top of the range, and about three miles in front of us.

We at once gave our horses the spur and went for them.

They reached the summit, paused for a minute or two to give their horses a blow, mounted and disappeared over the skyline. We reached the hill, jumped off, and hurried up it, leading our horses; but the gallop had finished the troopers' nags, and when we got to the top the officer found, with the exception of my party, he was alone. His horse was done, and even the hard-fed, splendid mounts of myself and mates had begun to show symptoms of distress. Quickly unscrewing the top of my flask, I emptied the spirits into my water-bag, and forced my horse to drink the contents. My comrades immediately followed my example and the noble beasts soon bucked up.

In the meantime the sergeant had reached the top, and with the officer and Blake held a consultation as to where we were, Jampot being called on to assist.

He spoke to Blake, who turned round and ejaculated: "My word, those hounds are making for Edwards' Station. It's only six miles off. The men are away; there are women and children there, and fresh horses."

The officer at once said to me: "You and your party are the best mounted and the lightest weights. Jampot may be able to take you a short cut. Ride like fury. You may be just in time, and if it comes to fighting you know all about that; but on no account leave there till I come." He said something more about not letting the bushrangers get fresh horses; but his words of wisdom were left behind us, for we were off, and I had the wildest ride I ever had in my life. The slope of the hill was steep and rough, but we tore down it at full pace.

Our horses, maddened with the spur, almost seemed to fly, clearing rocks and fallen timber as if they were simply straws, while we, rendered desperate by the thought of the danger of the women and children, urged them on with voice and spur, though we wisely gave them their heads and let their mouths alone.

They were all bush-bred horses, knew their work and did it without a fault or fall, which would have been certain death to both man and beast.

Well, we came to the foot of the hill and each man, taking his own line, although Jampot still led, galloped through the bush, every man riding all he knew.

Soon we came to the open and saw the house; yes, and we saw something else, for in front of it stood three knocked-up horses with hanging heads. A paddock with a heavy post-and-rail fence lay between us, so, catching hold of our horses' heads, we sent them at it. Over we went, in line, and charged for the house, a woman's scream causing us, if possible, to put on pace. Just then we saw a man coming from the stable leading three horses, and he saw us at the same time. Our appearance, from an unexpected direction, must have rattled him a bit. The horses he led, excited by the sound of our galloping hoofs, became restive and started plunging, so he let them go as Blake rode for him. I heard the pistol shots, but could pay no attention, as out from the French windows rushed two men. They made for the horses, then, seeing they had no chance, turned and opened fire on us.

The man nearest me had a big red beard, and I knew he must be Ginger, so I rode at him. Jampot rode at him too, firing as fast as he could; and this most likely upset Ginger's aim as, although I heard bullets whistle past me as I lay on my horse's neck, I was unwounded. When I was within twenty yards of him I fired twice and circled left, so as not to crash into the house. Both shots took effect. He fell, and was still trying to cover me when Jampot, jumping off" his horse, rushed up to him and shot him through the head. Blake now joined us, slightly wounded, having accounted for his man, and we found our other mate on the ground badly hurt; he had succeeded in also dropping his man, who, preferring to be hung instead of shot, surrendered.

I entered the house and found the ladies unhurt but badly frightened. They, however, with the self-control and handiness of colonial women, at once set to work to tend the wounded.

Jampot was still amusing himself with the remains of Ginger, but, as it is against my principles to allow heathen ceremonies to be performed on a white man, no matter how big a blackguard he has been, I made him desist and help me to look after the horses, the real heroes of the play.

The China boy-cook came out of his hiding- place and started to cook huge supplies of food for ourselves and the troopers, who turned up soon afterwards.

A swim in a water-hole, a good dinner, a long sleep, and on the following morning myself, Blake and Jampot returned home.

CHAPTER 6

The Scout That Failed

(Told by the Kia Tangata)

Scouting, like every other sort of business, has its ups and downs, and a scout may often fail to obtain the information he has gone out to gain, through no fault of his own. He may even lose the number of his mess, be captured, or have to ride or run for his life, notwithstanding the fact that he has played the right game from the start, until something happens, and he fails, frequently through bad luck, or because the vigilance of the enemy renders it impossible to achieve success. It has been my lot, as it has been the lot of many a better man, to fail frequently while scouting, and on more than one occasion I have been spotted by the enemy and have had to ride or run hard to save my bacon, without completing the duty on which I had been despatched. A yarn about one of these occasions may amuse you, although there is but little information as regards scouting in it.

It was in the year 1869 that we were after Te Kooti and the rebel Hau Haus in the Taupo district, and were building a chain of forts from Napier to Lake Taupo, so as to cut off the Uriwera and east-coast Hau Haus from the King Country and Taupo rebels.

Lake Taupo is a huge expanse of water on the high plateau in the centre of the North Island of New Zealand, and is fed by many rivers, creeks and boiling springs; but there is only one outlet to drain off its superfluous water, and this is called the River Waikato, which debouches out of the north-east corner of the lake in a deep and very rapid stream, running east, then bends north and north-west, forming a big bow; then turning to the north it eventually makes a sharp turn to the west, and flows into the Pacific Ocean south of Manakau Harbour.

This river, fed as it is from the big lake and also by innumerable tributaries, is, although not very broad, a most dangerous one to cross, especially while it is descending from the high plateau, as it either rushes through high banks or tumbles in foaming cataracts among large rocks until at last, as if tired with its exertions, it becomes a well-behaved, navigable river, and forms what was in early times one of the only roads into the interior of New Zealand; but during its whole course from the lake to the ocean it is a dangerous one to play with.

On the precipitous south bank of this river, some 200 yards from the lake, we were, in 1869, building a redoubt called Tapuaeharuru (the Place of Sounding Footsteps), and it was from this fort that I was ordered to ride to Te-Niho-te-Kiori (the Rat's Tooth), an enormous pinnacle of rock that springs from the ground just where the river starts on its long flow to the north. I was therefore, as it were, to ride along the string of a bent bow and, if successful in reaching this rock, to try and open communications with another column supposed to be in its vicinity.

It was not what some people might call a safe journey: road there was none, and the route I had to take was through country that, although it could not be called mountainous nor thickly bushed, was covered with *manuka* scrub and wire grass, with here and there a clump of heavy timber, while an occasional column of snow-white steam, rising into the air, denoted a boiling spring. These columns were of different magnitude, and as I knew which side of the river the principal geysers were on, and their situation, as seen from the river and fort, they proved most useful landmarks to me later on in the day.

At daybreak one lovely morning I plumped my saddle into a canoe and was ferried across the stream, my horse swimming astern, and on gaining the bank, after drying his back, I carefully saddled-up, lit my pipe and, with a cheery "So long" to the men who had paddled me over, mounted and rode away.

As soon as I was out of rifle-range of the camp I was in No Man's Land, and every native I met would be an enemy. I had twenty-five miles to ride to get to the Rat's Tooth, and had to depend entirely on my own wit and the good qualities of my horse to save my hair, in case I fell across any parties of wandering Hau Haus. My orders also directed me to look out for any signs of the enemy, and in case I cut a spoor I was to prospect it and try to ascertain if it were the track of a *taua* (war party) or not.

The horse I rode was indeed a noble brute. Standing fifteen hands, he possessed every quality that a scout's horse should. Not only was he very well bred, fast and strong, but he combined the manners of a lady with the courage of the lion, could scramble like a cat and swim like a fish; and all these qualities he was destined to display before that day was over. As, if possible, I was to return the same day, I rode light, carrying nothing on my saddle except half-a-feed for my horse and a couple of biscuits for myself. I wore neither tunic nor sword, but carried a carbine, with the usual revolver and knife, while my dress consisted only of a smasher hat, shirt, breeches and boots, with very short-necked spurs.

"There is nothing half so sweet in life as love's young dream," sings the poet, but I'll gamble that a smart canter on a high-bred, free-going horse beats dreaming all to fits, and is much better for you. Anyhow I thoroughly enjoyed the first part of that ride through the sharp, clear air, notwithstanding that I had to keep every sense on deck, and my thoughts, concentrated by looking out for an enemy or for hostile spoor, were occupied with far sterner matters than, love or dalliance. For the first six miles or so I made good progress, the ground being fairly open and the obstacles quite insignificant; but then I reached a part where a chain of heavily bushed hills ran on my left hand for some miles, the river being six miles to my right.

The pumice-stone flat over which I was riding was here much cut up by gullies running from the hills to the river; some of them containing creeks, the remainder being dry, but all of them with nearly perpendicular sides, which, except in places, were not to be negotiated by horse or man. As the depth of them varied so did the direction, some of them running into one another, while the others ran direct to the river. These I had to cross, and it was very nasty, dangerous work, in more ways than one.

First of all I had to look for a place where my horse could descend into the bed of the gully, at the same time looking out for a place on the other side up which we could scramble. This took time, as occasionally I had to ride a considerable distance up or down the edge before I could find a place suitable either to descend or to get out again; and it would have been an act of madness for me to have gone down into one of these ravines without having spotted a way of getting out again. Yet, at the same time, cross them I must. Again I had to make mental notes of every crossing, and take bearings, so that I should remember each gully and how to get back. I never forgot for a moment I was in an enemy's country and that perhaps my return journey might be expedited by a *taua*; besides, I had to keep my eyes open for an ambush, as it was quite possible I had already been spotted from the hills, among which many Hau Haus might be lurking, as the Maoris always make their plantations in the bush.

I had crossed some ten of these gullies when I came to a very big one, about forty feet deep and perhaps fifty yards broad. With trouble I could get down into this, but could not see, although I rode a considerable distance along its edge, any way of getting out on the other side. There was, however, another gully running into it that apparently took a northerly direction—the way I wanted to go—and if I entered this one and followed it I might be able to regain the level of the plain farther on.

It was a very grave risk to run, but it was a case of Hobson's choice, that or none; so, after a long look at the hills, to see if I could spot any signs of danger from them, I hardened my heart, descended with a nasty scramble and made for the entrance of the gully I had seen from the plain. I had no sooner reached the mouth of it than I reined up sharply, for there, clearly defined, and not twenty-four hours old, were the tracks of at least twenty, perhaps thirty, horses that, coming from the north, had turned to the right on reaching the big gully and proceeded towards the hills. As there was no spoor returning, it was evident that a number of the enemy must be located in their bushed recesses, and, in case they should have spotted me, they would most certainly do their best to cut me off. Yet, as their horses had used the gully, there must be a way out of it, and if I made a push for it I could take advantage of it to regain the level of the plain; anyhow it was no use staying where I was. I must go back, or go on.

Naturally, I was keen to complete my duty; so as soon as I had taken a good look at my carbine and revolver I entered the gully and rode forward at a steady pace. For nearly a mile it ran with a few bends due north, the bottom of it being smooth and the sides perpendicular. Then the bed began to rise with a gentle slope, until it eventually rose to the level of the plain. Its width was in no place more than ten yards across, and it had been formed by some convulsion of nature that had caused the surface to sink, and it looked as if it had been gouged out of the earth. There are plenty of these freaks of nature on the Taupo and Kaingaroa plains, sometimes like the one I was in, accessible at the ends, and others with precipitous sides all round.

Well, I had just got to where the gradual slope began when I heard a row behind me and, looking round, saw over twenty natives riding as hard as they could in pursuit. They were still some 300 yards away, and as soon as they saw I had spotted them they started yelling like over-tortured fiends. It was certainly time for me to hump myself, and I increased my pace so as to put a greater distance between us, while I rapidly thought out the best plan to shake off this undesirable company. Had I been on open ground I should have regarded the contretemps with placidity, and perhaps have enjoyed picking off a few of these howling sinners, but, mixed up as I was among the network of vile gullies, it was no joke, and the sun was on their side of the hedge.

The only feasible plan I could think of, was to follow the enemy's own tracks, as where they had travelled with horses so could I, until I was clear of these confounded gullies. You must remember I was quite ignorant of this part of the country, never having crossed the river before, and only knowing that if I kept due north I should cut the river; and on its banks was the Rat's Tooth I had to find. The Hau Haus, on the other hand, would know the country, and all the spots where they could cross the gullies thoroughly, and would, of course, try to cut me off. With these fiends in pursuit I should have no time to look for crossing-places whenever I came across a ravine, and I was sure these existed as far as the range of hills, which still extended for some miles on my left, ran. Therefore I must follow the natives' spoor, so as to strike their crossing-places, and make use of them. Of course I might fall in with a fresh gang of Hau Haus, but I had to risk that; needs must when the devil drives; and although I had not Old Nick behind me in *propriâ personâ*, yet those who were, so remarkably resembled him as to quite make up by quantity any deficiency they lacked in quality.

I had not the least fear, bar accidents, of their being able to catch me by riding me down, as my hard-fed, splendid-conditioned horse for pace and staying powers was far and away superior to their half-starved, grass-fed nags; and even if they had a good animal or two, looted from settlers, among them, yet these would have so deteriorated in their brutal hands as to be quite unfit to cope with my gallant mount; besides, in a long chase, like this might be, riding and handling would count a lot, and even if one or two did press me I could back my carbine against their guns, as a Maori is a vile shot. All these thoughts passed through my brain during the few minutes I was galloping along the gully and gradually ascending to the level of the plain. But Bobby Burns speaks the truth when he remarks that the schemes of both mice and men are liable to go crooked; for my hastily and maybe well-thought-out plan was all blown to blue blazes the moment I emerged from the gully, as it was all I could do to swing my horse to the right to prevent riding slap-bang into a big gang of Maoris, some of whom were mounted.

This party were making for the entry I had just left, for as I shot out of it the nearest of them was within ten yards of me. They straggled in a diagonal line, about 100 yards long, across to what was evidently the outlet to another gully, as in the hurried glance I took of them I saw a horseman emerging as if from the ground. The presence of these bounders, although not exactly astonishing, was most undesirable, and I sent my horse along, so as to escape nearer acquaintance with them; nor did they seem to be quite pleased with me, as they all started yelling like fiends, and those who carried their fire-locks capped at once fired them off in my direction, while with one accord they all began to chase me.

It was high time for me to get out of that, but my horse's pace soon carried me clear out of gun-shot danger, and I quickly edged away to my left to try and find, when I reached the gully, which I knew must be close in that direction, a crossing-place, so that I could get round the enemy's flank and still carry out my duty. One thing I was sure of, the Hau Haus would never give up the pursuit so long as there was the ghost of a chance of catching me.

As I expected, I soon came to a ravine running east, towards the river, and at the first glance saw that it was a teaser. Over twenty feet in depth, its sides, composed of hard pumice-stone, were quite perpendicular and unnegotiable, even by a monkey. I therefore had to continue along the brink, while a loud, jeering yell made me understand that the natives well knew there was no possibility of my being able to cross it. I was annoyed, more than annoyed, and I determined to solace myself by picking off one of the hilarious bounders, but decided first of all to try the other flank. Letting my horse go, I again crossed, diagonally, the enemy's front, only to find myself, after a gallop of not more than 400 yards, brought up by a similar gully. Again the jeering yell broke out, and I knew I was cornered between these infernal ravines and the Waikato River.

I halted and turned so as to take a good look at the pursuing Hau Haus, and determined to make it hot for the leading man, but was sold again, as I found they had extended in line between the two ravines. They were over a hundred in number, including at least forty mounted men, these latter being scattered among the footmen, with the exception of some eight or ten, who rode together about a hundred yards in rear of the line, with the evident intention of strengthening any part of it, should I charge and try to break through. This for a moment I thought of doing, but on looking towards the spots where the only two outlets I knew of were situated, I saw clumps of men stationed at them, so I was convinced it was no use charging, at least not at this period of the game.

The deliberate way the Hau Haus were advancing showed me that they knew it was impossible for me to break away to either flank, and that they were systematically going to pen me up against the river and try to capture me alive. This I determined they should not do; somehow I was convinced that my day had not yet come, and I had such an inner conviction I was going to wriggle out of my scrape that I felt quite easy about myself and only anxious about my horse.

The moment I halted the enemy began to poke fun at me. One shouted: "Get fins, like a fish, for yourself and horse, then swim the river." Another wag roared out: "Grow wings like a pigeon and fly back to your home." This was advice which, although not solicited, could scarcely be called rude. But another ribald ruffian was not only rude but grossly personal, for, running out in front of the line, he howled out, with the most insulting gestures: "Render yourself up to us; the women are making ready the ovens, and I hunger for your flesh."

I shouted back, and my voice carried far in those days: "You whose head is fit to be boiled" (the most awful insult in the Maori tongue), "thou at least shalt not partake of the feast; go feed on the spirits of your fathers." The old Sneider carbine, though laughed at nowadays, was true up to 300 yards, and the Maori was not more than 200 yards from me. He had just begun to make some nasty, uncalled-for remarks when I proved the correctness of my prophecy to him, by dropping him in his tracks, thereby cutting short what might have been a most eloquent oration.

A wild yell with a wilder volley answered my shot, and the line made a *kokiri* (short charge) in my direction. I only lingered long enough to shout in Maori, "I have caught the first man" (a most important and lucky omen in Maori warfare), then turned and cantered away out of rifle-range, as it would never do to have my horse wounded.

It was high time I should put on my considering cap and think out the situation and my future movements. It would have been far more to my advantage had they followed me in a straggling mob, as then

I could have picked off the leaders, and it would have denoted anxiety, on their part, lest I should find some possible crossing by which I could escape; but the quiet, methodical way they were going about their business showed me that they considered my chance of getting away was nil, and that they had made up their minds to risk nothing, that the gullies could not be crossed, so that their intention was to drive me before them to the river's bank, and hive me there at their own convenience, the river being uncrossable.

But halt! Was the river uncrossable? I knew it to be a very dangerous one, even for such swimmers as my horse and self, who together had crossed many a bad river before; but I was also aware that the natives' great dread of it was caused by superstitious nervousness, just as much as it was caused by its actual dangers. Of course there were very many parts of it quite impossible, but perhaps I might find a place where a determined attempt would have a chance of success. Anyhow I would go and have a look at it.

The river was not more than three miles from me and I cantered steadily towards it, so as not to tire my horse, but still give me time to examine the banks and select the best places to enter, and get out of it, provided I should make up my mind to risk the crossing.

It did not take me long to reach the bank, and I rode along it from one gully to the other. Both of these ran down to the water's edge, and the bank of the river near both of them was fully twenty feet high, and perpendicular; but half-way between them was a natural depression in the plain, that ran at a gentle slope down to the bank, where it was only four or five feet above the water, which was very deep right up to the bank. This depression slanted upstream, a point in my favour, and this was evidently the place I must take off from.

The river was indeed a noble one, quite 200 yards broad, and evidently of great depth. Its enormous volume of water, forcing itself along, confined by the high banks, reminded me of a big fat boy buttoned up tight in a suit of clothes far too small for him, wriggling and writhing about, trying to make them more comfortable.

I next turned my attention to the other side, to see if I could spot a place up which we could scramble. The far bank, though lower than the one I was on, was still very steep, and I knew there must be a great depth of water under it; but some 200 yards downstream the land ran out to a point, and there was just the possibility of my horse finding footing there. The current also seemed to set from my side of the river towards this point, and if so it would help me enormously. I tested this by tearing off a branch from a bush and throwing it in, when I saw it rapidly swept towards the spot I hoped to make. The rate at which it was carried also gave me some idea of the tremendous rush of water, the surface of which seemed to writhe and winkle as if in mortal anguish, while the numerous whirlpools informed me what a furious undertow there must be.

Great was the risk we should run in attempting to cross, yet under the circumstances I determined to run it. I felt certain I was not going under that day, and anyhow a clean death in the sweet, cool water of the river was far preferable to being turned into long pig by my brutal pursuers. Then again they might kill my horse and catch me with sufficient life remaining in me to make it worth their trouble to torture it out of me. No fear, I wanted none of that; the river was my dart, especially as my old nurse had always assured me of quite another kind of death than drowning, and, sure, she was known in my part of the world as a knowledgeable woman.

The few minutes I had sat and watched the stream at the taking-off place, I had talked to and explained matters to my glorious horse. What's that you say? a horse can't understand you? Rot! you taxi-cab, motor-busing new chum. A horse you have treated as a pal, and not as a slave, will understand any simple matter you explain to him, far better than the ordinary Englishman can understand the beauties of tariff reform. Bear that in mind, you mud-splashing, dust-creating greenhorn, if you ever want to become worth your salt on the frontier. Anyhow, my horse understood me, and I rode up to the plain again.

The Hau Haus were not far off, and when they saw me regain the level they evidently thought I had funked the river and was going to try to escape on *terra firma*, for they saluted me with loud laughter and jeers. Unbuckling my wallet straps, for I had them on my saddle, although I had left the wallets themselves behind me, I carefully fastened my carbine across the pommel of the saddle and also crossed the stirrups. Then, as a farewell to my pursuers, I shouted: "O ye slaves and dogs, I go to bathe in the Waikato; come with me, if ye be not afraid." I turned my horse and, gripping my saddle, with thighs and legs like a vice, I started at a canter down the slope, increasing my pace and urging him on with my voice, until at last we charged the river at full gallop.

The noble animal knew well what I expected from him, for as soon as I gave him his head he pointed his ears and, gathering himself together at every bound, without a swerve, the slightest balk, or the least hesitation, measured his take-off to a nicety, and leaped far out into the air. I was quite prepared for the plunge. I had twisted my hand well into his mane, and had taken a deep breath as we made the spring. I felt the rush through the air, and saw the shining water below us, that seemed to rise and meet us, but I felt no shock; for although we must have raised the deuce of a splash, and must have sunk somewhat, yet we seemed to come to the surface immediately, and the first sensation I noticed was the current tugging at me, as if trying to pull me out of my saddle.

We had taken the water exactly as I hoped we should do—that is, with the horse's head turned well upstream—so that the tremendous force of the current, although it swept us rapidly downstream, yet carried us diagonally across it. My horse was swimming deep but magnificently, and was not a bit flurried or nervous, and although the current kept tugging at me I had small trouble in retaining my seat, while I eased him in every way I could, talking to him and encouraging him the whole passage. The crossing seemed to take but a very short time, and I saw we should reach the bank above the point. I was very glad of this, as the current ran round the point like a mill sluice, and I did not know how it set on the other side, or what sort of a bank there was round it. We neared the shore, and I turned the good nag's head towards it, for him to make his effort, but feared the water would be too deep, as although the bank sloped, yet from the water it looked very, very steep.

Just as we reached it I felt the noble animal give a tremendous heave, with a mighty rearing plunge; his hind feet must have touched bottom, for he landed with both forefeet on the bank. Like a flash I was over his withers, taking the reins with me, and scrambled to my feet on the slope. It was with difficulty I could keep my footing, but I managed somehow, and, tugging at the reins, I shouted his name and encouraged him all I knew. Gathering himself together, he made another tremendous spring and, with me scrambling in front of him, in a few bounds he reached the top, where I lavished much praise and many endearments on him, these being cut short by the song of an Enfield bullet as it whistled over us; so I led him under cover, loosed his girths, unbuckled my carbine and returned at once to the bank.

We had crossed, they might try, and as I had had more of their company than I desired, I intended my carbine to dissuade them; I examined its breech and found that, notwithstanding its bath, it was in good working order, so that was all right. My appearance was greeted with yells, a straggling volley and a frantic war-dance. I never lack in politeness, so, to return their compliments, I danced a step or two myself, shouting, "Come to me, come to me"; then, dropping to a prone position, I took careful aim at a Johnny who was executing a *pas seul*. My shot spoiled his performance, for he sat down suddenly and was quickly removed by his friends.

I have heard that actors retire gracefully from the stage when the gods express their disapproval by heaving defunct cats and doubtful eggs at them, but I should think they would greatly expedite their movements if a man opened out with a carbine. Yes, they would quickly leave a clear stage; at least it was so in this case, as the company I disapproved of, cutting their dances short, dispersed in a moment, taking their wounded man with them, and hastened in their exits by two more bullets, both of which, I fancy, touched meat.

The Hau Haus having retired, I returned to my horse, removed the saddle and gave him a good rub-down with a handful of fern; then we lunched together. His oats were none the worse for their ducking, while my biscuits, if pulpy, were palatable, and we enjoyed them. The sun quickly dried me and we made for home. There was no chance of reaching the Rat's Tooth from the side I was on; besides, I considered it my duty to inform my colonel of the presence of the Maoris. Another thing, what were they doing there? I suspected they had large plantations of potatoes in that bush, and that when they blundered up against me they were on their way to dig them up and had brought their horses to carry them away on. If my conjectures were right, I now knew where to find them.

After a hard, scrambling journey over fern ridges we reached the fort, and I reported to the colonel, who babbled a bit at my failure to complete my duty, but was quite pacified when I told him my conjectures about the potatoes. He was not an Irishman, true, but he dearly loved a spud, and if my ideas about them turned out correct, the capture of these potatoes would be of enormous value to us, as the Government were at their wits' end how to keep us and our horses supplied with rations, while the loss of them, to the enemy, would be very severe.

That night a strong force, on foot, under my guidance, crossed the river and made for the big gully where I had first seen the spoor. We made a smart night's march, hoping to surprise the enemy and catch them on the hop. In that we failed, their outposts being well on the alert; but in the ensuing skirmish we killed a few of them, captured all their horses and an immense quantity of potatoes, large numbers of these having been already dug up and packed ready for transport, so that my friends the Hau Haus had worked hard for nothing, except our benefit, and I felt very pleased. Was I spiteful? I wonder.

But somehow, now I have spun the yarn out, something seems to have gone wrong with it; for when I come to look at the heading it distinctly states that the tale is to be a yarn about the Scout that Failed. And now I come to think it over, I was really not scouting at all, but only trying to open communications with another column, though to do that is certainly the work of a scout, and I moreover was a scout, but yet I was not scouting. Then as to Failure. Sure if I did fail to find the Rat's Tooth, faith! I found the spuds.

Therefore the title is a misnomer or I've put the wrong yarn to the right title, or the wrong title to the right yarn, but anyhow, failure or not, you've the yarn, so digest it and make the best of it, as we did the potatoes; and I assure you there was no failure about them. And as now this finale has bothered me as much as those confounded gullies did, I must confess that after partaking of perhaps too many of those spuds, and very good they were, I broke out into poetry in honour of my glorious horse. I will only give you one verse, so don't run away:

> A man may love a bow-wow, or a man may love a girl,
> He may prate on points of pedigree, or rave about a curl.
> But a trooper can love both of these, in a tiny way of course,
> For most of his affections are lavished on his horse.
> Oh, some men love a steamer yacht, and some love jaunting cars,
> And I hear that in a big balloon men soon will visit Mars;
> But here's a toast you all must drink, refuse it if you can,
> A health to the noble warhorse, God's greatest gift to man.

Don't throw pannikins at me, but blame potatoes and ration rum taken on an empty stomach. Goodnight.

Chapter 7

Some Miraculous Escapes I Have Known

There's a sweet little cherub who sits up aloft
And looks after the life of poor Jack.

Dibdin.

By miraculous escapes I mean those escapes from death that have been entirely engineered by the Power above, who has preserved the life of human beings when they were utterly helpless, and who, for some inscrutable reason, saves one life and allows others to be destroyed.

The yarns I am now going to spin will illustrate, I think, what I have written above.

About midnight on 6th September 1868 a New Zealand Field Force, under the command of Colonel McDonnell, consisting of 200 white men and 70 friendly natives, left camp, crossed the deep, rapid and icy-cold river Waingongora, and started to attack Tetokowaru in his stronghold Te-ngutu-o-te-manu.

I am not going to inflict on you the miserable yarn of the unfortunate fight, as I have written it elsewhere; suffice it to say that the great majority of the 200 white men were untrained new chums, and that over 40 of them bolted at the first volley. The remainder stood their ground, although they refused to extend; so we lost one-third of our number, killed and wounded, in less than a quarter of an hour, and had to retreat, leaving our dead and many wounded men behind us.

So that you can understand the position of affairs, I may tell you that Colonel McDonnell, retaining the command of 100 of the white men, had sent the remaining 100 under Major Von Tempsky, to act on the right of his own party, and, as soon as he saw that nothing but a retreat could save the remainder of his force, he sent Captain McDonnell, his brother, to Von Tempsky with orders for the major to retreat at once, and join up with his own party.

This order was delivered, but a few seconds later the Major was shot dead. Captain McDonnell then gave the order to Captain Buck, who promised to carry it out. Captain McDonnell returned to his brother, and the retreat began. Instead of immediately obeying the order, Captain Buck endeavoured to recover the Major's body, and was at once shot dead, without having passed the order on to anyone else. The next senior officer. Captain Roberts, took command of the party; but, as he was ignorant of the order to retreat, he still continued to hold his ground, until he was informed by some of his men that the Colonel had retreated. Joined by a few friendly natives, he retired by another route, and led the remains of his shattered and worn-out party into camp next morning.

Having given you a rough idea how things stood with our men on the afternoon of the 7th (please remember the date), I will now start the yarn.

It was late in the afternoon when Captain Roberts began his retreat, pursued by a party of Hau Haus. His men, nearly all new chums, behaved badly; but with a few good men, and the friendly natives who had joined him, he kept the enemy at bay till nightfall, when they drew off.

Now among his party he had a man named Dore, one of the Wellington Rangers. and a new chum.

This poor fellow had his arm, just below the shoulder, smashed to pieces by a bullet, fell, fainted from loss of blood, and was abandoned.

When he came to, he found himself stripped of everything, with the exception of his tattered and blood-stained shirt.

He must have been discovered by the pursuing Hau Haus, who had evidently thought him dead, but who, although they stripped him, forbore to *tomahawk* him or mutilate his body. This in itself was a marvel, and shows that that sweet little cherub must have taken his case in hand, as, with one other exception, the Hau Haus were never known to omit *tomahawking* and mutilating a dead body.

The poor chap hid in a hollow *rata*-tree, and when it was quite dark attempted to find his way back to camp. He, however, was a new chum, knew nothing of bush work, and consequently lost his way, wandering in a circle, and always returning to the vicinity of the bloodstained *pah* and ferocious Hau Haus. This he continued to do for three days; but on the evening of the 10th he managed to get out of the bush into the open country, and made for the camp. All this time he had been without a bite of food, with a severe raw wound, with only the fragment of a shirt to protect him against the icy-cold sleet and frost, and although all that time in the close vicinity of the Hau Hau *pah*, he miraculously escaped being spotted.

As I said before, on the evening of the 10th he found himself in the open country, and struck out for the drift across the flooded Wain-gongora River. He remembered reaching it, then lost recollection. How he crossed that drift, a very bad one even for a strong and healthy man to tackle alone, is more than a miracle; but he always asserted he was fired on while doing so, and fainted on reaching the bank.

Here he was only two miles from the camp; but his mind became a blank, for he wandered about till the evening of the 12th, when he was discovered by a patrol, coming out of a clump of bush, and he was brought into camp.

Now, just consider for a moment what this man Dore went through, and what awful dangers he escaped. Badly wounded and found by the most savage fanatics on the earth, yet, against their custom, they nei-ther *tomahawk* nor mutilate him. Then he wanders for over five days, through bitter frost and cold, with an open and untended wound; he escapes the notice of the enemy, crosses, while weak from the loss of blood, starvation and pain, a most dangerous river, and yet, when brought into camp, his wound heals long before those of men who are not nearly so badly hurt, and who have not been through his awful experiences. You may call it luck. I maintain it was the work of that sweet little cherub, who, for his own reasons, "bossed up the whole show!"

In many of my yarns I have mentioned the massacre at Poverty Bay that was engineered by that arch-devil, Te Kooti, and his gang of fiends, called Hau Haus. On 10th July 1868 Te Kooti and some 200 Hau Haus landed at Whare-onga-onga, having escaped from the Chatham Islands. They had overpowered the guard there, seized the schooner *Rifleman*, forced the crew to sail them to Poverty Bay, and had landed some fifteen miles south of the white settlements. Owing to the criminal negligence of the Government, who, because they wished for peace, persuaded themselves they had got it, the defence force had been disbanded, and even the arms and ammunition re-moved from the adjacent districts, so that the settlers were almost helpless, while Te Kooti was soon joined by all the restless fanatics in the country.

Major Biggs, who was in charge of the Poverty Bay district, made head against Te Kooti, with whatever men and arms he could scrape together, but with small success. He was also guilty of an unpardonable piece of folly, as he allowed the settlers to remain on their scattered homesteads, and delayed collecting them together for mutual support, although warned to do so by friendly natives, who offered to assist in building defensive works. For this delay he paid dearly, as he and the whole of his family were surprised and, with the exception of one boy, brutally murdered. It was on the night of 9th November that Te Kooti made his raid on Poverty Bay.

On that night Captain Wilson, second in command, was sitting in his house writing, when a party of Hau Haus, under a fiend called Nama, knocked at the door and informed him they had a letter for him from Hirini-Te-Kani, the head chief of the district. The captain, however, had his suspicions, and told them to pass the letter under the door, at the same time arming himself and calling his servant Moran to come to his assistance. Moran slept in an outhouse; but he succeeded in breaking through the enemy, and joined his master. The Hau Haus, seeing they could not deceive the captain, tried to force the door open with the trunk of a tree. The captain at once opened fire on them, and forced them to drop it; so they then set fire to the house.

The white men fought on until the house was in full flare, when Captain Wilson accepted the Hau Hau offer of life for himself and family, provided he surrendered. It was a choice of that, or being all burned alive; and as there was a slight possibility of the Hau Haus keeping their promise, Captain Wilson surrendered.

Carrying a little boy in his arms, and followed by his wife and Moran, with the other children, three in number, if I remember rightly, they were surrounded by the Hau Haus, who led them towards the river. *En route* he asked one of the natives where they were being taken to, and was at once shot, from behind, through the back.

Staggering to a bit of *manuka* scrub, the captain threw the child into it, telling him to run, and in the confusion the youngster was not noticed and hid in the scrub. At the same moment Moran was tomahawked, and Mrs Wilson and the children were savagely treated, bayoneted and left for dead. The children were dead, but Mrs Wilson still lived.

Te Kooti and his gang remained in the settlement till the morning of the 14th—mark the date—plundering and murdering all the women and children who had escaped the night of the 9th, and whom his men found in hiding. On the afternoon of the 16th a small patrol from Tauranganui visited the bloodstained settlement and found little James Wilson hidden with a dog in his arms. The boy told them how he was trying to get to Tauranganui to bring help for his mother, who was lying wounded in an outhouse at their late home, but he had lost his way. As well as he could, poor child, he also described his miraculous escape.

He had hid in the scrub, but next day came back to the spot where his family had been murdered. Here he found the bodies of his father, his brothers, his sister and Moran, but not that of his mother.

He had then wandered back to his old home, hiding whenever he saw anyone, and there, in an outhouse, had found his mother lying dreadfully wounded.

The patrol went on to the house and found the poor lady in a dreadful state, but quite conscious. She told them that after the murder of her husband and children she had been most brutally ill-treated and then left for dead. When she came to herself she struggled back to what had been her home, and had taken refuge in an outhouse, where she had been found by her little son, who had kept her alive by scouting for hens' eggs or anything else he could find.

Now I call the escape of that child miraculous. For a helpless youngster to get away in the first place is wonderful; but that he should have been successful in evading the Maori search, of five days, for stragglers, and after finding his mother, to have been able to feed himself and her for seven days, with the food he scouted for, is a bit more than miraculous, and I put it down entirely to that sweet little cherub who sits up aloft.

Mrs Wilson and her son were removed to Tauranganui and afterwards to Napier. For nine days after she had been found it was hoped she might recover, but her injuries were too great, and she died shortly after she reached the latter place.

The above short and very incomplete yarn may give you some idea of the reason why we, members of the Lost Legion, so cheerfully underwent the great hardships we did to revenge the Poverty Bay massacre of November 1868.

FOLLY, PLUCK AND ENDURANCE

It is wonderful what a great number of good scouts and men have jeopardised and even lost their lives and the valuable information they have obtained, by a small act of folly, or by refusing to endure hardships for a few hours longer, when by doing so they might have won through safely and have brought to their O.C. the information he so badly wanted.

I have known men who, despite years of experience, have rushed out of their camp to tackle a lion with only the one cartridge that was in their rifle; and there are plenty of men who go prospecting or even big-game hunting and have their rifle and ammunition carried for them by a *Kafir* boy. Trouble comes, the boy bolts, and they are in a mess. Again, I have known men throw away ammunition and rations, rather than endure the fatigue of carrying them on the line of march, and how often has not a night's march or a premeditated attack on an enemy's position been spoilt by some man lighting his pipe or letting off his rifle that he has been told to carry unloaded?.

The yarn I am going to spin you now will perhaps bear out what I have just written, and though the man who committed the folly extricated himself by a deed of heroism never surpassed and seldom equalled, yet the act of folly he and his mate perpetrated might have led to the loss of three lives, their own included.

It was in November 1865. The Hau Haus (fanatical and rebel Maoris) had received a severe defeat at the hands of the Colonial forces and friendly natives at Waerenga-a-Hika, which so broke them up that they were unable to face the music in that district (Poverty Bay) for a few years.

Over 400 of them had surrendered. Of these some 200 had been transported to the Chatham Islands, the remainder settling down peacefully for a long time. There were, however, still a large number of the most fanatical and bloodthirsty of' the savages who, although unable to make a stand, yet roved about the country in small bands, seeking opportunity to destroy any white man or friendly native whom they might come across.

Now among the Defence Force, scattered at posts built for the protection of the settlers, was a big, raw-boned Irish sergeant named Walsh, who had heard very many extraordinary yarns about some petroleum springs at a place called Pakake-a-Whirikoka, situated some thirty miles from the post he was in charge of I do not know what his reasons were; perhaps it was only curiosity, or perchance he had ideas of becoming an oil king. But as things looked quiet and peaceful, he determined to visit them, and persuaded an old settler and his son, named Espic, to guide him to the locality.

Well, they started early in the morning, the time being summer and the weather very hot, and after a long ride of nearly thirty miles reached the steep hill leading to the springs. Here they dismounted, and, because they had seen no signs of the enemy, decided to leave their horses in charge of the boy, while they went up the hill, on foot, to examine the springs.

This in itself was an act of folly; but they went one worse, for, the weather being hot, and meaning only to be absent a very short time, they left their carbines, coats and all their ammunition at the foot of the hill, rather than endure the slight trouble of carrying them, and started the ascent with only their revolvers.

Now they had been spotted by one of these bands of Hau Haus, who, as soon as they saw the two white men go up the hill, crawled up to the horses and captured them, with the arms and ammunition. The boy, however, although fired at, escaped and got away. The Hau Haus, thinking they had their prey secure, tied up the horses to a tree, and went up the hill after the white men, who, having heard the shots, were returning.

As soon as they met, the natives fired a volley, which broke Espic's arm and wounded Walsh on the forehead and hand. The white men returned the fire, and in the skirmish that followed Walsh was again wounded and, the white men's revolvers being now empty, the Hau Haus, nine in number, rushed them with the *tomahawk*, to finish them off.

In the hand-to-hand scrap that ensued Walsh was again twice wounded; but he still fought on, and a Hau Hau, determining to finish him, put his cut-down gun to Walsh's chest and fired.

Fortunately the bullet must have fallen out of the gun, as Walsh only sustained a bad burn on the chest. Springing in, he felled his assailant with a tremendous blow from the butt-end of his revolver. This was too much for Maori superstition. That a man whom they had badly wounded five times should be able to continue to put up a fight was bad enough; but that he should be able to floor their best man just after that best man had shot him through the chest was more than any decent Hau Hau could understand. Leaving the horses and the stricken man behind them, away they fled, only too anxious to put as great a distance as they could between themselves and the awful *tohunga* (magician), who refused to be killed. So much for folly and pluck. Now I will go on to endurance.

No sooner had the astonished and affrighted Hau Haus bolted

than Walsh and his mate kicked their prisoner into convalescence and proceeded down the hill, where they found their horses tied to a tree, but the carbines, ammunition, and even saddles, taken away. Both men were badly wounded, Walsh in five places; but he would neither kill his prisoner nor let him go. Passing a rope round his neck, they made shift to mount their horses, bare-backed, and, forcing him to accompany them, they led him that long, hot ride of thirty miles, back to Tauranganui, where they arrived that night. Yes, faint though they were with the loss of blood, racked with the pain of untended wounds, without a round of ammunition, and hampered by an evil brute of a Hau Hau, who did everything in his power to retard their progress. Yet they would neither kill him nor let him go.

That I think is a yarn that illustrates folly, pluck and endurance.

CHAPTER 8

A Tough Swim in Bad Company

If you look at the map of the middle island of New Zealand you will see the north coast of it, washed by Cook's Straits, is deeply indented by fiords running inland, and that Tory Channel and Queen Charlotte's Sound are two of the principal ones.

These run in separately for some miles, and then join together and form one sound, which continues for a considerable distance, having on one side, some miles farther south, the important seaport of Picton.

The island, surrounded by the water of the aforementioned fiords, is known as Alapawa or Arapawa Island, and in the year 1872 was divided into two sheep runs and occupied by two firms of squatters who had already acquired a large number of sheep.

The scenery up these fiords is magnificent, the densely bushed mountains coming down to the water, which is deep to the very shore, so much so that the largest ship can sail close in and, if her skipper wants to, can make fast to the big trees growing down to the water's edge. The tide runs up and down these fiords at a tremendous rate, and this must be remembered when you read the yarn I am now going to spin you.

Arapawa Island is a range of high mountains, and on the side facing Queen Charlotte's Sound I was staying at one of the sheep stations for the purpose of recuperating my health after a rather long spell in hospital.

The year before I had foolishly got in the way of a small piece of lead that, being in a hurry, was travelling very fast. I had stopped it, and had been punished for my imprudence by having to lay up while doctors sunk shafts and drove drives in my corpus and generally prospected me for a lead mine.

True, they had not struck the reef; but then they had not succeeded in killing me, and when I got out of their hands I called it a drawn game, and started to get well in my own way.

The shafts and the drives had filled up, and I had finished the cure by staying two months in the glorious climate of the sounds, first knocking about in a sailing-boat in the management of which I was a dab, and then assisting my friends by running over the hills after sheep. This exercise, with plenty of good mutton and damper, turning-in just after dark, and turning-out just before sunrise, had perfected my cure, and I was as strong as ever, and in good training. At that time I neither used spirits nor tobacco; I was as hard as iron and as tough as whipcord, and had, moreover, practised swimming, boxing, fencing and other gymnastics from early childhood. The awful hardships of the past wars had done me no harm, but rather good, as they had squeezed the last soft drop out of me, and I was fit for anything.

I should have rejoined my troop on the frontier of the North Island a fortnight before, but waited to help my friends through with their yearly mustering and sheep-shearing. Hands were scarce, and I had never before seen a muster or sheep-shearing, so, my traps having been sent on to Picton, I waited for it. Well, the shearing was over and the men temporarily taken on for it were paid off.

In those days, on the last night before the extra hands were dismissed it was considered the right thing to do for everyone to go on a big burst, and men who had worked hard for weeks, and not touched a drop of spirits, would get blind drunk. So it was at this station, with the exception of myself, who did not touch grog; all hands, masters and men, had a tremendous burst, drinking up every drop of strong rum laid in for the occasion.

The following morning at daylight I started for Picton in a boat, accompanied by one of the partners and four of the extra hands, all of whom were what is known as suffering a recovery, which means they were very ill from the effects of the previous night's debauch. I had roused them up, got the boat out, and we started on as lovely a morning as I ever saw in my life. My crew, very ill and sulky, lay down in the bottom of the boat, a roomy craft of about twenty-three feet in length, and tried to sleep.

Well, we made our offing, the sun rose very hot and the wind died away. It was by this time slack water, and, as the men refused to pull an oar, we lay motionless. Suddenly I noticed the day darken and the mountains of Arapawa Island covered with a dense black cloud that

102

was rolling rapidly down them, and knew in a moment we were in for a southerly buster.

The air grew rapidly colder, and I shouted to the men to get up and shorten sail; but they would not move. I saw what resembled a dense cloud of dust raised off a very dry road in summer-time coming at us. In a moment it was on us; it was a spray torn from the sea by the force of the squall, and it stung and blinded me. As the squall struck us broadside on, it simply sunk us, turning us over at the same time.

I stuck to the tiller until the boat turned turtle, when I was, of course, thrown out, and was swimming at her stern as the keel rose from the water. The boat had a very deep false keel, and I saw that everyone had got hold of it. Just as the squall was thinning the boat rolled over and righted herself, and in the lull I shouted to the men to leave go their hold on the gunwale and join me, so that we could try and swing the stern to the wind, when perhaps one man could get in and bail her out. But they would not listen. They all tried to scramble into her at once, and over she went again. This happened twice, and I could not get the men to obey me, or try to do anything to save themselves. They all seemed to be mad with fright; one even kicked savagely at me as I tried to get him to leave go his hold on the keel. I saw the only chance to save my own and their lives was to try to swim ashore, and get help and another boat from the station.

I had at least two miles to swim; and that in the teeth of a southerly buster, which I could see was now coming on in full force. I was dressed only in a thin flannel shirt and trousers; the latter I easily tore off, but I determined to keep on my canvas shoes, as I would have a long run round the beach to get to the house—that is to say, if I ever got on shore. This was very problematical, as not only had I the gale to contend against, but I knew the bay and sound swarmed with sharks; and the evening before I had sat on a rock and shot at the brutes as they were tearing to pieces the bodies of a lot of old and worthless sheep that had been killed and thrown into the sea.

Well, the sharks would have their chance at me now, and turn and turn about is only fair play. In tearing my trousers off I sank a bit, and on coming up I shouted to the men I would try to bring them help, and started. Just then down came the true gale. The wind rushing through the tops of the mountains struck the water as if forced through a funnel, and tore it into foam and spray, which not only blinded me, but simply drove me under the water, and I quickly saw I must dodge the fierce blasts by diving. I was a very powerful swimmer and had the lungs and wind of an ostrich, so that, whenever I saw a cloud of water dust coming at me, down I went and swam under water for all I was worth. Then, when I had to come up for air, if there was a lull in between the squalls, 1 would strike out with a good long side-stroke, and make all the way I could.

This sort of thing went on for a long time, and I thought of and used every dodge I had ever learned or heard of to save my strength and use it to the very best advantage. My long experience in scouting and despatch-riding had trained me to think quickly and to act decisively. I was as cool as a cucumber and as hopeful as a boy setting out to rob an orchard. The water was warm. I was in splendid fettle, and I had a wild feeling of elation, as I dodged the squalls, that was simply grand, although my eyes ached and smarted with the spray. If it had not been for the danger of my helpless mates I should have simply revelled in my struggle against the elements. As I rose for air, during a lull, I took a good look at the land, and was surprised at the very rapid progress I was making.

For a minute I could not understand it. I was certainly drawing more under the lee of the land, and the squalls were not so fierce as at the first start, but still I was quite a mile off, and they were bad enough; but all at once I understood what was befriending me; it was the tide.

It had been slack water when the accident had happened, and the tide had turned and was simply helping me all it knew; now I felt certain of getting ashore, bar accidents. Yet, bar accidents, I was all right; but there were other things also, as I quickly discovered, for when I determined it was no longer necessary for me to dodge the squalls, and had settled down to a long, steady side-stroke, I glanced to my right, and there, not thirty feet from me, was a long, triangular fin sticking out of the water, which I knew belonged to a shark of the largest size. Instinctively I turned to the left. There was another one; and as I raised myself in the water and looked astern of me, there was a third.

To say I was in a funk is not to tell the truth; funk does not fully describe my feelings. I knew what funk was; I had been in a funk before, plenty of times. I had been in many a tight and hot corner before. I had often looked at what might be certain death, but then I had weapons in my hand and the prospect of a good fight before I went under; but now I was helpless. There was to be no fight, there could be no fight. I had not even a knife, and had I possessed one I was outnumbered and outclassed.

As I trod water for a few moments I knew what real fear was. I had never felt it before, and, thank heaven! I have never felt it since. I can't describe my feelings, and I would not if I could. Certainly it was not the fear of death that caused these sensations; but it seemed so hard that I, who had almost overcome my danger, should be turned into long pig for a beastly shark.

But my cowardice did not last long. I was still at least three-quarters of a mile from shore; the good tide was still sweeping me in, and my wild Irish blood all at once boiled up in me. My duty to myself and mates required me to get on shore, and get on shore I would. If a shark took me, well and good, *kismet*. Stick to my work I would, shark or no shark; so I fell into my stroke, and swam as if there had not been a shark within a degree of latitude of me, escorted by a guard of honour I never want again.

Yes, I got ashore, those d——d sharks keeping company all the way; and when my foot hit bottom and I stumbled through the shallow water and fell on the sand there they still were, cruising about, not a stone's-throw away, as if they were the most harmless beasts in the ocean. Why did they not go for me? I don't know; certainly my time had not yet come, *kismet*. As soon as I had taken a few breaths I looked for the boat, but could not see her for the dense spray which the gale, now at its worst, was kicking up; so I started to run the four miles round the bay to the station. The rough beach and rocks soon cut my soaked shoes to pieces and, as the soles became detached, I had to run with bare feet, and suffered awfully. Fain would I have halted and rested, but my mates' danger spurred me on, and I ran as if a Maori, with his *tomahawk*, were after me.

I came to the head of the bay and suddenly remembered that between me and the house there was another very deep indent of the sea. At the mouth it was not more than 250 yards across, but it ran very far inland, and with my feet in the state they were it would take me hours to get round. No, I must swim it; and I was just plunging in, notwithstanding the squalls, which were tearing the surface of the water into dust, when I was struck with the horrid thought of sharks, and for a moment I paused like a coward on the brink.

It was only for a moment. Curse the sharks! my mates were on the boat; and in I went and crossed after a hard swim. To get to the house, rouse up the other partner and the one remaining man, and to get out a small whale-boat did not take many minutes. We manned the boat, peaked the oars and ran before the gale. We came up to the derelict in mid-sound, rolling over and over, but not a sign of a man was on her, nor was a single body ever found. We ran across the sound, beached the boat, and, when the gale subsided, pulled back.

This is, I think, the nearest call I have ever had, and if there is any moral in my yarn it is to leave drink alone, keep in training, do your duty by yourself and mates, and trust to your luck while doing so. Since then I have always hated sharks. The curse of Cromwell be on them.

CHAPTER 9

Held Up By a Bushranger
(Told by the Old Identity)

It took place in the early seventies. I was in Australia, and was temporarily in command of a body of Mounted Police, doing duty as gold escort—a very necessary precaution in those days. On one occasion I was travelling upcountry, accompanied by four troopers, when a big squatter, a friend of mine, asked leave to ride with my small party, as he was carrying a quantity of gold upcountry with him to his station. Of course I was delighted to have his company, and we set out.

All along the road there were plenty of shaves (rumours) of bushrangers, but for three days we never saw one. At noon on the fourth day we halted at a bush shanty to feed, water and rest our horses.

The bush shanties, in those days, were as a rule vile poison shops, the owners and their employees being usually hand in glove with every scoundrel, cattle thief and bushranger in the country, giving them information as to the movements of the police, and in many cases sharing with them their plunder.

However, with a party like ours there was nothing to fear, at least so I thought; so when we dismounted and handed over our horses to the troopers to lead to the stockyards, some little distance from the house, myself and my friend entered. It was a long, one-roomed building, with a bar running the whole length of it, and the only door at one end.

There was no one inside but the bar-tender, as hang-dog-looking a ruffian as I have ever set eyes on. Foolishly, as it proved, as I entered I unbuckled my belt with sword and revolver attached and threw them on a bench by the door. Then we strolled together to the far end of the bar and, hot and thirsty with our long ride in the burning sun, called for drinks.

Glasses in hand, we stood with our backs to the door, and were just about to sample our poison when we heard the ominous words: "Bail up!" Turning round, I saw a wicked-looking devil standing in the doorway.

He had me covered with the heavy revolver he carried in his right hand, while its mate, ready for action, was gripped in his left by his side.

He was a well-made, tough-looking chap, very muscular and strong, without carrying an ounce of superfluous flesh, and dressed in the ordinary up- country dress. His face, clean-shaven, was covered by a black mask, but I noticed a well-cut mouth, a determined chin, and his eyes gleamed through the holes of his visor with a glint there was no mistaking, while the hand that held the gun was as steady as a rock.

Then I realised that he was between me and my weapons, which lay on the bench by the door.

A man who has passed years in bush-fighting, scouting and despatch-riding thinks quickly and acts decisively. Had there been the slightest tremor in wrist or lips I should have slung my glass at him, and risked a rush; but there was not a sign of a tremble, and I knew that the slightest hostile movement on my part would not only lead to my certain death, but would be quite useless.

My friend and the villainous bar-tender, the latter with a broad grin on his ugly mug, had at once bailed up, and as there was no chance of help from my troopers, who by that time must have off-saddled and be attending to the horses at the stock- yard, some way off, I knew we were cornered and beaten.

"Captain," said the bounder, "I guess I've got you. Bail up."

"I'll see you d——d first," I replied.

"I've got you," he retorted, "and I'm on the shoot. Sling your money on the counter, and"—this to my friend—"sling that bag down too."

The squatter was standing with his hands above his head, so evidently could not do so, and the bushranger said to me: "Captain, sling that bag over here."

"Rot!" was my discourteous reply; so he turned to the blackguard behind the bar, who was probably in league with him, and said, "Joe, you do it." And the bag was promptly thrown to him.

Then he said to me, and I noticed he changed his voice, dropping the Yankee slang and idiom he had previously used, and speaking with a well-modulated and refined accent: "Captain, I don't want anything from you." (This was just as well, as I had nothing.) "But," he continued, "how long start will you give me?"

I said: "Five minutes."

"Word of honour?"

"Yes."

"So long." And with that he backed out, and in a moment I heard the beat of a horse's hoofs starting at a gallop. My friend was raving mad, and wanted me at once to alarm my troopers, but I said: "No; you'd got your gun with you just now, why did you not use it?" When five minutes had passed I gave the order to saddle up; but of course the man had got clear away. I never knew who he was, but a man shot shortly afterwards by one of my troopers was believed to be he, and most probably was.

CHAPTER 10

On the Scout In New Zealand
(Told by the old Kai Tongata)

It was in June 1869 that Te Kooti, chief of the rebel Hau Haus, caught a party of mounted volunteers on the hop, at a place called Opepe, on the high plateau near Lake Taupo. The men, worn out by a long march, and soaked through by the cold winter rain and sleet, had taken shelter on some old whares (huts) and were trying to dry themselves when a few Maoris came up, and, declaring themselves to be friendlies, joined them at their fires.

More and more of them gradually arrived, until the volunteers were outnumbered, and then, on a signal being given, the natives sprang on their unsuspecting victims, and the tomahawk did the rest. The victors did not stay long at the blood-stained spot. They knew that Colonel McDonnell, Colonel St John and, worse than anyone, Major Ropata Te Wahawaha, with his friendly Ngatiporou, were not far away, and that it behoved them to hump themselves and travel before the avengers could reach them. Some of the volunteers had escaped, and two of them joined up with Colonel St John's column, with which I was serving, the same evening as the massacre took place.

It was at once boot and saddle, and before nightfall we had marched to Opepe.

Colonel St John had reached the spot before us, in fact the men cut up belonged to his column, and he had only left them the morning of the massacre to rest themselves and horses, while he went on to visit a Maori chief about ten miles away.

Next morning we were on the spoor, and followed it through rough pumice-stone gullies for some miles, in pouring rain and sleet, then lost all trace of them in a dense scrub of *manuka* bush, so we returned to Opepe for the night.

The following day it was determined to send scouts out to find where the enemy had retreated to.

We had followed Te Kooti since July 1868, when he had escaped with 160 fighting men from Chatham Islands, had landed at Whare-onga-onga, close to Poverty Bay, and had gathered all the disaffected Maoris in the country to him. He had sacked Poverty Bay, murdering about ninety helpless settlers. He had fought us twice at Makaretu and innumerable other places, had captured a convoy of ammunition, had fortified himself at Ngatapa, where he had repulsed, with heavy loss, two assaults and had only evacuated the *pah* when starved out for want of food and water. And although we had, in the pursuit, captured and killed 136 of his men, yet he himself escaped and reached the fast-nesses of the Uriwera country.

In April 1869 he had swooped down on the Mohaka settlement and had murdered in cold blood seventy whites and friendly natives, and then retreated to Taupo country with us at his heels.

In fact he had kept us lively for a year, and was going to prevent us getting rusty for two more, until, having lost nearly all his men, he retired into the King country, where we could not follow him; and he lived there quietly for twenty years, and at last died in the odour of sanctity, highly respected by all who knew him. For nearly four years we were on his track: his escapes were numerous and miraculous, we destroyed band after band of the desperate savages who joined him, but although he was wounded twice we never got him.

Bad luck to it, I'm off the spoor. To get back.

It was determined to send out scouts to locate Te Kooti, and I was chosen with two men to do the job. It was a big contract to handle. One glance at the map will show you Lake Taupo. We were at the north-east corner, about ten miles from the semi-friendly *pah* at Tapuacharuru (Sounding Footsteps), our base was at Opotiki, eighty miles away, on the Bay of Plenty coast. There were at that time no roads, no bridle-tracks, no paths; no game existed in New Zealand, and there was no food to be procured for man, and but little for horses.

No white man, with the exception, perhaps, of a stray missionary, had ever penetrated to that part of the country, which was composed of dense bush, mountains and broken ground covered with *manuka* scrub, or long fern, which grew from six to ten feet high, and it was in the depth of winter, bitterly cold and wet. The enemy had retreated in the direction of the great volcanoes Ruapehu and Tongeriro, at the south-east end of the lake, about thirty-five miles from where we were camped, and in an awful country, quite unknown and hostile to us. This country had to be searched, Te Kooti found and attacked before he established himself in another stronghold and recruited his murderous band of bloodthirsty savages. The columns could not advance and look for him; they had no food to feed man or horse during the time it would take to find him. No, they must fall back nearer the base, and the scouts must find him, and then the troops and horses, well fed, could make a rush for him and perhaps put an end to his career. My orders were that I was to find Te Kooti and return to Opepe, the Colonel promising he and the column would meet me there on the sixteenth day, when I was to guide him up to the quarry.

How I was to find the bounder, and how we were to live while we were looking for him, was left to me. It was certain that Te Kooti would be looking out for anyone who might be impudent enough to look for him, and if he caught us our fate was certain, though, of course, we could only guess at the nature of the torture to which we should be subjected. Even if we were lucky enough to be able to blow our own brains out before we were captured, the Colonel would lose the information he required, and more men would have to be sent; so that it behoved us to keep ourselves and our tracks hidden, and to see without being seen.

How we were to live I left to Providence; it was beyond me. We were all hardened bush-fighters, and we must take our chance.

My two companions were queer characters; both of them had been sailors: one of them, Pierre De Feugeron, a Frenchman, the other a Kantuarius Greek. They had been mates for years, were both splendid scouts, expert bushmen, good shots, and utterly fearless. Well, no sooner had I got my orders than we started. Our field kit consisted of smasher hats, dark blue serge jumpers that reached to the knee, but during the day were drawn up and fastened round the waist; we wore no trousers, but had shawls round us like kilts. I wore shooting boots and socks; the others went barefooted with sandals. Our arms consisted of carbines and revolvers, and we each wore in our belts a *tomahawk* and sheath knife. On our backs we carried a blanket rolled up, in which was some very bad bacon and worse biscuit, four pounds of each; and with this we were to penetrate thirty-five miles or more into an unknown country, as rough as any in the world, find a wily enemy and, above all, get back with our information.

It may not seem much to the man who has never been out of Britain, but a Colonial will appreciate the job at its true value.

We left the camp from the north side, and made a wide detour to the north-east, before we struck to the south-west, to touch the lake. The enemy had retreated almost due south, through a number of rough pumice-stone gullies, and it was more than likely that a sly old bird like Te Kooti would leave an ambush on his spoor to cut off any scouts that might be sent after him, or, in case a strong party followed him, to give him news of their movements. I did not want to fall into that ambush. I had been in a few before, and did not like them; and so went round to try and cut his spoor a good way south of where we had abandoned it on the previous day.

All that day we tramped across deep gullies and through *manuka* scrub, very often having to head off our road to examine the ground on either side of us, and to take bearings to our rear as well as to our front.

A good scout should always do this, as he may have to return a sight faster than he went; and he must remember which way he came; he has no time to think much when a war party is after him.

Well, as night fell we came to a range of mountains covered with bush, and I reckoned that, with our detour, we had made quite ten miles to the south of Opepe, and were well on our way. It had rained all day, except when it sleeted, and of course we were wet through, yet we dare not light a fire. For all we knew we might have been spotted and followed; so we entered the bush, and as soon as it was quite dark moved carefully a mile away and, eating a small handful of biscuits, wrapped ourselves in our shawls and blankets and slept as well as we could.

It froze hard that night and the cold was intense; in the morning we were up as soon as a glimmer of day came, and started to cross the range of mountains. The bush was a regular New Zealand one, composed of trees of gigantic size, and with a dense undergrowth that nothing but a pig or an elephant could get through. We therefore had to take to the bed of a creek and follow it up to the ridge. The water was icy cold, and the cold drip from the trees and bushes wet us through, although it did not rain. With nothing but a few bits of flint-like biscuit to chew, up we went, and came to the top of the range, and there we rested and got a view of the country.

To our west was the lake, and to the south was the cone of Tongeriro and the three peaks of Ruapehu; between us and them was range after range of hills, below us lay a deep valley, and, tough as we were,

I almost feared the job was too tough for us. To despond is one of the last things a scout should do; so after more biscuit off we went again, and, striking another creek, we descended the bed of it till we came to the river that ran through the valley and entered the lake at the foot of it. I determined to descend the bed of this river, as I thought I might cut Te Kooti's spoor on the beach of the lake, which I determined to examine next morning. I feared to do so that evening, as they might have ambushed the drift, and there was also the dread of the ambuscade he most likely had left behind to watch our camp.

This party, after they had watched the column move away, would most likely, provided they had not seen us, be on the march to catch up Te Kooti.

We therefore hid on a fern ridge with the drift in view of us, and fortunate it was for us we did so.

We had not been there long when we saw coming from the north, along the beach, a party of twelve natives; and I felt much relieved, for I knew at once that they had not seen us, or they would have been after us, and that I had been quite right to make the detour I had done.

They marched quite carelessly, evidently thinking no white man was nearer them than the retreating column, and when they had crossed the drift lit a big fire, cooked food and warmed themselves; then, leaving the fire burning, started at a rapid pace for the south.

We watched them round a far cape of the lake, then down we went to their fire and warmed ourselves and cooked a bit of bacon. Thankful we were for the warmth and food; but we dare not stay long.

I wanted to get the benefit of the open beach, and also to spot their camp fire that night; so, as soon as our frozen limbs were thawed and our food swallowed, we were off, hiding our spoor as well as we could.

That night we saw their camp, and envied them as we lay hid in the fern shivering with cold; for again we had a hard frost, and our clothes were far from dry; but a scout must put up with cold, heat, hunger, thirst, and be ready to face, smiling, anything that falls to his lot.

The earlier in life he hardens himself to do without rotten sweet stuff the better, and always remember that cigarettes are the invention of the evil one.

Well, day after day this sort of life went on. If I were to try to describe our adventures day by day they would fill a book; let it suffice that for ten days we lurked through tangled and dripping bush, waded up the bed of mountain torrents, crossed snowclad ranges, and struggled through matted fern, soaked with rain and sleet during the day, and frozen stiff during the bitter nights. Our miserable rations were gone. Sometimes we found a rotten *matti*-tree, and from it extracted the white grubs, which we ate thankfully. Once we found some potatoes.

At last we discovered Te Kooti, and where he was building his new pah.

For one night I prowled round it, and long before morning we were on our way back. For the first two days the same care had to be taken to hide our spoor; it would never do to be caught or killed after all our troubles and sufferings.

On the third day I moved down to the lake.

We were starving: not just hungry, but absolutely starving. As the evening was coming on, in a small bay I saw the smoke of a fire; that meant Maoris camping. They had food of some sort, and we decided to have it.

The bay was an inlet, into which a small creek emptied itself, between two low ridges of fern. A short detour led us to the bed of the creek, down which we descended as quietly as otters, while the noise of the stream drowned any slight noise we might make in wading down it. The creek ran into a small clump of tree ferns, and we crept on till we came to where the party was encamped at the mouth of the creek.

There were four fine-looking big Maoris. Their canoe was drawn up on the bank of the creek with the paddles leaning against it. Had there been more than four paddles it would have meant that some of the party were absent; but now we knew we had only the four in front to tackle. We dare not use our fire-arms on account of the report. No, the job must be done with tomahawk and knife. We were within twenty feet of them.

A glance at my companions and we laid down our carbines, slipped off our blankets and drew our *tomahawks* and knives.

One more look. The four Maoris were sitting by their fire, unconscious of our presence. A nod to my mates and we sprang at them. *Whiz, whiz* went my men's knives—they were both past masters at the art of knife-throwing—and over went two Maoris with the knives buried up to the hafts in their bodies.

I rushed my man, but, surprised as he was, he was a splendid, tough old warrior, and jumped at me, his *tomahawk* swinging loosely in the air above his head.

I had practised hard with the *tomahawk* for the last two years, but I knew I was no match for the old man. I therefore determined to rush in on him, guard his first blow and use my left fist. (I was very strong in those days, and a good boxer.) Throwing up my *tomahawk*, I guarded a smashing cut at the left of my neck, and although I felt the keen edge of the blade cut my flesh on the left shoulder, the impetus of my charge carried me in, and lashing out with my left I struck him full on the throat. Down he went, astonished by this novel mode of attack, and in another moment the head of my *tomahawk* was buried up to the eye in his brains.

When I looked round the fight was over, the only unwounded Maori falling an easy prey to the combined attack of my two *desperadoes*.

Pierre, a splendid cook, was already looking into the pot that was on the fire, and, declaring the contents to be good pork, not long pig, we were soon enjoying it. To get rid of the bodies did not take long. The marks of the struggle were obliterated, and we were off. Two days more and we reached Opepe; and, true to his word, my colonel met us with a strong patrol. We were thin, foot- sore, our legs torn, our kit in rags; but what mattered that? We had done our duty and had got back with valuable information, and as we swallowed some hot tea we did not care for the past—it was past. My wound was nothing— Pierre had stitched it up—and as I once more donned my breeches and boots, a clean shirt, and threw my leg over my dear old horse, I was as happy as the day was wet.

CHAPTER 11

The Colonels Fiery Tot

(Told by the old Kai Tongata)

During the east coast war the division in which I was serving landed on the beach to seize a "*pah*," or native stronghold, two days' march inland. As usual we carried four days' rations, including rum. We were led by a fine old colonel, a distinguished Crimean officer, who was much liked by the men. He was one of the old "two-bottle men"—or, rather, he was contented with two bottles when he could not get three.

At that time I had not acquired a liking for ration rum—raw, fiery stuff—but by the end of the second day's march the colonel had consumed his own allowance and mine too. At daylight on the third day, when we had fallen in beside a creek, and were preparing to attack, he said to me: "Give me a tot" (calling me by a nickname I acquired early and retained throughout my active career).

"I haven't any rum, sir; you finished mine last night."

He bubbled like a furious turkey-cock, and swore I'd drunk more than my share. As I had not tasted a drop, I thought this unfair, but wisely said nothing. It is bad policy to argue with a liverish colonel, when he is two days' march from the nearest drink.

Then he said: "I must have a tot. I wonder whether the men have any left." I was just promising to inquire when he exclaimed excitedly: "Look there!" And lo and behold, a man stepped out of the ranks, then standing easy, and took from his haversack a bottle containing something that looked like rum. He poured some into a pannikin, poured in some water and drank it off. "By heavens," said the old colonel, "I've struck oil." Just then I called the men to "attention," and as we went down the ranks inspecting the colonel kept saying: "Deuced bad pain in my stomach."

As we got opposite the man with the bottle—he was, by the way, the most temperate man in the corps—the colonel's groans became heart-rending. The man thereupon brought out the bottle from his haversack, and said to him: "Do you think this would do you any good, sir?"

The colonel's face was wreathed in smiles.

"Aha, my man, just what I wanted," he exclaimed. "Give me your pannikin." And he proceeded to pour out for himself a strong "tot."

"Be careful, sir," said the man, "it's very strong."

"Ah!" said the colonel, "when you're as old a soldier as I am you'll be able to take your 'tot' neat." And with that he tossed it down.

The change that came over his face was marvellous! The smiles were replaced by a look of agonised surprise. He coughed and spluttered, and ejaculated: "Shoot the blackguard; he's poisoned me!" Then he rushed to the creek and drank more water in ten minutes than he had drunk in the ten previous years. "What have you given the colonel?" I asked the man.

"Perry & Davis's Pain-killer," he replied. "Will you try some, sir?"

I put my tongue to the mouth of the bottle and then said, "No, I'm blowed if I do." For the stuff was like liquid fire, and was hot enough to burn the entrails out of a brass monkey, and if applied externally would have blistered the halo from a plaster saint. It also claimed to cure everything. In that it lied, for it did not cure the colonel's propensity for ration rum, although I must admit it made him very careful for some time to sample his tot before he swallowed it.

CHAPTER 12

Lost in the New Zealand Bush

In spinning this yarn I wish to warn all new chums that, no matter how clever you may fancy yourself to be, you must, when you enter a bush, keep all your senses on deck, or you will run the chance of finding yourself bushed just as easily as the greenest tenderfoot ever exported. True, an old hand will, as a rule, pull through, while the green- horn will go under; but yet the number of old bushmen who have been lost and who have died is very great, and no one, no matter how experienced he is, or what his training has been, has a right to enter the bush without taking every precaution. This was driven into me very early in my frontier education, and I have saved myself frequently if not from death, yet from many hardships, by always ascertaining I had sufficient of the indispensable articles about me, without which no man should enter the forest or wilderness.

Perhaps, right here, I may enumerate them. In a dry country a man should always carry a water-bag or bottle, and see that it is in good order and full; he should never stir without plenty of matches, carried in a damp-proof box or well-corked bottle, a flint and steel, a burning-glass, or some means of making a fire. A *tomahawk* and sheath knife are indispensable; and of course, in Africa and countries where there are lions, etc., see that you have plenty of ammunition with you—remember you may want to signal with your rifle—and if possible shove a couple of ship biscuits into your haversack: you may want them, and they do not weigh much.

Now for the yarn. In 1874 I was located at a place called Wai-Tangi (Murmuring Water), a native *kainga*, on Lake Tarawera, and one day determined to go pigeon and kaka (New Zealand parrot) shooting in the densely bushed ranges on the east side of the lake. The lake is a very beautiful one, of large size, surrounded by mountains, among

119

which is the volcano Mount Tarawera, and at the south-west corner is the creek that leads up to Rotomahana and the wonderful terraces.

At the date I write about Mount Tarawera was quiet, and everyone thought it had retired from the volcano business; but some years afterwards, 1886, it took a fit, broke out, blew the terraces galley west, destroyed a great deal of property and killed a good few people, among others my quondam hosts at Wai-Tangi. Now the New Zealand *kaka* and pigeon are, in the fall of the year, very toothsome birds indeed; they get very fat on the berries of the gigantic trees, and the Maoris have a very good way of preserving them. I mention these last facts, as, previous to my departure from the *kainga*, I had told my host, the chief of the place, that I was going to try to kill a great many birds, had requested him to order a woman to make a couple of large bark buckets to preserve them in, and had also intimated I might camp out or stay for a night or two at one or other village on the lake.

This was unfortunate, as, subsequently, the Maoris took no notice of my prolonged absence and did not come to look for me, as they concluded I was staying somewhere else; and it was only on the day of my return the old chief, having become anxious, started a party of young warriors to paddle round the lake to find out if I were all right.

Well, I started off in a canoe, taking with me my gun, fifty No. 4 shot cartridges, some tea and sugar, a couple of blankets and half-a-dozen ship biscuits. I should also have taken a young warrior, but as all the natives were engaged on their plantations, I went alone. It was a lovely day, the lake as calm as a millpond and the splendid scenery most entrancing. I paddled slowly out of the little bay at the head of which the *kainga* stood, and after a few minutes' contemplation of the glorious bushed mountains, whose beauties were reflected as in a mirror on the glass-like water, I struck out across the north-east corner of the lake and made for the east shore, where I meant to beach my canoe in some small bay at the mouth of one of the numerous creeks that ran into the lake, then ascend the bed of the creek, get on the top of the high ranges, where there is comparatively little undergrowth, and shoot my game. After a few miles steady paddling I reached the shore, where there was rather a deep inlet, grounded my canoe on the beach at the head of it, where a fair-sized creek entered the lake, and landed.

Now I mentioned before that I had made the best use of my frontier education; so at once I dragged my canoe out of the water as far as

I could and made fast the painter to a stout tree, then overhauled my belongings. I was dressed in proper bush outfit: a serge jumper, flannel shirt, smasher hat, good strong shooting boots and a shawl round my waist instead of trousers. In my belt I wore a tomahawk and sheath knife, and slung on to the back of it was a strong tin pannikin. I also carried on my belt a leather pouch containing a metal damp-proof box full of matches, a burning-glass, a plug of tobacco and my pipe. My cartridges I wore in a bandoleer over one shoulder, and over the other I wore one of the old-fashioned game bags.

I was very strong in those days and did not mind a little extra weight; so after I had lunched on a biscuit and a lump of cold pork I put the remaining biscuits, a tin containing tea and sugar mixed, and a small one holding salt and pepper mixed, into my bag, hid my blankets and paddle, and after a glance to see that my canoe was all right, I entered the creek and started up the range. For some distance the brushwood and undergrowth were too thick for me to be able to see a bird on the tree-tops, but as I got higher up the range the bush thinned out, so that I could occasionally get a shot, and I found when I came to the summit I had bagged three brace of birds. These I hung up on a rata-tree and I out *tomahawk* and blazed it well, so as to let me know, on my return, it was the point at which I was to descend to the lake. The country I found myself in was very broken, and what had appeared from the lake to be a straight range of mountains running from north to south I found to be a regular jumble of broken ridges, cliffs and spurs that seemed to be mixed into several ranges that took no definite direction at all.

This sort of country is very dangerous to explore and, knowing the fact, I ought to have taken precautions and exercised the greatest care. I did neither; for I wandered on after the birds and presently began thinking about some important letters I had lately received from home, and other matters, without even noting any of the salient landmarks, or the turnings and twistings of the broken ridges and spurs I was walking among. Nor did I turn round and spot landmarks to guide my return journey. This was an act of folly unpardonable for a scout who knew his work and who was quite aware of the danger he was running. Yet the very best and most experienced bushmen sometimes commit an act of folly, and, not being infallible, I had in my turn committed a very grave one. For when the approaching dusk warned me it was time to regain my canoe I turned round, and in a moment knew I was lost. You may ask how it was I knew at once I was lost. I will tell you.

Every scout worth his salt should carry in his head a map of the road he has been traversing that day, and when he is about to return on the back track he should at once be able to see that road with his mind's eye, its salient points, its landmarks, its difficulties, and everything worthy of note along it. Well, when I turned I naturally cast my mind's eye on to my map and found a blank. I had noted nothing from the time I had hung up the birds and blazed the first tree; and I cussed myself for my folly. It was now I felt bush fear; for a desperate longing came over me *to run* and try to find my way; but this I combated with all my will-power, and after a minute's struggle forced myself to sit down under a tree and think if I could not remember anything that might recall the road to mind; but in vain. The only thing to guide me was that I had shot a pigeon which had fallen into a fork of a tree and stuck there; that incident could be of but little use to me, yet I treasured it. Again the desire, stronger than ever, came over me to run and look for the tree I had blazed; and again I had to fight it away.

Was I, fool as I had been, to lose my head and run mad through the bush like an untrained new chum? Not by a jugful. I would camp where I was, and next morning, with a clear head, would try to unravel the puzzle. Work was the thing for me, and I turned to. It did not take me long to collect plenty of firewood and make down a good fern bed. Water I could hear close by, and when I had filled my pannikin I lit my fire, for night falls quickly in the New Zealand bush, and over- hauled my stores. I had my gun and over thirty cartridges left, and, besides what food I had brought with me, I had ten fat birds; so there was no fear of starvation for a long time. I had also no fear of thirst, as there is always plenty of water to be found in a New Zealand bush; so I was well off, though I could not disguise the danger.

Anyhow I would have supper and think matters out, over a pipe, afterwards. In next door to no time I had two birds plucked, cleaned, and spitted on a splinter of wood, with a biscuit on a clean piece of bark under them. My pannikin, full of water, on some embers, soon boiled; to this was added some tea and sugar mixed, and I had a feast for the gods. True, I only had my sheath knife and fingers to eat with, but what of that? I was an old campaigner and could dispense with luxuries. Then, my meal over, I lit my pipe and thought out my position. I was in a hole, that I knew, and I should require all my bushcraft to get out of it. It was not as if I was in a forest on a plain, but I was in a regular jumble of broken ridges, valleys and spurs, all of them heavily bushed. The only thing I had to look for was a blazed tree with some birds hanging on to it, and I did not know if I were north, south or east of it; nor could I judge my distance from it; for although I knew I had walked about four hours and a half, and that I had turned south when I left the tree, yet, for all I knew, I might have worked round in a circle and at the present moment be due north of it, or have turned farther to the east.

My pipe finished, I determined to sleep if I could, so as to be fresh in the morning, and also to try to get rid of the feeling of solitude that now attacked and surprised me. I had frequently had to pass the night alone, aye, many a time, without fire or food, not daring to light the one and having none of the other; yet I had never felt so lonely or deserted before; for although I well knew there was nothing in the New Zealand bush that could hurt me, still I kept on looking over my shoulder, or glancing to right and left into the darkness, and I could now realise the feelings that men who had been lost and found had tried to describe to me. They had been tenderfoots. Faugh! I was an old hand; I had never funked the Hau Haus when they had been on the warpath after me. Why now should I let these childish qualms assail me and funk shadows? Yet they were there; and I confess them to you so that you may know how absolutely necessary it is for you, in case you should ever be in the same fix, no matter how experienced you are, to keep a tight hold over yourself, and not let your nerves get away with you. Rolling myself up in my shawl, I lay down on my fern bed (a very comfortable bed it is too, if you know how to make it properly) and, thinking over my plans for the morrow, went to sleep.

I awoke at daybreak refreshed and fit. A cold bath in the creek. A good breakfast. Then selecting a huge tree, I climbed it by shinning up one of the big pendent vines, and had a good look round. I had hoped to be able to see the lake, but could see nothing of it; nor could I recognise any of the loftier mountains; but I knew the lake must be to the westward of me, and as there seemed to be a higher range in that direction I determined to make for it, though I could see no spur running in a direct line towards it. I therefore descended and, carefully blazing the big tree under which I had camped, started, taking care to blaze all the trees on my line. My reason for doing so (and bear it in mind) was, I had reached the spot where I found myself lost, without going down into any of the deep valleys that surrounded me. Had I done so, I must have remembered the fact, as all the valleys were full of dense undergrowth, and I should have had to cut a road through it.

I had not used my *tomahawk* on the previous day, except to blaze the first tree, therefore there must be some way of getting back without using it—if I could only find that way. I was making for the west. Suppose after a time I should be certain I was going wrong, I could return with ease along the blazed track back to my camp, and start a new line, which I should also blaze, using a new tomahawk cut on the trees, and if that line failed, return and try again, always using the tree under which I had camped as a starting-point. I might fail half-a-dozen times or more, yet, with patience, I had a good chance to come out right in the end.

Again, although I did not reckon on it in my case, as I had no hopes of a search party coming to look for me, if you should ever be bushed, and you think it possible for a search to be sent to find you, it is a very good thing to carry out the above plan, and always return to your first camp, as most probably it will be the nearest spot to help; and if you pass your time in blazing lines (being careful to keep your lines distinct) the party looking for you will most likely strike one of your tracks and easily follow it to your assistance.

Knowing all this, I started, taking a course due west. I had no compass, but as a trained bushman I wanted none, and with all my senses on deck I began blazing trees on my line, taking care to spot every noticeable thing *en route*, and frequently looking back to see my track ran straight. Sometimes I fancied I was going right and I felt the impulse to run; but this feeling I at once suppressed, and determined I would play the game to the end. Past midday I knew I was wrong, as I came to a steep cliff descending perpendicularly into a deep valley, so I knew I could not have crossed it before. I was disappointed but by no means disheartened; so after a good look around I turned in my tracks and easily regained my camp, where I cooked more birds, had a good supper and slept without any bogeys coming to trouble me.

On the morning of the third day I started again and blazed a new line, in a north-west direction; but again I met with disappointment and returned to my base.

You may ask how it was that, as a trained scout, I did not try to follow my own spoor back to my starting-point. I will tell you at once. I was far too old at the game to waste my time by doing so. Of course I was always on the lookout for any trace I had left; but there is very little soft ground on the top of New Zealand ranges, and although I was in a daydream on the first afternoon, yet I knew that, instinctively, I should have avoided any soft or damp ground, also the gloom in a bush is not a good light to track by. An Australian black fellow might have been able to follow my spoor, but no one else, so I did not try to.

On the morning of the fourth day I started on what I thought to be a hopeless line nearly due north, as I expected to be shut off quickly by a deep valley I had noticed on the previous day; still it was the right game to play and I played it. Strange as it may appear, I was not shut off as I had expected, but continued on till I came to a couple of large trees growing so close together that they seemed to spring from the same root. These attracted my attention, and although they were out of my line I went to them. I seemed to remember them in a dim sort of way, and I examined the ground carefully, going on my hands and knees to do so. I also took a good steady look at the country I had just passed over, to see if any glimmer of remembrance would dawn on me; and it did, but so faint that I feared the wish was father to the thought. But yet, those trees! A certainty came to me that I had seen them before, and I crawled round to the other side of them, scanning every foot of ground, and found what might be the spoor of one of my boots.

At once I began to feel elated, and again the mad impulse to run came on; but I crushed it back, marked the spoor and forced myself to sit down and smoke a pipe. When I was quite cool I again examined the spoor, determined to restart my line from there and use the trees as a base.

I started a new line and had not gone very far when under a tree I saw a lot of pigeon feathers. I at once went on my hands and knees and after a few minutes' search found undoubted spoor; so I knew I was on the right track; and again the desire to run came on, but I squashed it and, blazing the tree well, had a good look round, but could get no certainty as to my route, so went on with my line and during the afternoon found myself blocked, and had to turn back. That evening I shot three birds, and camped at the tree where I had found the feathers.

Next morning I was off, after a good breakfast, taking a new line west of north, thinking it would only be a short one; but yet I got on farther than I expected, and with my eyes glancing everywhere, all of a sudden I spotted something in the stunted fern, and going up to it found a dead pigeon. Looking up, I noticed a fork in the tree close by and recognised it, as the one in which my bird had lodged. I at once tore the feathers off the bird. Yes, there could be no doubt, it had been killed by No. 4 shot; and now I was certain I was more than halfway out of the fix. Again the crazy desire to run, this time crushed with more difficulty and requiring a pipe. Then more blazing, until I began to think I must again be wrong and found myself unduly hastening my steps, and had to use the curb of my will to rein in. I had reached a place where I was thinking seriously of turning back, as I was convinced I had gone wrong, and had in fact halted when I noticed something waving in the wind about 150 yards away to the south. I could only now and then catch a glimmer of it through the trees, but I went towards it. I lost sight of it in the bush, then saw it again, and in a few minutes was standing in front of a blazed rata-tree with six pigeons hanging on it.

Here was my starting-point; but I was so convinced I had gone wrong that for a minute or two I could not believe my eyesight, and fancied I had gone mad, in fact was so surprised that I had to argue with myself that someone had not moved the tree and the birds. This folly did not last long, and I was quickly in the bed of the creek, descending to the lake. I had just reached the foot of the hill when my foot slipped on a boulder and I came an awful cropper. In a moment I realised I had sprained my left ankle badly and had hurt my left side and shoulder.

Groaning and cursing with pain, I managed to crawl the remaining way to my canoe, untied the painter, crawled to the place where I had hidden my paddle and blankets, and with much agony got my right shoulder to the bow of the canoe and launched her. It made me shudder with pain to use the paddle—for a Maori paddle requires both hands—but it had to be done, and I slowly worked out of the inlet, when to my horror I found I had a strong head wind to contend against.

I could never do it, and was painfully turning my canoe to get back to the beach when I heard a deep-chested Maori shout come pealing over the water, and looking in the direction from whence it came, I saw a large canoe with a dozen sturdy paddlers bearing down on me. In a few minutes I was in it, lying down on a heap of fern; and I must have fainted, but soon came to, to find the canoe tearing through the water, while fourteen stalwart warriors howled a canoe song to bring me back to life and give time to the paddles. We soon reached Wai-Tangi, and I was carried up to my hut, all the Maoris holding a big *tangi* (weeping match) over my accident and blaming themselves for the misadventure that had happened to their guest.

"Te Parione "(my Maori name) quoth the chief, "your *mana* (luck) is very great. If you had fallen three days ago where would you have been now?"

It was not a nice conundrum to puzzle over, so I went to sleep instead.

CHAPTER 13

A Trooper's Regard For His Trust and Horse

Years ago on the Taupo line (the road running from Napier to Lake Taupo) everything used by the men garrisoning the forts on the line had to be carried on pack-horses from the town of Napier up to the headquarters (Opepe), and this necessitated hard work and required hard language on the part of the troopers escorting the pack train, which consisted of some sixty horses and mules.

Of course the men were held responsible for the goods or valuables entrusted to them, and they regarded this trust as a point of honour that must be guarded even with life.

Now why a pack-mule or a transport ox won't go without the strongest language I don't know; but they won't; and in making this assertion I am only stating a well-known and proven fact. No matter how good a man may be with a stock-whip, or a waggon-whip, he will not get a journey or trek out of his beasts unless he beguiles them with the most powerful and sultry talk.

I have never known a man to love a pack-mule, nor to caress one, and although you will find a trooper fond of and kind to most animals, yet somehow he draws the line at a mule. For his horse he will do anything—beg for it, lie for it, steal for it, halve his last bit of bread with it, and willingly risk his life for it—but not for a pack-mule. No, a pack-mule has few friends, and though men do their duty by them they don't give up their only blanket to them on a bitter cold night; and I have known many a trooper do that for his horse. However, I am getting off the right spoor, so must try back for the yarn.

On the Taupo line, at the time I mention, about 1872—the exact date I forget, and is of no consequence—the forces were rationed by a firm of contractors who had the right to run a canteen at each of the forts.

The rations were good, but the liquor was bad; and when an old campaigner calls liquor bad, it must be very bad indeed. There were plenty of rows about it, and changes were promised, but somehow it never improved. This being so, it was the usual thing, when the pack train went down-country, for two or three of us who could not face the filth supplied by the contractors to send down a private horse and get up a couple of cases of spirits fit to drink.

I was quartered at the time at an outlying station that the pack train did not pass, and one day received a note telling me to come to Fort Tarawera and get my share of two cases of brandy that had reached there.

This I did, and rode over next day, accompanied by a very smart trooper named Steve—at least that name will do for him, as he left the Lost Legion and has been for years a parson in the Church of England. Good luck to him!

Now the road, or rather the bridle-track, was a sinful one, partly through bush and partly along the bank of the Waipunga River. At one place the path had been scraped out of a very steep hill of loose shale sloping down to the river, which ran about eighty to one hundred feet below it, and it was so narrow that, once on it, you could not turn your horse, nor even dismount.

The length of this very bad bit was not more than two hundred yards, but there was a nasty turn half-way, so that it was necessary for you before you entered on it to give a loud shout in case anyone was approaching from the other end; and altogether it was not the sort of road to entice a nervous old gentleman to ride a restive horse along for a constitutional.

We reached Fort Tarawera in safety, and I put in a very pleasant afternoon, hearing the news and yarning with my pals there. Towards evening we left with my share of the plunder, which consisted of four bottles of brandy, to ride back the fourteen miles to my station. These bottles we carried in our wallets in front of our saddles, and after a parting drink and cheery good-night we rode gaily away.

It was quite dark when we reached the worst part of the road; but in those days neither of us cared for anything, so that after a loud *coo-ee* we filed on to the bad track, myself leading.

Previous to our quitting the firm ground, I had said to my companion, in a joking manner: "Take care you don't tumble over, Steve;

remember you are carrying precious brandy."

He answered: "All right, I'll look after it." And we started the crossing.

Just as we got to the very worst part of the road I heard a scuffle, an oath, a rattling crash, and knew in a moment that Steve with his horse had gone over the cliff, and rolled down the slope into the river.

I was close to the end of the bad part; so, pressing my horse on to the firm ground, dismounted, and led him back to the place of the catastrophe. Peering over, I could see nothing, so shouted: "Steve, are you much hurt?"

The answer came back and there was an exultant ring in the voice: "The brandy is quite safe."

"D—the brandy! Are you much hurt?"

A mournful reply came back: "Poor Darkie [his horse] is dead."

"But yourself?"

"Oh, I've only broken my leg," was the answer, given in a tone of the most utter indifference; "I'm all right."

"Is your head well above water, and can you hang on till I get help from the fort?"

"Oh yes; I'm all right."

So I told him to open one of the bottles and have a nip when he felt he required it, then led my horse to the firm ground, mounted and rode back to Tarawera at a gallop.

On my return with a party of troopers, ropes and torches, it took us a long time to extricate the poor fellow from his dangerous position, and he must have suffered great agony in being hauled up the steep bank of shifting shale; but at last we managed it, and got him back to the fort, where he soon become convalescent, his only regret, which was very deep—*viz*. the loss of his horse—being tempered by the fact that he had saved the brandy which had been entrusted to him. As for his own severe and painful injury, he cared nothing: it was certainly a nuisance; but it came in the day's march, and, as there was no fighting going on at the time, was not to be grumbled at.

Well, as I said before, good luck to him. If he is half as good in the pulpit as he was in the pigskin, the Church gained what the Legion lost, by his exchange of regiments.

CHAPTER 14

A Gruesome Flute
(Told by the old Kai Tongata)

There was nothing of a picnic about the wars in New Zealand.

The cold-blooded massacres at Poverty Bay, Mohaka, and scores of other places, as well as the vile tortures practised on any of our men who were unfortunate enough to fall alive into their hands, made us treat the Hau Haus with very scant mercy; and this savagery was not diminished by the brutal hardships, hunger, cold and toil we underwent while in pursuit of Te Kooti and his bands of bloodthirsty and fanatical followers.

Among these was a half-caste, the son of a very prominent white official. As a boy he had been sent to school by his father, and had been highly educated. He had then been entered for the law, but, committing a forgery, had fled to the bush and joined his mother's tribe, then in rebellion.

To show and prove his Maori blood, on joining them he had murdered, with his own hand, in cold blood, a number of helpless white women and children who had been taken prisoners; and this horrible crime, together with his ferocious courage in action, and further murders, perpetrated whenever he had the chance, caused him to be held in high repute by the Hau Haus and in bitter detestation by us.

To such an evil notoriety had this fiend attained that his father, then high in the Government, sent the unnecessary and quite superfluous order, that if his son were captured he was to receive no mercy. This order I carried myself to the officer commanding one of the flying columns that was then operating against rebels who by that time were getting considerably knocked about.

It was most dangerous work, despatch-riding in New Zealand. You had to travel through a rough and hostile country to find a moving column, or perchance a place the position of which was not known, and even the direction to it most uncertain. The Hau Haus, always on the lookout to catch the unfortunates employed on this job, would lay ambuscades in the long fern, alongside the footpaths, in such places as it was impossible to avoid passing, or at a ford you were obliged to cross.

Their dart was to kill your horse and take you alive, if possible, and then God help you if you were unable to blow your brains out—your death would be a very, very hard one.

We lost numbers of men this way; and although no officer or man was ever known to shrink the duty, yet we hated it. On the arrival of this most unnecessary order to the column with which I was serving, being first for duty, it was my fate to have to carry it on to another column and then, provided I lived, to rejoin my colonel at the earliest possible moment.

Now I was aware of the contents of the despatch, and it did not make me more pleased with the job, as I knew I was running the most desperate risks to carry an order absolutely superfluous.

Long before the despatch had even been penned, had either of the three white columns been lucky enough to catch the bounder whose name was mentioned in it, he would have been shot on the spot; while if Rapata and his friendly natives had rounded him up his end would have been quite as certain, though probably more complicated; and any orders on the subject were quite superfluous.

Well, I was warned to go, and went. I started at daylight, and after a long day's ride, during which I had a few squeaks for my bacon, I fortunately, just as evening was coming on, fell in with the column I was in search of, and delivered my despatches to the O.C.

This column was composed of friendly natives, of course on foot, so I dismounted and joined the O.C, who was making for a camping-ground on which to pass the night.

We had nearly reached the desired spot when a body of the enemy who, unaware of our presence, were making for the same place opened fire on us.

The O.C. and myself were some short distance ahead of the majority of his men, who, after the usual way of native contingents, straggled a good deal when marching into camp.

We, however, at once charged, and the enemy gave ground until we came to a long natural opening in the *manuka* scrub, through which we were moving, and which was about twenty yards across. Here we halted and took cover, as we heard the Hau Hau leader shout to his men to turn and come back quickly, as there were only two white men by themselves and they, the Hau Haus, could kill them before the others came up. We stood our ground, as we knew our men were close up, and we both carried carbines.

All at once I saw a man on the other side of the opening aiming at my companion, and I at once fired and knocked him over; at the same moment my companion fired and hit a man I could not see, but who was aiming at me. Our men just then rushed up, and we continued the charge; but the enemy had bolted, and as night was falling fast we did not pursue them, but went up to the two men we had put out of mess. My man was quite dead, and was quickly recognised as a man of no great consequence, though of some reputation as a fighting man. The other one, however, was only wounded, but refused to tell us who he was, and to our questions replied by using the greatest insult in the Maori language—*i.e.* called us boiled heads. Having a suspicion as to his identity, the O.C. tore the breast of his shirt open, and there across his breast was tattooed the much-cursed name. Well, if he had lived like a beast, he met the death of a beast without flinching.

Two years later, after the wars were over, I was again crossing that part of the country and rode a little out of my way to the scene of the fight, to see if there were any traces of the men we had killed. Sure enough the skeleton of the half-caste was at the very spot on which he had fallen. Dismounting, I picked up a leg-bone, slipped it under my wallet straps and rode away. Later, I had it made up into a Maori flute by an old native—they used to make all sorts of useful and orna-mental instruments out of human bones—and hung it on the wall of my quarters among other trophies and curios.

Sometime after I was visited by the very official who had been fa-ther to this half-caste. He examined my collection of curiosities with some interest, and catching sight of the flute, said: "Oh, I used to tootle a bit on a Maori flute in my young days." Then taking it down he tootled a "*wyetta*" (a Maori song). Little did he think he was playing a tune on the leg-bone of his own son; and I was not such a bally fool as to tell him.

Let sleeping dogs lie is an old and true aphorism, and I did not wish to stir up bitter family recollections by reminding him of a dead one; besides, he was a very big pot indeed, and the head of my department, so that a discreet silence as to who had been the original owner of that flute was sound policy.

CHAPTER 15

The Doctor and the Sentry

Years ago in New Zealand there was a chain of forts stretching from the sea to the centre of the island. These forts were intended to keep open the road that had been constructed at great trouble and expense, on which a coach ran every week, conveying the mails and passengers to and from the wonderlands of Taupo and Rotomahana.

The headquarters of the district was at a place called Opepe, and consisted of a strong stockaded fort on the top of a pumice-stone hill, or, rather, I should say on a flat piece of ground surrounded by steep-sided gullies, which made it into a hill, and contained sufficient area for the fort and a parade ground.

Through the gully in front ran the road, and on the other side of the road were the troopers' stables and a hotel for coach passengers, which also held the troopers' canteen. The fort was approached by a zigzag path cut out of the hill, which was here perpendicular, and on the top of the path was posted a sentry.

Now among the officers stationed at headquarters was a doctor who had medical charge of the district. As far as his profession went, he had scarcely anything to do. The men were all picked men, most of them young; and in that splendid climate, with plenty of good, healthy work to do, sickness was almost unknown. This was very fortunately the case, as the doctor, having, perhaps, too much spare time on his hands, and caring nothing for sport, devoted that time to the worship of Bacchus and, at the time I write about, had become scarcely fit to attend to a crocodile, much less a human being.

Had he not given the regimental sergeant-major a dose for a cold that made that ancient warrior tie himself into complicated knots, then dance and squirm for a week, and even curse him for a year afterwards with a fervency that made the atmosphere tingle and the blue sky grow cloudy? Yes, it was fortunate the men were a healthy lot, and the doctor's medicine was not in demand. The medico's appearance was also decidedly against him. He wore his hair and whiskers, which were white, very long. His face was very red, and his nose, bulbous in shape, was purple in colour. He was, moreover, very slovenly in dress and dirty in his habits. It was strange he, being an Irishman by birth, should be morose and ill-tempered when sober (I beg his pardon. I don't think I ever saw him really sober), and far from amusing when drunk. So, taking him in the large, he was neither popular nor respected by his brother-officers nor by the men. He had never been on active service, was very nervous of being sent on it, and had a holy dread of fire-arms of all sorts.

Well, this beauty made it his habit to go down to the hotel every night and booze there by himself. The men's canteen was closed at 9.30 p.m., and lights-out was blown at ten. The doctor would leave the hotel at 10.30 and proceed up the hill to his quarters; and as by this time he was quite full up, he would climb the steep zigzag path on his hands and knees, and refuse to answer the challenge of the sentry. This caused trouble; he was reported over and over again and the O.C. reprimanded him once or twice, till at last, determining to give him a fright, he ordered the sentry to be served out with some blank ammunition, and that if the doctor again refused to answer the challenge, he was to let rip at him with a blank charge.

The following night the doctor began his crab-like ascent. "Halt, who goes there?" rang out the challenge. No answer. Twice again the challenge was repeated. Still no answer. Bang went the carbine. A loud yell from the medico, and he rolled over and over to the foot of the hill. Promptly the guard turned out. Down the hill they ran and found the doctor much shaken by his roll, and sobered by his fright.

They brought him up, and next morning at office he complained to the O.C, and charged the sentry with trying to murder him, swore that he had heard the bullet whiz just past his ear, and that it was dangerous to trust a sentry with such a thing as a carbine.

The O.C. listened to him and told him he could not punish the sentry for firing at him, as he was performing his duty by doing so, but he would severely reprimand him for making such a bad shot, and the next sentry who missed him would be severely punished.

This put the fear of the Lord into the doctor; but the force of habit was too strong for him, and the following night he was down at his usual haunt, filled up, and started at 10.30, his usual time, to return in his usual manner; but he took unusual precautions. No sooner had he crept across the road than he started howling at the top of his voice: "Friend, friend, friend"; and so on up the hill, past the laughing sentry and guard, across the parade ground and crawled into his quarters, still yelping his protecting cry.

This went on for a few nights, until one day he had to visit an out-station. He stayed there that day, got full up and started to return home that night. He must have fallen off his old pony and slept in the fern, for he did not turn up till 6 a.m. next morning. Then, having handed over his nag to the stable orderly, he immediately made for the hotel, and began to freshen his nip with more liquor. That day there was a commanding officer's parade, and at 10 o'clock all the officers and men fell in. By 10.30 the inspection was over and the men standing at ease, previous to the drill commencing, when the howl of "Friend, friend!" was heard coming nearer and nearer. It seems that the doctor, true to the clock, had filled up, and at his usual time, but, oblivious to the fact that it was 10.30 a.m., and not 10.30 p.m., was making the best of his way to his lair and, by way of protection against the possible murderous attack of the sentry, was singing his usual ditty of "Friend, friend!"

Presently he appeared over the crest of the hill on his hands and knees, crawling across the parade ground towards the quarters, still uttering his doleful howl, when, glancing up, he saw the long line of men looking at him. He staggered to his feet and gazed at them for a full minute, with horror and consternation depicted on his face, then yelled out, "O blessed St Bridget, they mean to kill me this night. Sure, they've mounted one hundred bally sentries, and they can't all miss me." With that he reeled away, looking over his shoulder and, still yelling his shibboleth of "Friend, friend!" ran to earth in the welcome portal of his stronghold. This spectacle was too much for the risibility of the parade; officers and men went into a roar of laughter, which could not be checked for some time.

Next morning the doctor was informed he must resign or stand a court-martial. He did the former, and we got rid of him, while he retired to some place where he could indulge in his favourite pastime without running into dangler from a murderous sentry or of the un-kind remarks of a censorious commanding officer.

CHAPTER 16

How Kiwi Saved His Clothes

New Zealand is, of course, famous for its natural beauties and wonders, among them the hot lakes and the terraces of pink and gleaming white stone. The latter, unfortunately, were destroyed by volcanic eruption in the eighties, but, I believe, are forming again, (as at time of first publication).

On one occasion when I was located in the hot lake district several prominent Colonial officials, with their wives, came up, and I had to show them round. On Lake Rotorua we had two large whale-boats, and it was arranged that the party should be taken along the lake in these, to the island Mokoia, the scene of the romantic story of O Hinemoa and Tutanekai (the Maori Hero and Leander). The Maori yarn differs from the Greek, as it was the young lady who did the swimming part of the business, and the hussy was not drowned.

Mokoia has also been the scene of ruddy war, for it was on this island the Arawa tribe took refuge from a dreadful raid of the Ngapuhi tribe, under that bloodthirsty monster Hongi, who, from the year 1818-1838, raged through the North Island of New Zealand like a plague, and destroyed over one-fourth of its inhabitants.

He was one of the first Maoris who visited England, having been brought there by Kendal to help Professor Lee with his Maori grammar and dictionary. While in England he was much lionised, and received many valuable gifts.

He was presented to George IV., who made him presents of a suit of armour and other valuable articles.

On his return to Sidney he sold all his presents, with the exception of the suit of armour, and bought 300 muskets with ammunition. While in Sidney a grim story is told of him. At Kendal's dinner-table he met another Maori chief belonging to a tribe hostile to the

Te Tarata: The famous white terraces, Rotomahana

Ngapuhi. Quoth he to his fellow-guest: "Go home, make ready for war, and prepare to be killed and eaten." Landing in New Zealand, he swept the country bare, killing thousands and eating all he could. At last came the turn of the Arawa.

Sweeping down the east coast, he landed at Maketu and twice defeated the Arawa, who retired inland and took refuge in their stronghold, the island of Mokoia. He followed them and camped on the edge of the lake. Every morning the Arawa, confident in their fancied security, used to paddle past his camp and cheek him. I do not know if they used to place their thumbs to their noses and stretch their fingers out at him, but they poked fun at him and asked him rude questions, such as: How did he expect to come to Makoia? Was he growing wings like a duck, or, perchance, fins like a fish? etc., etc.

Naught would reply the grim old warrior, as he sat, surrounded by his cannibal chiefs, on the high bank of the lake, to his enemy's ribaldry; but he took the opportunity to *tapu* the splendid canoes as they dashed past him, the jeering crews showing them off to the best advantage.

"My skull is the bailing pot of that canoe," said Hongi, pointing to the largest and best one. This was a most awful assertion, but it rendered that canoe sacred to Hongi, as who, at the division of spoil, could claim a canoe the bailing pot of which was Hongi's skull, the most *tapu* part of his body.

This went on day after day, while Hongi was having his big war canoes transported from the sea, up creeks, across land, over a range of bushed hills, and through lakes to the scene of action.

First of all up a creek, then he had a road cut through a forest, covering a range of hills, until he launched them on Lake Roto Ehu. Again, he cut a road through a forest, and launched them on Lake Roto Iti and then up a rapid creek till they emerged on Lake Roto Rua. Now, poor Arawa, you will find out to your cost how Hongi is coming to Mokoia!

One morning, as the Arawa were preparing for their usual daily amusement, they saw, to their horror and consternation, the advancing fleet of their bloodthirsty enemies. The time for jeering and laughter had passed, some tried to escape and a few succeeded, the others stood and fought the hopeless fight of spears and stones versus muskets. The canoes drew near the island and Hongi opening fire on the hapless defenders, shot them down in heaps, then, landing, killed or enslaved all that remained of the Arawa tribe. The ovens, surrounded with the crumbling bones of the victims, remain still to mark the spot where scores of the unfortunate Arawa were cooked and eaten; and these, with Ohinemoa's natural hot bath, are the two show places on the beautiful green hill that sits like a gem on the bosom of the dark blue lake.

After we had visited Mokoia we were to descend the rapid creek up which Hongi had brought his canoes and inspect Roto Iti. The boats were manned by young Maoris of splendid physique, whom I dressed for the occasion very prettily, in shirts and trousers of white cotton, with black silk neckerchiefs. They were very proud of themselves in these smart, unaccustomed clothes.

When we came to the shallow water, at the head of the creek, it would be necessary for these fellows to jump out of the boat to lighten her, and drag her over into deep water; and I warned them that as English ladies did not like to see men without clothes on they must jump overboard in their smart suits. The three officials went into one of the boats by themselves, with a crew that knew no English, as they wanted to discuss important business, and I escorted the ladies in the other boat. We landed at Mokoia, and I showed them the bath and the gruesome ovens, and told them the tales of love and war, and then we re-embarked to visit Roto Iti. All went well till we reached the shallows at the head of the creek; here the boat grounded and I ordered the crew overboard to push her along.

All obeyed and plunged in with their clothes on, as instructed, with one exception. This was the stroke oar, a fine young Maori named Kiwi, who spoke broken English and was the son of a principal chief. He was very proud of his smart new clothes, and when the other fellows sprang into the water he sat tight. His mates called to him for help, and seeing he did not move I ordered him overboard. But he meant to preserve that suit. With a deep sigh he took off the black silk neckerchief, next he stripped off that immaculate white shirt. He looked at the water, and then at his lovely white trousers.

Then, with sudden inspiration, he touched the principal lady on the shoulder and said in a deep whisper of despair: "You no like to see me: you look that way." And in another moment he had whipped off his last thread of clothing and joined his comrades in the water.

THE LOST DINNER

Sometime after the New Zealand wars ended Pierre de Feugeron settled down at a Maori village called Wairoa, situated at the head of

Lake Tarawera, and there built himself a two-roomed shanty, which he called the Maison de Repos, and offered to entertain any tourists visiting the wonders of Rotomahana.

Now Pierre was a miraculous cook. He could make a good dinner out of anything, and there is no doubt he would have done well but for his great failing, Drink—in his case spelt with a very, very big D. For no sooner had he been remunerated by one lot of tourists than he would at once make off to Ohinimutu, where there was a drink shanty, and blow the lot.

He was indeed a queer character. In appearance, he was big enough, and looked ferocious enough, for a stage brigand, wearing his hair long and a huge beard. In reality he was as kind-hearted and simple as a child, and, notwithstanding his past life of bloodshed and adventure, he was just as harmless as one.

Pierre was also great on politics, in more ways than one, for his special brand would depend on the number of tots he had absorbed.

When sober he was a Legitimist, after he had had a drink or two an Imperialist, a few more made a Republican of him, and as he got full up he became a Communist, an Anarchist and a ruddy Red. At this stage he would become an awe-inspiring object indeed. Armed with a tomahawk in one hand and a huge knife in the other, he would dance a war-dance of the most bloodcurdling description, and with rolling r's emit horrible wild yells, in French, broken English and Maori, sufficient, unless you had known him, to daunt the courage of Bayard himself. Yet when the non-com. on duty considered that Pierre had *ranged* himself enough, he only had to send a Maori kid to him, with the intimation that the guardroom required him, and Pierre, dropping the Bombastes Furioso business, would immediately make a bee-line for that hospitable abode and fall asleep, sobbing over the sorrows of *La Belle France*.

Well, it was my duty to escort round the hot lakes any big pot the Government chose to send up to me, and the governor, once a year, used to come round, with a large party, and visit the wonders of the district, which, of course, included the marvellous terraces.

A noble marquis was at this time proconsul in New Zealand, and when I received warning of his advent I also received the straight tip that his Excellency, a *bon-vivant*, dearly loved a good dinner, so I determined he should have nothing to complain of while under my care.

Now it was customary for the governor to camp a night at Wairoa *en route* to the terraces, and also to stay another night there on the return journey, so I determined, albeit with grave doubts, to engage Pierre to take charge of the culinary department for the two nights we should be there.

For the first night I had no anxieties, as I had kept Pierre closely confined to the guardroom for the preceding fortnight; but I was very nervous about the day that I should be at the terraces with the party, when Pierre, perchance getting hold of some of the liquor, might raise Cain and wreck the dinner. However, I put my trust in Providence, and also in the discretion and vigilance of the reliable old non-com. who would be left in charge of the camp during my absence, and to whom I gave instructions to keep a very sharp eye on Pierre and his movements; so, hoping for the best, I received his Excellency with equanimity.

The first night all went well. Pierre served up such a *recherché* dinner that the governor sent for him to be congratulated, and in his enthusiasm offered the old chap a drink. Alas! I dare not interfere, though well I knew this meant trouble; for the first tot to Pierre was like the first taste of blood to a tiger.

Pierre picked up a bottle of brandy, and pouring out a bosu'n's nip, drank it off to the health of ze Governor, ze Great Queen Victoria, and ze Great Napoleon, and then took himself off, but, *horrible dictu*, he also took the bottle with him.

Unfortunately, just at that moment my whole attention was drawn from him by a lady questioning me about his adventures, so he escaped with his plunder without my observing the act.

I left the table as soon as possible, and sought out Pierre, whom I found walking about on his tiptoes, looking scornfully at the troopers, while he informed them that he himself was Pierre de Feugeron, ze grand scout. He also demanded their attention, that he himself, and no other man, was Pierre de Feugeron, ze grand *cordon-bleu*, who had cooked dinners for the Emperor, and that the great Reine Victoria had sent for him to cook ze dinner for herself *Le Bon Dieu* save ze Queen, ip ip—

He had just reached this stage when I reached for him, and ze grand *cordon-bleu* retired at the double to his hut; but, alas! I knew nothing about that plundered bottle, which he had planted before my advent.

The next morning, after an early breakfast, and after I had reiterated my cautions to the non-com., and my warnings and threats to Pierre, we started in canoes for Rotomahana, where the governor and his party enjoyed themselves thoroughly, returning in the evening to Wairoa.

Now I must confess that although I placed great faith in both Providence and the non-com., yet Black Care sat on my soul like a wet blanket; and this would have been considerably enhanced had I but known that a sudden stampede of the horses had forced away the non-com. and his men, leaving Pierre alone in camp to work his wicked will. All the way back in the canoes the conversation turned on gastronomy, and His Excellency, well pleased with the day and having a forty-dollar appetite, looked forward to his dinner, and hoped it would be as good as the one on the previous night. I hoped so too; but coming events cast their shadows before them, and I had my doubts.

At last we landed and climbed the steep hill that led to the flat on which the camp was pitched. Alas! while still afar off I heard the wild war-whoops and bloodcurdling yells I knew so well, and was assured that my very worst apprehensions were more than justified.

I at once pushed on, the governor accompanying me, and on our reaching the camp there was our *cordon-bleu*, armed as per usual, dancing a war-dance that would have excited the envious admiration of a crazy Hau Hau.

The governor paused for a moment, and stood aghast in astonishment at the horrible-looking object before us, then full of pluck, for of course he did not know how utterly harmless the old fellow was, rushed up to him and said soothingly: "Pierre, how goes the dinner?"

Pierre briefly answered that the dinner had gone to a place where it must have been overcooked and spoilt long ago.

But quoth His Excellency: "I am so hungry."

"And a ruddy good job too," howled Pierre. "It is good for kings and governors to be hungry. I myself am Pierre de Feugeron, the great Communist. I myself am Pierre de Feugeron, the noble anarchist, and I scorn to cook the dinners of kings and governors."

Then seeing the rest of the party, who by this time had arrived and were regarding him with awe and astonishment, he at once consigned the governor and the rest of us to the same place as he had committed the dinner, and was proceeding with his *pas seul* when some Maoris, acting on my instructions, took a hand in the game. Exit the noble anarchist, to be tied to a tree for the night, to regain his loyalty, while I had to bustle about to knock up an impromptu dinner for my sorrowing and shocked guests.

CHAPTER 17

A South Sea Bubble

So we found no copper island, nor rapid fortunes made,
But by strictly honest trading a dividend we paid.
And Maori Browne converted, with an ancient flint-lock gun,
A mob of ruddy pagans, beneath the southern sun.

I was in Auckland with a lot of spare time on my hands, I had come down-country intending to go over to Australia, but, having been stuck up by a flooded river for two days, I had missed my boat, and consequently was planted there, as boats at that time were neither so numerous nor ran so often as they do now.

On the morning after my arrival I was strolling down Queen's Street, wondering what I was to do with myself, when I was hailed from the other side of the road, and, looking in the direction from which the *coo-ee* came, I at once recognised the long red nose and brilliant scarlet hair of a man who had been our regimental surgeon during the past wars. His had been a hard case. Out and out the best medical man we had in our service, as far as professional knowledge and skill went, he was still a born fighting man, and was always more anxious, while under fire, to damage the enemy than to repair friends. This inclination was somewhat held in check and restrained by the Roman Catholic chaplain, a great pal of his who was always in the firing line doing the best he could for any wounded man, be he papist or heretic.

Well, one day while on a patrol along the east coast, we had a scrap with a few Maoris, and the doctor, who happened to be with us, to his huge delight, killed one. Now I do not for a moment want to assert that this was the first man the doctor had ever killed. He had, doubt-less, during the practice of his profession, killed very many, but it was the first Hau Hau who had ever fallen to his carbine; for, although a brilliant medico, he was a vile shot, and the dear doctor was greatly elated, so much so that he determined to have a trophy in commemoration of the event. Now the Maori was a fine big fellow of some rank, and had the skin on his thighs magnificently tattooed, so the doctor, wanting a *spolia opima, faute de mieux* flayed off and preserved the tattooed portions of the bounder's epidermis, which he cured and subsequently had made into a tobacco pouch. He was very proud of this pouch, and was fond of exhibiting it and making people to whom he showed it guess from what material it was manufactured.

He did so once too often; for one night after dining well, though not wisely, he exhibited it in the smoking-room of the club at Wellington. The same official was present whose son's leg-bone was afterwards annexed and turned into a flute. He was at that time posing as a goody-goody minister; and, pretending to be shocked, brought such pressure to bear that he forced the medico to resign; and so we lost the services of our best doctor, and the company of a thundering good fellow. All this had happened some time before, and I had not seen him for over a year. We had been great friends, and I was under great obligations to him, as he had on several occasions mended me after I had been broken, and had even saved me my left leg when two other sawbones wanted to amputate it. So you can easily understand I was delighted to meet him, and we at once adjourned to Perkins's saloon and proceeded to wet this auspicious meeting.

Well, no sooner had we lowered our first cocktail than the doctor demanded what I was doing in Auckland, and on my telling him I had lost my boat he expressed unfeeling delight and thanked Providence for sending and detaining me, as I was the very man he wanted, and I must take charge of a party he had raised to search the South Seas for a copper island.

Now I had not lost a copper island, and should not have known what to do with it if I found one, yet the very mention of the South Seas allured me like a honey-pot to a wasp.

Then as he went on to open out his plans, and tell me the names of the men who had joined him in his scheme, most of whom I knew well, I saw at once, copper island or no copper island, there was every chance of a rollicking good time. So when the men dropped in by twos and threes, Perkins's saloon being their rendezvous, and all of them joining the doctor in persuading me, I quite gave way and consented to join with them and take command.

A case of champagne was quickly ordered and consumed, drinking luck to the venture, and I found myself chief of forty as reckless, devil-may-care filibusters as ever banded themselves together. Do not think, dear reader, we were going to hoist Jolly Roger, or anything of that sort. No, we were going to search through some of the least-frequented groups of islands to find one of pure copper, and we were all to return fabulously rich.

If we could not find the copper island, we might yet find something else of value, and even failing that we would trade with the islanders, gentle or otherwise, for *bêche-de-mer*, whales' teeth, or anything else we thought could be disposed of to our advantage. Trade, I say, not take; we signed articles as Gentlemen Adventurers with every liberty but no licence.

We were, moreover, all of us highly respectable, very moral and well-brought-up young men. Every one of us had served and seen years of active service, so all knew the value of discipline. Most of us were public schoolboys, and although we might have found ourselves *de trop* at an Exeter Hall spring meeting tea-party, yet we were quite fit to take our places and shine in the *beau-monde* that at that period graced the South Seas.

Our party for the above purpose had chartered a very large and powerful American schooner, with a skipper, a Yankee who knew the South Seas well, and who turned out to be a rattling good fellow, two mates, a brace of cooks, a few China boys as flunkeys, and we worked her ourselves. Strict discipline was to be maintained. Every one of us had put a considerable sum of money into the venture; we all knew one another well, and two days after I had met the doctor we went to sea well armed, well found, and as good a crowd as ever set sail, without a single rotter amongst us.

Well, one lovely morning we got our anchor and glided out of the splendid harbour before a fine, fair wind, made our offing, then, setting every inch of muslin, started on our quest.

The schooner proved herself to be very fast, and also, a few days afterwards, in a bit of a blow, showed herself, although a trifle wet, yet on the whole to be a really good sea boat. The skipper and mates not only proved themselves good seamen, but good fellows; so we were all well contented and looked forward to great profit and more fun.

Those were the days when a man yearning for excitement could have his fill in the South Seas. Everyone there did what he liked, unless a stronger man prevented him.

Those were the days when Bully Hayes, in his lovely brigantine, *Leonora*, swept the seas and established a funk in everyone not too strong or too poor to fear him.

Bully Bragg was still to the fore. The infamous brig, *Karl*, and the psalm-singing Scotch scoundrel who owned her had not yet been found out, and there were plenty more black bird-catchers, sandal-wood traders and others always ready to grab and take anything, provided they were strong enough to do so.

We had, however, nothing to fear from savage or picaroon: we were a strong party, with plenty of arms, and all of us well able to use them. We wished to interfere with no one, and whoever interfered with us must take the consequence. So we sailed on, enjoying the day and careless of the morrow.

If I were to write half of what happened to us on that glorious trip it would fill books.

We met Bully Hayes and hobnobbed with him, finding him the most obliging and courteous of men. But then we carried two twelve-pounders and fifty good rifles, so we deserved fair treatment, and received it. We landed on very many of the islands, and saw a good deal of the natives. Their conduct was mixed. So was ours. We paid well for everything we required in the way of wood, water and fresh provisions, when they were civil to us, and when they were the other thing we still took our requirements, and they took the other thing. So we sailed on, strong in the knowledge of our rectitude and integrity, and confident in our ability to take care of ourselves.

Well, we had a rollicking good time of it. But we did not find that copper island, nor anything else we wanted of any great value. We therefore turned our attention to trading, in which peaceful pursuit we were very successful.

Our strength in numbers, our discipline, and our skill with our weapons, overawing most of the savage islanders, enabled us to put in with impunity to places where smaller parties dared not have ventured, and also ensured us fair treatment, a good market and prompt payment. So we prospered as gentlemen adventurers of a highly moral tone deserve to.

One day we put in to an island where half the people, under the guidance of an old American missionary, had turned into what they called Christians, the remaining half still retaining their ancient superstitions.

The missionary was a dear, good old chap, as simple and confiding as a child, and it was very difficult to understand how such a cute nation as America could have produced such a man. I do not know to what brand of fancy religion he belonged, but he was not Church of England or Roman Catholic. Anyhow, he was a good man, and we respected him accordingly.

Now in a bit of a blow we had had a few days before we had been somewhat damaged, and seeing that the lagoon in which we were anchored was a very safe one, and the natives fairly civil, our skipper determined to remain a few days to complete the necessary repairs. So we landed a lot of stores, and started trading for *bêche-de-mer,* which animal the natives caught in large quantities.

During our trading I made the acquaintance of the head devil dodger of the pagan crowd, and found him to be not half a bad old fellow. He was, naturally, rather bitter at the desertion of the half of his parishioners, and gave me to understand that his tithes had so decreased that he could barely make a living, and that the island was not, in his opinion, large enough to support two rival churches. So, judging I was a knowledgeable man, he asked my advice on this point. He also requested my active assistance to aid him in his endeavours to regain his rightful emoluments and status.

His first proposal was that he should kill his rival sky-pilot; but that I forbade, and impressed on him the fact that if he hurt the missionary a ship of war would quickly come and blow him and his island galley west. He next proposed that I, to show my friendship, should oblige him so far as to kill the missionary for him. This proposition was, of course, decidedly negatived. Then he suggested that I should at least shoot the boss convert, the next cause of my old friend's trouble. Again I had to refuse, and explained to him that the quarrel was not mine, and that the white man's God only allowed us to kill one another in *pukka* (war).

Then he requested the loan of my rifle to do the deed with himself; but I opened the breech and let him look down the barrel, explaining to him that only a Christian could use that weapon, as a heathen, not possessing the spirit of the true faith, might receive damage from the breech. He shook his head and intimated that it was a weary, weary world and full of disappointments. But an old flint-lock musket among the trade goods catching his eye, he begged to examine it, and seeing it had no opening at the breech he at once said that it was the very weapon he had dreamed of with which to right his wrongs. Would I give it him?

I am not a business man, but yet I suggested that I should like payment for it in *bêche-de-mer* or whales' teeth. Alas! he was a poor man, he had none; but would I not lend him the gun, just to shoot one Christian with? I pointed out the dangers he ran in attempting to do such a thing. The *mana* (spirit) of the Christian God was far stronger than the *mana* of his pagan ancestors, and most likely if I lent him the musket it would only bring trouble on himself, and he would be sorry for it. He, however, refused to grasp my reasoning, sound as it was; so knowing quite well what would happen, I lent him the old flint-lock. He was delighted, and promptly borrowed two handfuls of coarse black powder to feed it with. These he carefully poured down it, then rammed home various chunks of coral, pebbles, etc., topping up with a fid of rag.

At my earnest request he moved a short distance from my camp, to a spot where he dug a shallow hole in the sand, in which he lay dogo, and waited with great patience for his Christian friend to come along. Towards evening come along he did. I knew the bounder by sight and I did not admire him. Christianity, as a rule, does not improve the manners of the gentle savage, and it certainly had not added to this Johnny's stock of humility, for he swaggered along with as much side as a new-made Lance Jack, bumptious cheek being written all over him, in fact he looked the very quintessence of insolence and cheap pride.

Presently he arrived within a few yards of the spot where Nemesis awaited him, and where he was to receive a shock that was to fill him with the fear of the Lord for a considerable period of time.

Yes, indeed he was just within a yard or two of the little heap of sand that masked the old devil dodger's ambush when that ancient worthy rose up and, holding the old gun out at the full stretch of both arms, shut his eyes, pulled the trigger and let go. For a moment the powder fizzled in the touch hole, then off it went with the report and recoil of a 32-pounder. Where the charge went the Lord only knows, but the report, flame and smoke were quite enough for the Christian. He turned and fled, and went round the bay, at a pace that would have won him any Marathon race record in the world; and the last thing I saw of him was a black dot on the white beach, disappearing round a far cape and still travelling as if the devil had kicked him edgeways.

If the report had upset the equanimity of the convert, the recoil had been equally deadly to the equilibrium of the pagan. Struck full in the face by the heel-plate of the old gun, he turned at least three back somersaults; and when he came to the conviction that he was still on this planet he rose up, and after straightening out and arranging his scattered features, he went and looked at the old musket, and solemnly cursed it for at least ten minutes. Then seeing it was now in a state of quietude, he gingerly picked it up and, holding it at arm's-length, brought it to me and handed it back, remarking sadly, with a shake of his head: "This gun is no good."

Here I joined issue with him, and declared it to be a very good gun indeed. Had it not knocked him over and over again, and that with the peaceful end of it? Had it not made him see more stars in a few minutes than he had ever before seen in his whole life? And if that was the case to himself, had not even the talk of it caused his enemy to run faster and farther than any mortal man had ever been known to run before? Well, then, how much more damage would it not have done, with its business end, had it only been directed by a man who possessed proper *mana* in proportion to the strength of the gun? No, the gun was a good gun, and the fault clearly lay with himself.

Again, had I not pointed him out the dangers he ran in attacking a Christian? Had I not assured him that the *mana* of the white man's God was far stronger than the *mana* of his pagan deities? Had he believed me and taken my advice? No. Then who was to blame? Why, undoubtedly himself; and consequently he had suffered for it.

This he was forced to allow, but then the same question cropped up again. What was to be done? Could I not give him some sound advice? Why, certainly. The best course he could pursue would be for himself and people to at once turn Christians, and then, if they obeyed the missionary implicitly, they would soon make up the leeway of *mana* that the others had acquired, and he would be on the same plane as the other josser.

To this he agreed, and swore he and his people would be converted right away, and started off hot-toe to summon them.

I had just finished telling my comrades about my first attempt at converting the heathen when who should appear but his Reverence himself, in a terrible state of fluster.

Approaching me, he said sorrowfully: "Surely I am misinformed: surely you did not lend a musket to one of these heathens with which to kill one of my dear Christian converts."

I pleaded guilty. "Is it not written," I said, "*He that lendeth to the poor giveth to the Lord*'? This poor chap hadn't a musket of his own so I lent him one."

The dear old fellow was very much shocked, but I convinced him that I was fully aware no harm would come from my perhaps injudicious kindness; and finally, on the appearance of my old friend, the knight of the rueful countenance, with his leading people, who one and all declared that they were convinced of the power of the Christian God, and that they were all both anxious and willing to join his flock, his sorrow turned to gladness, and he declared that Providence worked in wondrous ways, and that now he was convinced that our visit had been a great blessing to his community, although he had had at first grave doubts upon the subject. He also returned thanks for the sudden and wonderful conversion of the heathen, and declared that now the whole island would become the home of one happy family, living together in peace and harmony. I had my doubts; but he was such a good old fellow that we all turned to and built him a swagger church, and endowed it with a spare ship's bell we had on board.

So that when we left the dear old innocent took a tearful farewell of us and gave us his blessing; and a really good man's blessing, like a tinker's cuss, does no one any harm. He also prophesied we should all meet again in heaven; but there again I have grave doubts, as I fancy most of our crew were making for a more tropical latitude.

Well, I have never heard of that island since the day we left it, and I have even forgotten its name; but I have always felt uncertain about the happy- family part of the business, and fear his Reverence was premature in the thanks he gave concerning it. For on the day we left, on my presenting the ex-devil dodger with an American axe, as a parting gift, he gravely informed me that he felt the *mana* of the Christians rising so strongly within him that as soon as he had acquired a few more hymns and prayers he should feel strong enough to have another go at his enemy, and he thought, this time, he would fetch him, especially as my beautiful present would provide him with a *beau-ideal* weapon that would do its work quietly and not kick back and destroy its innocent proprietor. I may therefore be forgiven for my doubts on the brotherhood, peace and harmony of that happy family.

I have never tried to convert any heathens since, but I sincerely hope that my one attempt proved, in the long run, as profitable as our trip to the South Seas did for us. But may I again remark, I hae ma doots.

Yarning round the camp fire

PART 2

CHAPTER 1

The Debut of the Lost Legion in Natal

There were giants in the earth in those days.
Moses.

Of course ninety-nine out of every hundred old war dogs who have the misfortune to retain their pristine longing for hard work and an active life, when they are rapidly approaching the allotted three-score years and ten of their existence, and maybe, like the writer, are incapacitated by rheumatism, sciatica, *tic-doloreux*, housemaid's knee, liver and the hump from ever participating again in such sports as their hearts yearn for but their age and infirmities render impracticable, sit down, and, instead of employing their remaining years in making their souls, grouse and grumble at their bad luck, blaming everyone except themselves (*bien entendu*) for their bad luck, and maybe poverty, entirely forgetting the glorious years they put in when they were able to lead a charge, rush a *kopje*, or back a bucking horse with the best.

Yes, and they are prone to belittle, and perhaps to undervalue, the men who have shouldered them out and taken their places in the fighting line, and who are at present responsible for and are upholding the honour of our gracious King and glorious old flag on the frontiers of our splendid Empire. "Yes, by gad, sir," growls one old war dog to another, "these present men are not worth their salt, sir. They should have been with us, sir, fifty years ago, then they would have known what privations and hand-to-hand fighting meant. Nowadays, (as at time of first publication), they are fitted out with flat trajectory magazine rifles, Maxim guns, pom-poms, and the Lord only knows what else, while we had to fight with old muzzle-loading rifles, Sneiders or Martini-Henry's that were always jamming, etc., etc., etc." Grouse, grumble, grouse: and so they go on *ad infinitum*.

Yes, it is very true men who are approaching the age-limit of threescore years and ten had in their early manhood to fight with inferior rifles to those that our gallant troops are armed with at present, and, speaking from personal experience, deuced good weapons we thought them, and were always game and happy enough to use them when luck sent any fighting our way. Well, I have no doubt that in those days our seniors were making the same remarks and passing similar strictures on us, that we nowadays are passing on our successors, and as they in their turn will bestow on theirs.

Still there is no doubt that, thanks to science and the enormous expenditure of cash, the lot of the present-day fighting-man is infinitely better than it was fifty years ago, (as at time of first publication), while far more men and much better material were employed on a war of conquest during the sixties and the seventies of the last century than were deemed necessary fifty years previously; in fact you may say it has been so way back to the days of romance, when Samson used to play a lone hand against the Philistines, or even when Sir Galahad and his compeers used to start out holy-grailing, giant-killing, dragon-hunting or lovely-maiden-rescuing. True, there are nothing like the hardships in modern wars there were in those of the past, although I opine that the Turks have just had about as bad a time of it as ever men wanted to face; but then it has been sharp, quick and soon over, and entirely due to their rotten government allowing them to be caught on the hop. (Please God the precious gang who at present misrule our country will not put us into a like hole.)

Still I doubt very much at the present day if you could get troops of any nation to voluntarily face the hardships that Pizarro's men had to undergo during the conquest of Peru, or any of our young sybaritic loungers to don aluminium waistcoats (much less steel ones) and go for a jaunt crusading as their hardy ancestors did. But, mark time, the majority of the progenitors of our nowadays gilded youths were in those times trading in old clo's or doing a bit of stiff and not wearing metal vests and unmentionables at all at all.

However, we will pass over the good ould toimes, when a rale fighting-man had no need to insure himself with Lloyd George against unemployment, and comedown to the nineteenth century—in fact the years 1838- 1839, when there were but few English in Natal, and the black fiend, Dingaan, who had murdered his brother Tshaka, ruled the roost in Zululand with his army of 50,000 bloodthirsty warriors. I am not writing a book on the history of Natal, but, as 999 out of every 1000 Englishmen have probably never heard of Tshaka or Dingaan, and are just as ignorant of the struggles of the early Settlers in the garden colony of South Africa, I may state that, although Natal was not officially occupied by British troops till 1842, when Captain Smith of the 27th Regiment marched there with a portion of his corps and a detachment of artillery and built a fort near Kongella, in which he was speedily surrounded and besieged by the trek Boers under Pretorius: yet small parties of Englishmen (good Lost Legionaries every one of them) had years previously taken root in the vicinity of where Durban now stands, where they carried on the usual pioneer pursuits, such as hunting and trading with the natives.

Yes; they had taken root, and meant to hold their own and stick to their foothold in the country, notwithstanding the jealousy and secret enmity of large parties of trek Boers, who were crowding into Natal for the purpose of forming a Dutch republic there. Well, the year 1838 had been a hot one for the Boer trekkers, as in the early part of it Pieter Retief, a chief, one of their most influential commandants, together with seventy picked Boers and from thirty to forty picked Hottentots, having visited Dingaan's *kraal* for the purpose of making a treaty, were inveigled, unarmed, into the cattle enclosure, overpowered and brutally murdered.

This act of treachery the savage monster quickly followed up with a lightning raid into Natal, during which over 600 Boers, men, women and children, were butchered with fiendish barbarity. This raid he continued down to Port Natal, where the aforementioned few Englishmen were forced to take refuge on board two ships that, providentially, happened to be in the harbour. Later on in the year the Boer War punitive expedition, under the celebrated commandant Piet Uys, were ambushed and badly worsted, having to fall back, with the loss of their O.C. and many men, so that the year 1838 is still regarded by the Dutch inhabitants of South Africa as a very black year indeed.

Now the Zulu raid to Port Natal had upset the equilibrium of the English settlers, who, being moreover very savage at the losses they had sustained, determined to pay back the Zulu potentate in his own coin. First of all they volunteered to join Piet Uys' commando, but as he entered Zululand from the north they were left behind, and so determined to form a punitive column of their own.

And, now I have reeled off this prosy prelude, let me tell you how it was I first heard of the exploits of the first band of English Lost Legionaries, who, although fighting for their own hand, made the English pioneers in Natal respected and feared by both Boer and savage, while the story also convinced your humble servant that, no matter how good he fancied himself and his lambs to be, still, in the near past, there were better and more daring men tailing on to the halyards of the Old Rag than either he individually or all his flock collectively were. And now let me trek.

It was during the latter end of December 1878, just previous to the Zulu War, and forty years after the aforementioned incidents had occurred in Natal history, that I was trekking through the Thorn Country from Grey Town to Rourke's Drift, together with the staff of the 3rd N.N.C., and we were camped for the day on the banks of the Tugela River, when there arrived, at the same outspan, an old interior trader, trekking out of Zululand. Now, as I was particularly anxious to gain all the information I could about that country, I entered into conversation with him, and eventually he accepted my invitation to come over to my waggon, have some lunch and a yarn. *Tiffin* having been discussed and pipes lit we were chatting on the probabilities of the coming war when he noticed my M.H. sporting carbine and heavy B.L. revolver that my servant had just cleaned, and at once requested permission to examine them.

After he had done so, and I had explained to him the mechanism of the carbine and the flatness of its trajectory in comparison with the sneider with which he himself was armed, he heaved a sigh, and handing back the weapon said: "Ah, if the first English army that invaded Zululand had been provided with such guns, instead of old flint muskets, they might have won the day."

Smelling a yarn I replied: "I thought no English army had ever invaded Zululand up to date."

My guest smole the pitying smile that an old timer usually employs when a new chum exhibits his ignorance or puts his foot into it and queried: "Did you ever hear of Cane?"

"Oh yes," quoth I; "if you mean the cockatoo agriculturist who had the first row with the boss of the original sheep-raising industry, I have heard of him."

"No," responded my companion; "the party I allude to was no relation of his—did not even spell his name the same way, though both of them were handy with their dukes, and prone to go for their neighbours when riled. By the way, what is the strength of your invad-

156

.

ing force?"

"Oh," said I, "about 6000 white men and an equal number of natives."

"And I suppose," queried he, "all your white men are armed with M.H. rifles, and that you will take three or four batteries of artillery, rockets, etc., and that a percentage of your natives will be armed with rifles?"

I nodded assent.

"Well," he continued, "the first English army which invaded Zululand, when Dingaan was at the zenith of his power, consisted of 18 Englishmen, perhaps half-a-dozen Dutchmen, 30 Hottentots and about 3000 Natal Kafirs, and they had only 400 old M.L. muskets to the whole outfit."

"Oh, come," said I; "you're trying to pull my leg."

"Devil a bit," said he. Then he spun me the following yarn, which anyone may verify by perusing the late Mr D. C. F. Moodie's book, *The History of the Battles and Adventures of the British, the Boers and the Zulus in South Africa,*[1] from which volume I have not only refreshed my memory, but have cribbed many paragraphs, which I shall quote during my narration, as I consider the whole story to be so incredible that it requires the evidence of an historian who, although not present himself at the battle, was yet alive at that time and who both knew and conversed with the survivors of the invasion.

After the raid made by Dingaan on Port Natal, in 1838, two Englishmen, named John Cane and Robert Biggar, together with a few other British adventurers smarting under the losses they had sustained, determined to retrieve them and avenge their injured feeling by making a raid into Zululand, for which purpose they mustered 18 Britishers, 5 or 6 Dutchmen, 30 Hottentots who were first-class, up-to-date fighting men and less than 3000 *Kafirs*.

The number of firearms this motley outfit possessed was 400 old-fashioned muskets, which number included a few rifles and sporting guns of that epoch, the great majority of the *Kafirs* carrying only their shields and assegais, and this expeditionary force they called the Grand Army of Natal. Thus equipped, these daring Lost Legionaries crossed the Tugela in February 1839, and entered a mountainous broken country, where one of the most bloodthirsty despots that Providence ever allowed to exist awaited them, with an army of over 50,000 highly trained warriors who had never before been beaten.

1. Republished by Leonaur under the title *Zulu 1879*

Long odds, my gentle reader? Yes; too long odds even for a bellicose Irishman wid his back teeth awash wid the crater. Still, they did it, and now I am going to quote Moodie.

Having crossed the Tugela River the advance guard encountered some Zulu spies, and fired upon them, thus opening the ball. Ascending the opposite hill they came upon the *kraal* of "Endonda Kusuka"—that is, tardy in starting—and surrounded it before daylight. A detachment of Dingaan's army was lying there, upon whom they opened fire with their guns; when the inmates of the huts, finding the firing directed low, took hold on the tops of the huts, holding by the sticks which formed the wattle-work. This plan was, however, quickly detected, on account of the huts sinking with the pressure, when the settlers directed their fire higher up, and the people fell, wounded or dead. The whole *kraal* was destroyed, the people being killed and the huts burnt.

As the morning of this awful day dawned, many of those who were attacked lying dead and others being in the pangs of death, one of them said: "You may do with me as you please, and kill me; but you will soon see and feel the great Elephant"—meaning Dingaan's army. The Elephant soon appeared, and crushed them to death under his ponderous feet. The land was very hilly, the hills stretching out something like the fingers of a man's hand when extended, rising to ridges in the centre, and descending to deep ravines on each side; the kraal being near the top of one of these ridges and reaching down the slopes on each side. It was at a short distance from this *kraal* that the great Elephant presented himself and uttered his piercing cry and terrific scream, which, coming from thousands of infuriated savages, wrought to the highest pitch of frenzy, must have had an appalling effect, being enough to make the stoutest heart quail.

Dingaan did not appear in person in this notable battle, nor were the old warriors allowed to fight, the young men being destined to win the highest honours, and take the weapons of their foes as trophies to perpetuate the memory of their conquest.

The Zulu captains commanding were Umahlebe, Zulu and Nongalazi. These, with the old warriors, took their stand on the hill, from whence they could see all that passed, and issue their commands accordingly. Seven Zulu regiments were brought into the field of action. They were flushed with three successive victories—first, the cutting-off of Retief and his party at the great place; second, the slaughter of the Boers in the Weenen district; and third, the defeat of Uys and the dispersion of his people. Besides they were full of rage at the loss of their cattle, women and children at Utunjambeli, and the destruction of the *kraal* before their eyes, for which they were burning to be revenged. These circumstances led them to fight with a fury which could only be quenched in death. When they were shot down, if they could crawl, they would take an assegai and try to inflict a fatal stab on one of their bitter foes, rendering it needful to fire upon them again and again until dead.

The Natal army had therefore to fight with the vigour of men whose lives were in a fearful balance, and who were made desperate by the greatness of the impending danger. They were drawn up near the kraal in question, the English and Hottentots with muskets in front, and the native aids with assegais in the rear. The first division of the Zulu army came on with a fearful rush, but were met by the steady fire and deadly shots of their foes, which cut them down like grass. They were checked, broken, driven back and defeated, many lying dead and dying at the feet of the settlers. Robert Joyce, or, as he was called, Bob Joyce, a deserter from the 72nd Regiment, had ten men under him with guns, besides *Kafirs*; and such fearful execution did they do that they cut a pathway through the Zulu regiment as they approached, until the Zulu commanders ordered a change in the mode of attack.

The first division, however, only retreated to make way for the Zulu forces to come from different points favoured by the formation of the hill. Cane sent Ogle's *Kafirs* to attack the Zulus on the south-west, whilst he, with the main body of the Natal army, took the north-east. When Ogle's *Kafirs* had dispersed these, they were to come round and take the Zulus in the flank; instead of which, the hour of revenge being come for some affront which they received at Cane's hands, when they had dispersed the Zulus they fled to the drift, on which the Zulu chiefs exclaimed: "*O ganti baka balegane*"—i.e. "They can run, can they?" The sight of them running inspired fresh courage into the Zulus, who now closed in from all quarters upon the diminished Natal army, coming down as an overwhelming flood, the mighty masses of which it was impossible to resist. The strife was deadly in the extreme. The Zulus lost thousands of their people: they were cut down until they formed banks over which those who were advancing had to climb, as well as over the wounded, crawling and stabbing, tenacious of life, and selling it dearly.

Cane fought hard and died of his wounds. A fine old *Kafir* who was present gave me a description of his death. He was questioned about other matters, but as soon as he came to this his eyes appeared to flash with excitement and his hands moved in all forms to express the firing of the guns and the stabbing with the *assegais*. He took a stick and held one point to his breast to show where the *assegai* entered Cane's chest. He then gave his companion another stick, to show how a second *assegai* was buried between Cane's shoulders, Cane's gun was lying on his left arm, his pipe in his mouth, his head nodding until he fell from his horse and died. His horse was killed close by.

The last deed of this man was tragical. One of his own people who had thrown away his badge was coming to snatch the *assegai* from his back when Cane, supposing him to be a Zulu, shot him at once over his shoulder. Stubbs, another of the Englishmen, was stabbed by a boy, and when he felt it was his death wound exclaimed: "Am I to be killed by a boy like you?" Biggar fell close by. The Natal army being surrounded and cut up, heaps of slain lay dead upon the field, to be devoured by beasts of prey, their bones being left to bleach under many summer suns. The work of destruction was, however, not yet complete. No sooner had the leaders fallen than the Natal *Kafirs* threw away their badges and shields, and seized the shields of the Zulus in order to favour their escape, whilst the swiftness with which they could run was their best defence.

But in making their escape the Zulus knew their ground, and that the river must be crossed, and they therefore so surrounded them as to compel them to take one only course. In flight then these wretched beings had no alternative but to take a path at the bottom of which there is a descent of 100 feet perpendicular to the river, having deep water at the bottom, and so numerous were the bodies heaped upon each other in this great grave that at length, instead of leaping, they walked over the bodies of those who filled the chasm. One of those who made the leap was Upepe, who was stabbed as he went under water by a Zulu, who cursed him and said: "I have finished you"; but the death wound was not given, for the man escaped.

In order to complete the dire destruction of this day of blood and death, a division of Zulus were sent round to cut off those who might escape by the river. These men were to be seen up to the armpits in the stream, stabbing any who might be in danger of escaping; and very few gained the opposite bank and lived. It was here that another leader, Blankenburg, was killed. Of the few who escaped, some swam, some dived, and some floated along, feigning to be dead. One Goba crossed the river four times and was saved at last. Petrus Roetrzie, or "Piet Elias" as better known by many, entered the river lower than most of the others, and got into the long reeds of the opposite bank, where the Zulus searched for him in vain.

In this terrible battle fell John Cane, Robert Biggar, John Stubbs, Thomas Garden, John Russell,—Blankenburg, Richard Wood, William Wood, Henry Batt, John Campbell,—Lovedale and Thomas Campbell, with two or three other white men, leaving not a dozen to return and tell the tale of woe. Of the Hottentots three or four returned; and of the *Kafirs* very few except Ogle's. The few who escaped arrived at home singly, many of them having been pursued nearly to the Bay of Durban, owing their deliverance to the shelter of the bush and the darkness of the night.

Most of the particulars herein recorded I can vouch for as being correct, having conversed with several who were engaged in the transaction, and others who were residing in Natal at the time.

Here endeth the extract that I have taken from Moodie's aforementioned history.

Now, judging by the foregoing account of the Battle of the Tugela—which it must be remembered has been extracted, word for word, from a history written by a knowledgeable gentleman of undoubted veracity, who not only knew the survivors of the action, but had heard the yarn from their own lips, and that the story told me by the old trader who also had been acquainted with the majority of the men composing the English army, he being a full- grown boy at the time, and resident in Port Natal, coincided and agreed with Mr Moodie's narrative in all the principal details—I think I am not far wrong when I assert that the battle of the Tugela was a scrumptious one, in which every man engaged must have enjoyed himself to the utmost of his ability, and no one could subsequently grumble at not getting his fair share of the fighting.

Yet when you come to consider the numbers and equipment of that invading force, and compare them with the resources at Lord Chelmsford's disposal when he began to play the same game, just forty years afterwards, and which were then declared to be inadequate, you are forced to come to the conclusion that Cane and his Lost Legionaries were a bit over-venturesome. For looking back at my own experience in the Legion, I do not think I could ever have found twenty men daring enough to undertake the same contract, and I am quite certain that, even had the men been willing, I individually should never have possessed sufficient pluck to have bossed the show.

The story of Cane and his daring companions, unheard of in England, is, I fear, being rapidly forgotten in South Africa, but should any patriotic Natalian with imperialistic convictions wish to perpetuate the memory of those gallant adventurers, who, in despite of Boers, savages, the devil, and the gas-bags of Downing Street, formed the advance guard of the settlers in his lovely country, and see fit to raise a subscription to build a cairn in commemoration of the pluck, or call it foolhardiness—if you like—of the first army of Natal, I, poor old sinner as I am, will gladly plank down my mite. Yes, by gad! I will, even if I have to forgo my baccy for a month to raise the oof. For, by the great gun of Athlone! those men were men, and died like men, and may the British Empire never run short of Lost Legionaries of like kidney!

And now, before the call of "lights out" is sounded, let me relate briefly another deed of daring, performed by one of the old-time Natal settlers, and as I am not writing a history of Natal, but only recounting a few well-authenticated facts of heroic bravery, carried through by a handful of Lost Legionaries, it will suffice to remind my reader that Port Natal was occupied for the first time by British regular troops in May 1842, when Captain Smith (27th Regiment), with 200 men and two field pieces, arrived there. He at once entrenched himself on the flat ground near where the city of Durban now stands, in which camp he was speedily surrounded, and cooped up by an overwhelming number of trek Boers. This rendered it absolutely necessary for the beleaguered O.C. to communicate with his superiors at the Cape, so as to warn them of his dangerous position, and to request immediate reinforcements. But how to communicate was the problem that required solving, and it was solved, thanks to the devotion and undauntable courage of one of the early settlers, who promptly volunteered to carry the despatch.

Now despatch-carrying during wartime is by no means a salutary occupation, even when the distance is short, and the country over which it has to be carried is open, with decent roads. What then is the said duty to be called, when the bearer has to traverse a distance of 600 miles, through thick bush, dangerous swamps, rugged mountains, and across innumerable rivers, very many of which have to be negotiated by swimming.

Also please bear in mind that this delectable country through which the orderly must travel swarmed with hostile tribes, and was infested with wild animals, such as lions, leopards, elephants, etc. Troth, I call such a contract a decidedly unhealthy one. Yet such was the nature of the road Richard King had to travel alone, and bedad! he did it so successfully, for after being ferried across the harbour with two horses, on the night of the 25th May 1842, he slipped past the Boer pickets, and overcoming all the difficulties, and passing through all the manifold dangers met with on the journey, he delivered his despatches ten days after his start.

I regret exceedingly I am unable to recount the details of that wonderful feat of skill, pluck and endurance, although I was told them by one of King's relatives, nor am I aware that the yarn has ever been written; for I remember, having done a bit of despatch-riding myself, how much I was entranced by the narrative, and have always considered Richard King's exploit to be a record worthy to be treasured in the annals of the "Legion that never was listed," and I am sure that most of my readers will allow I am right when I again assert "*there were giants on the earth in those days.*"

CHAPTER 2

A Queer Card

Yes, you are quite right in saying that there must have been many queer as well as hard cases in South Africa during the seventies and eighties of the last century. Some of these I met, and knew well, and if I had been asked, during that period, to assign the biscuit to anyone of them in particular, I should without hesitation have handed it to one whom I shall call Mad Conway: a sobriquet he had earned by his wild pranks and escapades. As I said, this was not his name, but anyone who resided either in Kimberley, Free State or Transvaal, during those years, will at once recognise who is hereby designated, or at all events will do so when they have read a few lines further. Now Mad Conway had also another nickname, as he was likewise called, especially by the Boers, Vrei Stadt Conway; the prefix having been earned by his numerous deeds of reckless gallantry, performed while fighting for the Free State against the Basutos, during the war of 1865- 1868. Yes; Mad Conway was a caution, and in his own line of business stood out unique. Let me describe him, and recount a few incidents in his wild career.

To begin with, he was a cadet of a fine old English county family, some of the members of which were celebrated in the world of English sport during the early part of the nineteenth century, and whose name, like that of Osbaldistone, is still treasured by all true votaries of Diana. Well, Conway in no way disgraced the family reputation as a horseman, he being one of the very best I have ever seen, and would, provided his lot had been cast in the shires, have gained a place in sporting song and story as well as his ancestors. After having been sent home from Eton for some mad escapade, he joined a crack cavalry corps, and had to send in his papers, owing to his having mistaken his colonel's pet charger for a horse belonging to a newly joined cornet.

Now this charger was held as sacred in the corps as the mares of Mahomet were held by the Moslems, but Conway, after a heavy night in the mess, converted it, with considerable artistic taste and skill, and a couple of pots of paint, into a zebra.

On leaving the service—as he was over head and ears in debt to the Jew sharks, who in those days battened on the follies of young officers—troth! they do it still, when not more lucratively employed in the art of bogus company promoting, and other congenial pursuits—his people thought a *tour du monde* would be a salutary exercise for him, and that if he could pick out some salubrious spot about half-way round, and make a permanent camp there, why, so much the better for them. So Mad Conway landed in South Africa sometime in the fifties. Now what he originally intended to do there I don't know, and I don't think he knew himself; but he certainly wandered all over the country, taking a hand wherever the chance occurred in any *Kafir* fighting that might be going on, and putting in his spare time big-game hunting and exploring.

In both these congenial occupations he quickly gained the reputation of being a man utterly devoid of fear, while the wild and fantastic pranks he would play when he happened to be in a town made him an object of wonder and astonishment to both the phlegmatic Boers and the lazy Portuguese, some of them even causing his own more up-to-date and reckless countrymen to open their eyes. During this period of his existence he accompanied two successive expeditions that were organised for the purpose of searching the lower reaches and delta of the Zambesi for a gold-laden *dhow* that the Portuguese had sunk in the early part of the century, so as to prevent her capture by an English cruiser.

On both these occasions Conway was the only European who survived the attacks of fever and wild beasts, and although, on the second trip, they actually located the dhow, still, before they could clear the drifted sand from off her his last surviving mate died. Conway always declared that, notwithstanding the awful hardships he had undergone, he would have stuck to the job, lone handed, and would have scooped the jack pot himself, but the *dop* (common Boer-made peach-brandy) cask gave out, and as that and quinine were his sole diet, he had to chuck the contract before he could touch the *geldt*. Darned bad luck, he called it, especially as the long war waged by the Zambesi natives against the Portuguese, at that time breaking out, prevented him from having another try for the plunder. Reaching Delagoa Bay, thanks to the kindness of the officers of one of H.M. cruisers, he wandered up to the Transvaal, and took a turn on the early goldfields. Doing no good, he drifted away to the Free State, where, as aforementioned, he earned the name of Vrei Stadt Conway by his feats of reckless daring. Let me recount one of them.

During one of the numerous unsuccessful attacks made on the impregnable mountain Thaba Bosigo, the principal stronghold of the great Basuto chief Moshesh, a gallant Dutchman was wounded and captured by the natives. This poor chap, having been duly tortured, was crucified on the very summit of the mountain. Moshesh at once declared that the poor remains were to be regarded as his standard, and at the same time sent an insolent message to the Boers, stating the fact, and challenging them to come and pull it down. This brutal and contemptuous message deeply enraged the Boers, and was all the more galling as the poor fellow's remains hung in full view of the Dutch *laagers*. Something must be done at once; so the farmers' war council determined to recover the body, and called for volunteers to do so.

These being forthcoming, the attempt was made, but the party, after fighting its way about half the distance up the mountain, having suffered heavy loss, halted. They caved in, declared the undertaking to be impossible, and point-blank refused to make any further effort. This sensible determination, or pusillanimity—call it which you like, but remember a Boer is no coward—did not coincide with Conway's temperament, he being one of the leaders. He had declared he would bring that crucified corpse down, or would bust in the attempt, and if his men refused to come any further, why, he and his Hottentot arterrider would go on alone; and, faith! the two of them went. Troth, I forgot to tell you before that his mother was Irish, and when the best of English hunting blood is crossed with the best of Irish fighting blood it is deuced hard to stop the owner when on the warpath.

Well, subjected to a *feu d'enfer*, these two beauties scaled the almost perpendicular cliffs, and reached the cross, which they pulled down, and removed from it the battered remains. They then turned to descend the mountain, only to find their one path down it blocked by a strong party of the enemy, who had allowed them to do so much, to make sure of capturing them alive, and then the following morning there would be three crosses on the mountain instead of one.

This strategy on the part of the natives would have caused most men to despair, and even the bravest of the brave, if cornered in a like manner, could have only hoped to enjoy a last good fight, and sell his life as dearly as possible. Mad Conway, however, thought otherwise. He had declared he would bring the body down the mountain or bust, and as the Basutos had blocked the only path down which he could carry it, why naturally he could only keep his word by throwing it over the *krantz*, and then, by following it himself, he would at all events balk the enemy of their anticipated fun, and save himself from the horrors of the torture stick.

He and his faithful *Tottie* boy, therefore, expended their remaining cartridges, and then, bundling the corpse over the edge of the precipice, jumped after it themselves. No one looking at Thaba Bosego would believe the possibility of a man going over the edge of its perpendicular *krantzes* ever reaching the bottom with a semblance of humanity left, much less that he could survive the awful fall without every bone in his body being broken and life crushed out of him. Yet Mad Conway and his *Tottie* boy did so, and miraculously reached the foot of the beetling precipice, not only alive, but comparatively unhurt. Then picking up the corpse they carried it, under a hail of bullets, back to the *schanze*, where the rest of the party awaited them. Now these men must have been blessed with charmed lives, for although their scanty clothing was nearly shot off their bodies they only received a few slight flesh wounds, until they were just reaching the safety zone, when Conway was knocked over with a bullet through his left leg.

Well, now I have given you a glance at the heroic side of this queer card, let me turn the tables and spin you another yarn, so as to give you some idea of the mad pranks he was capable of playing. Here goes.

At one time, during the long protracted struggle between the Free State farmers and the Basutos, Conway was commandant of a small Dutch *dorp* situated close to the border which, like all other Free State villages, during wartime was *laagered*. Now Conway's commando had in their possession an ancient six-pounder ship's cannon so honeycombed that, had they fired it off, the probability is they would have made a considerable hash of the gun's crew that served it. Still, it was a real cannon that, when polished up and mounted on a pair of waggon wheels, looked formidable.

Well, mad Conway had this piece of antique ordnance in charge, and being in his usual state of impecuniosity, and the said cannon being the only available asset he could lay his hand on, he one fine day determined to raise the gentle breeze of affluence and also to remove a possible danger to himself and men by disposing of the ancient bombard to the enemy, whose paramount chief, Moshesh, was most anxious to obtain artillery at any price, be it ancient or modern. This nefarious idea having been conceived, he at once sent a message over the border to Moshesh offering to sell it for 100 head of prime cattle. Moshesh was delighted. All the preliminaries were arranged: the time and place for the transfer of old scrap iron for live stock was fixed upon, and the transaction was carried out, a small party of Basutos bringing 100 head of splendid oxen across the border, which they handed over, receiving the old carronade in return.

Mad Conway, many years afterwards, declared to me that it was only when the cattle were safely in his hands that the shameful wickedness of his act struck him, and he realised that, no matter how worthless the cannon might be, still he was an officer in the service of the Free State, that he had sold their war material to their enemy, and that by doing so he had forfeited his last shred of honour as an English gentleman. In fact his conscience reminded him that he had placed himself on the same low level as Mr Judas Iscariot, so he at once turned-to, like the Hebrew traitor, to purge himself of his shame.

Now, my gentle reader, don't, please, imagine that Conway handed back the cattle, or expended a shilling in buying a rope wherewith to hang himself. No, not by a jugful; for he differed in very many respects from the Hebrew gent and when his qualms of conscience became too poignant for him to bear he turned out his commando, made a tremendous forced march, overtook the gun escort, which he surprised and routed, on their own side of the border, and brought back the old thunderer in triumph.

Now some people may say that Conway had been guilty of decided sharp practice over this gun deal, but he always asserted that if old Moshesh could not keep possession of a purchased article after it had been delivered to him, and he had taken it across the border into his own territory, then he (Moshesh) was the only one to blame, and that he had no cause to grumble. Anyhow, the recapture of the gun reinstated Conway in his own self-respect, and as the sale of the cattle brought him in some £500, I think you will agree with me that he fared much better than the late Judas Iscariot, Esq.

Through the unjustifiable interference of the British Government, the long war between the Free State farmers and the Basutos was brought to an end in March 1868, so that Mad Conway must needs look out for something else to do. He had gained great kudos in the field, and the Free State Government not only passed a vote of thanks to him, but also determined to add a more substantial token of appreciation, by presenting to him a large farm, the title deeds of which were to be delivered into his hands on the occasion of the last parade of the Bloemfontein *burghers*, previous to their disbandment.

Well, the function was held, President Brand made his speech, and at the end of it Commander Conway's name was called. The hero of the hour rode to the front, to be welcomed by the plaudits of the men, and the handkerchief-waving of the women. A fine figure of a man, and a superb horseman. Mad Conway looked well as he reined up beside the President, and one would have thought that the bestowal of such an honour would have made even the most reckless dare-devil in the world conduct himself with decorum. Moreover, Mr Brand was perhaps the one man in South Africa who was highly respected, both by Briton and Boer, and had frequently befriended Conway in many ways.

But alas! the Fates willed otherwise, for the reckless child of impulse, prompted by Ate or Old Nick, as usual, fell away and behaved in a most shocking manner. I said prompted by either Ate or Old Nick. Well, maybe they were the original instigators, but they used deputies to carry out their designs, for you see Conway had that morning imbibed many *klein soupjies*, and President Brand was wearing a tall bell-topper hat. Of course you will understand in a moment that a multifarious number of tots might excite a hot-tempered, reckless fellow such as our friend, but it may puzzle you why the hat of a respectable old gentleman should arouse the somnolent devil in Mad Conway. Let me explain.

A tall bell-topper hat was, at that time, and for many years afterwards, an aggression that upcountrymen, be they Boers or Britons, could not stomach, for even in the latter eighties only two men were allowed to wear them in Kimberley—one, as old hands will remember, being Chief Justice Buchanan, and the other Donald McKai, the De Toits Pan market master. No one else, no matter what his status might be, possessed the temerity to appear in public wearing one; for, had he done so, it would have suffered the same fate as the presidential Golgotha did, on the occasion of which I am writing.

Yes, bedad! and it did suffer, for Mad Conway had no sooner been given the title deeds of the farm, and had uttered a few words of thanks for the complimentary speech, and the honorarium he had received, than he waved his right arm wildly over his head and brought his fist down flop on the presidential bell-topper, which after emitting a drum-like thud, collapsed over the ears of its portly wearer. Then there was the deuce to pay and no pitch hot.

Had anybody else been in Conway's boots he would have been massacred at once by the infuriated *burghers*, but seeing it was Conway, and being accustomed to his crazy vagaries, they sat on their horses and stared open-mouthed at the extraordinary spectacle, while the President attempted to struggle out of the ruins of his battered *chapeau*. In a moment Conway was himself again, was off his horse and assisting the President in getting rid of his encumbrance, at the same time pouring out a volume of excuses, and censuring himself for his confounded clumsiness. These excuses the dear old man accepted, and, in fact, in a few moments was acting as comforter to the brazen scallywag, so that the latter emerged from what might have been a desperate fix with honour and emolument.

Now let me tell you how I fell across this queer character. I think it must have been about the end of the year 1883 that I, who was at that time working as a digger in Bullfontein, received an invitation to dinner from an old brother officer residing at the New Rush, for the purpose of meeting Mad Conway, who had drifted down to the diamond fields from the Transvaal. Of course, like everyone else in South Africa at that time, I had heard heaps of yarns about him, but although we had both served in the same wars we had somehow or other never met; so I joyously accepted the invitation.

On my arrival at my friend's house I was introduced to this noted madcap, who turned out to be a well-dressed, well-groomed, well-set-up man, who, although past middle age, looked as hard as iron and tough as whipcord. The dinner passed off well, myself and others being kept in a roar of laughter by the extraordinary yarns he related, together with the inimitable pantomime with which he illustrated them. Mad Conway had sojourned on the diamond-fields in the earlier days, and had literally been hunted from off them, his exodus being so thoroughly in keeping with the man's whole career that I think you will pardon me should I digress and recount it. You see, it was in this way. Conway was as usual over head and ears in debt, and one fine morning he heard that writs were out against him for civil imprisonment.

This was an indignity that sent him hopping mad, so jumping on to his horse he galloped to the courthouse. *En route* he encountered the bum-bailiff, who, mounted on an old pony, was looking for him, and who was fool enough to try and stop him. Waving a sheaf of blue papers in his hand, he called on Conway to pull up, at the same time turning his nag athwart the road in an attempt to stop him. It was only an attempt, for the next moment the messenger of the court and his gee-gee were heaped up in the *sluit*, while his scattered documents were being rapidly torn up by a mob of laughing, cheering diggers. After his successful charge, Conway cantered on to the courthouse, through the sacred portals of which he rode his excited and plunging horse. Scattering the limbs of Satan and the grimy scum usually to be found in such establishments to the four winds of heaven. "———" shouted he to the horrified magistrate. "I heard you had been signing some d———d arrest papers against me, so I just dropped in to tell you, you can shove them where the monkey shoved the nuts. So long."

"Stop him! Arrest him!" cried his outraged worship, as Conway swung his horse round, and two policemen made a half-hearted attempt to do so, but were ridden over and dispersed.

"Whoop, gone away," yelled Conway, as he emerged into the Free State road and burst through a squad of mounted police. "If you want to catch me try to."

They wanted to catch him very badly, and tried very hard to do so, but the *veld* was close handy and. Lord bless you! they might as well have tried to rope a sunbeam as to round up Mad Conway once he had gained the open plains; so that after he had played with them until, I presume, he got thirsty, he just turned his horse's head for the Free State and cantered across the frontier, leaving his baffled pursuers to ride their knocked-up horses back to the disgruntled beak. This escapade took place just before he joined the irregular forces who were carrying on a desultory sort of warfare with Sekukuni. It was while serving with this disorganised crowd that Conway mated with an ex-naval lieutenant as like himself in character as two peas are in appearance. Faith, they made a bonny half-section, for what one did not know in the way of devilment, the other could teach him.

Well, it was just before the time when the aforesaid irregular forces were to be reorganised. Sir Garnet Wolseley was on his way up country, so were strong reinforcements, and the atmosphere was thick with shaves as to what was going to happen. Now, it was just at this moment this brace of beauties found themselves to be in a dilemma: they were both stony-broke. True, they were accustomed to be so, and as they had both been appointed to irregular corps about to be embodied, possessed smart uniforms and first-rate horses, they thought it would be a hard matter if they could not manage to raise a fortnight's board and lodging of the best, together with the necessary liquid, in liberal quantities, *bien entendu*, from somewhere or other.

Now half-a-day's ride from where they were located was an up-country *dorp*, in which was a canteen of such pretensions that the owner, a leery old Scotsman, called it a hotel. He was, like many of his countrymen, exceedingly avaricious, and prided himself on his cuteness, making a brag that no one could impose upon him. For many years he had enjoyed the monopoly of such trade as passed through the little township, but latterly another individual had opened an opposition shop, which, as it was slightly more up-to-date, filled the old sinner with apprehension, and rage, especially as hard cash was very scarce in the Transvaal at that date. Well, it was this close-fisted old Boniface that our brace of worthies determined to victimise, although to anyone else an attempt to do so would have looked very hopeless indeed.

Now mad Conway was so well known in the *dorp*, especially by the said Boniface, that it was utterly useless for him to try to obtain credit for a tot of *dop*, as the publican would sooner see the liquor on his shelves than trust anyone for a shilling. But at the same time he was well aware that Conway had held, and was likely again to hold, a fairly high position in military circles. The other partner, however, was a perfect stranger. So this was the way the two scamps worked the oracle.

One fine morning Conway cantered up to the old Scotsman's hotel, into which he strode with a bustling, dutified air. "Swan," quoth he, Colonel —— (mentioning the well-known name of one of Sir Garnet's principal staff officers) will be here in a few minutes. He is riding in advance of the general, so as to make arrangements for the accommodation of Sir Garnet and his whole staff, who will be staying in this *dorp* for some considerable time. The colonel was recommended to go to the new hotel, but I, who am acting as his guide, have persuaded him to try you first of all, to see if you can furnish the necessary requirements. Of course you will have to do your very best, furnish the best rooms, supply the very best food and liquor, and all that sort of thing, and the colonel will require a private sitting-room, in which to carry on his correspondence, while he is awaiting the general's arrival."

Old Swan nosed what he thought was going to turn out to be a most profitable bit of business. He had heard of the enormous sums of money- squandered by the Imperial Government during the late

Zulu war, and his fingers fairly itched at the chance of being thrust into the plunder pot. In a moment he was all smiles and attention, even going so far as to promise to turn out, at a moment's notice, all his usual guests and to reserve the whole of the house for the great man and his staff. Throwing open the door of his own cosy sitting-room, he inquired if Conway thought that would do until a better one could be provided, and also asked if he should be doing right to invite the colonel to have a drink on his dismounting.

"Well," said Conway, "I should hardly do that, as perhaps Colonel —— may be one of those rabid teetotallers who do not like to drink in public, but you had better place a bottle of whisky, one of brandy, yes, and perhaps one of gin, together with some soda-water, and a box of your very best cigars on that buffet, and if he should help himself you will then know whether he drinks or not. Ah, by Jove! here he comes."

A fine stalwart figure, clothed in undress uniform, rode slowly across the big market square and, reining up at the front door, leisurely dismounted. Handing his horse over to the grinning *Tottie* hostler, he coolly scanned the front of the premises and the surroundings. Out rushed the obsequious host, more leisurely followed by the debonair but still respectful Conway.

"Ah, Conway," drawled the newcomer, "so we have arrived at last, and this is the hotel you recommended, is it? Well, perhaps it will do, though I must confess I like the appearance of the other one better. Still, I have no doubt our worthy host here will do his best to make us all comfortable, especially as our stay here may be rather a long one. Let us step inside and see what accommodation he has to offer, as you know how particular Sir Garnet is."

Enter the bandits, who are shown over the house by the palpitating innkeeper, whose ears at the illusion about the more attractive appearance of the rival house are aching as if struck by an acute pang of *tic doloreux* and he forthwith promises at once to carry out the most frivolous suggestions, and there were many of them, of the somewhat haughty and exacting S.O.

"And now you have shown me the house," quoth the latter, "perhaps you will be good enough to show me my private sitting-room, in which I think, Conway, as I am somewhat fatigued by my long ride, we might indulge in a biscuit, and on this occasion, although I hardly ever take anything stronger than tea, I think I will venture, Mr Swan, on a glass of your best sherry or *pontac*; and by the way, Mr Swan, at two o'clock you will be good enough to let us have the best and most substantial lunch you can furnish at such a short notice. Ah, this will do very nicely"—as the deluded innkeeper threw open the door of his own snuggery and ushered his stony-broke guests inside. The room looked like a cosy miniature bar, for the small buffet was loaded with bottles, plates of delicately cut sandwiches, biscuits, and a big box of extra-special prime cigars, while the canvas water-cooler was full of bottled ale and soda water.

Well, our two adventurers were in clover, and so well did they employ their opportunity that old Swan, who had been bragging to all his usual bar frequenters about having secured the general's custom, and chuckling to himself over the huge bill that, in the future, he would present, which would be duly paid in bright English gold instead of in worthless Transvaalian greenbacks, was fairly wild with greed and pride. There was, however, one small cloud on the horizon: the colonel had stated that he rarely touched anything stronger than tea, and the tea-drinker is not nearly so profitable a customer to an upcountry innkeeper as one who imbibes expensive drinks at short intervals during the day.

This gloomy conjecture he confided to his circle of cronies, who condoned with him, but the cloud, however, was to be quickly blown away, for after he had summoned his guests to their lunch he rushed back into the bar and exclaimed: "Tea-drinker, does he call himself? Tea-drinker, *ma certes!* Why, they have finished the sherry; they've finished the *pontac*; they've finished the brandy and more than half finished the whisky, and the colonel has ordered two big bottles of champagne for their *tiffin*. Yes, and I'm blest if they've turned a single hair. Tea-drinker indeed! My word, if the general and the remainder of the staff drink tea like the colonel, and are half as drouthy, they will drink the *dorp* dry in less than a week," And the old fellow rubbed his hands as he booked the amount for the liquor consumed and chortled over the anticipated profits.

Well, to cut a long story short, our two penniless heroes lived for over a week on the very fat of the land, their Gargantuan repasts and the amount of liquor they consumed causing wonder and astonishment in the quiet *dorp*. But the end of their bean-feast was at hand. Sir Garnet, they knew, was in the vicinity. Prudence warned them to, and they determined to cut their lucky, before the inevitable denouement. One evening, therefore, they informed old Swan that the expected great man would arrive the next day, that they were riding out in the morning to meet him, and they conjured him to have things ready for his reception. Next morning, with their wallets filled with the best cigars, and their flasks full of the best cognac, they rode gaily away on their quest, and, bedad! it was high time for them to do so, as they had not proceeded two miles out of the *dorp* before they met the real Simon Pure, with all his staff, escort and mule waggons *en route* to the village they had just quitted.

Well, they were all right: the paymaster had arrived, all arrears would be paid up, the war would start again, they had had a high old time of it, and they lapsed into roars of laughter when they thought of old Swan and the fury he would be in when he found out he had been hoaxed. Yes, old Swan's consternation and rage were beyond description when the general's cavalcade, instead of pulling up at his highly decorated house, proceeded to that of his hated rival, from whence, after a short interview between Sir Garnet and the *landrost*, it continued its way to parts unknown. Truly the old fellow's provocation was great. Not only had he been put to much expense by the alterations to his house, but the bill run up by the two marauders was a very big one, and then the chaff that he would have to submit to, because he, who fancied himself to be more than cute, had allowed himself to be taken in and done down by a well-known bad hat like Mad Conway.

No; it was not to be tolerated, so he called for his horse and his two-shot scatter gun, for the purpose of going in pursuit, but on second thoughts that was far too risky a job, so he got drunk, and goaded at last to desperation by his wife's clacking tongue tried to beat her, but she, being a strong-armed suffragette, took the contract out of his hands and gave him the devil's own thumping. So the poor old fellow subsided and submitted to having his leg pulled with the best grace he could muster. There was, however, a little balm in store for him, as after the two freebooters had had some financial dealings with the paymaster they sent him a good round sum of money; for they were both men who did not object to paying their debts when they had the coin, and remembered to do so. This remittance, although it brought relief to his avarice, still did nothing to assuage his injured self-respect. He had been taken in and hoaxed.

The yarn spread all over the country, and he was unmercifully chaffed to the day of his death about the way he had entertained Mad Conway and the counterfeit colonel. It was, however, to be the last escapade of the latter, as the poor fellow was shortly afterwards killed while gallantly leading a desperate rush at Sekukuni's Mountains.

I, however, had started telling you about my personal experiences with Mad Conway. Well, after I met him at dinner, I saw a good deal of him, and one day he asked me to come for a drive with two of his friends, who owned a very smart turn-out, to a well-known drift across the Vaal River, where there was an hotel. We were to start on a Saturday afternoon, stay there the night, and return the next day. He promised me a lively time, as two of the team of four horses were un-broken, and the other two, although splendid animals, possessed all the vices that gee-gees can be either born with or acquire.

The distance was about twenty-five miles, the road was good, across a dead-level flat, which, like most of those in Grigualand West, was thickly sprinkled with ant- heaps, from about a foot to two and a half feet high. Well, perhaps the characters of the horses and that of the two other men who were to accompany us, both roaring blades, to say nothing about the well-known recklessness of our Jehu, might have made a nervous old gentleman give pause and refuse the invite; but then you see at that time I was not a nervous old party, and although I have no wish to claim an inordinate amount of pluck or reckless-ness still as I was blue mouldy for the want of a bit of divarsion, and knew Conway to be one of the best whips in Africa, I gladly accepted. The start was a trifle exciting, our two companions turning up just about half- seas over, while the horses promised to act up to their evil reputations.

However, the trap was a brand-new Cape cart, and the harness of the very best, so that after some little circus play Conway managed to get the nags to move off, and we started. The drive through the dig-gings was accomplished, thanks to Conway's masterly management, in safety, for although we scattered like chaff many groups of niggers, we only upset two Parsee pedlars and one Chinaman, the balance of the damage done being the demolishment of a coolie's habitation, which was constructed out of material that at one time had been paraffin and sardine tins. This accident caused the pious Hindoo who owned the shattered tin-heap to swear horribly and spit just like an angry cat; but I don't think we killed anybody.

When we reached the *veld* and were on the broad, open waggon road, the horses, thanks to the splendid handling of our charioteer, settled down to a swinging pace. There was but little chance of our meeting anyone, the scores of high-heaped produce and wood wag-gons trekking into Kimberley being, at that time of day, all drawn off the road and outspanned, as were also the empty waggons homeward bound, and I firmly believe we should have reached our destination in safety had it not been for the conduct of the other two passengers.

The drive was most exhilarating as we rushed through the glorious air, and there was plenty of excitement in it too for a man who was not a glutton; for although the road was a first-class one, and quite flat, yet frequently, when we passed a group of outspanned waggons, the Dutchmen's dogs would rush out and bark at us, a proceeding that drove our unbroken and vicious horses nearly mad. Yet I thoroughly enjoyed the drive, and no doubt should have done so to the end, as the change from the slogging hard work of the mine, with its dust and dirt, was delightful, while the slashing pace we were going and the wild, fresh, *veld* wind roused my animal spirits till I felt as exhilarated as a penniless small boy does when he is presented with an unexpected half-crown.

But, alas! we had other spirits on board, and our two companions, who occupied the back seat in the cart, partook of them freely, nor did they partake of them in the orthodox manner, as the motion of the swinging cart made the use of a glass and a mixing of *aqua fortis* with *aqua fontis* a somewhat difficult matter; so they dispensed with the usual accessories and swigged the whisky neat out of the bottle. Now this was a very dangerous proceeding, especially as they had imbibed a fair skinful previous to starting, and what with the natural high spirits engendered by the drive, and the other spirits they loaded up in the aforementioned manner, they became very tight indeed, and decidedly uproarious.

First of all they began to sing a song. That was a failure. Then they began to chaff old Conway, which was dangerous; and then they began to rattle and stamp their feet on the floor of the cart, so as to make the horses more restive, which was both unnecessary and foolish. Conway, the muscles of whose arms were swollen to nigh breaking-point, took no notice of their crazy antics, except to order them to stop monkeying, as it was all he could do to hold and guide the half-maddened animals, but they paid no heed to his admonitions. Then he cursed them with unction, but that succeeded no better, till at last, thoroughly angry, he shouted out: "Oh, you want a smash, do you? Well! by gad, you shall have one."

And without another word he bundled up the reins, which he threw on to the leaders' backs, at the same time letting go a letter "S" cut with his whip which impartially stung up every horse in the team, and then sitting back he let go one of his well-known wild bursts of laughter. At the moment this happened we were about five miles from the drift. The road was perfect, but some two miles or more farther on there was a sharp bend in it, and the problem to me was, would the maddened horses keep to the road or take to the *veld* when they came to it. I had not to wait long for the solution. The horses, the moment they felt the whip, and found their heads loose, at once broke into a tearing gallop. Reaching the bend in next door to no time, they took to the *veld* and tore wildly across it, making straight for the long line of willows that marked the river's bank.

Here we were bound to come a most unholy smash, provided we ever reached it, but I knew there were far too many ant-heaps on the way, and to run against any one of these, which we were sure to do, would be quite enough to upset our apple-cart. From the moment Conway threw away the ribbons I knew I must come an awful mucker, and had philosophically prepared myself for the inevitable smash. He simply leant back in his seat, giving vent to his peculiar bursts of laughter, while the other two, sobered up by the danger, howled curses, entreaties and pious ejaculations in a duet that would have been highly diverting under other circumstances.

Now events that are inevitable usually happen—at least, that is my experience—and we had not travelled far across the *veld* when the off-side wheel of the cart struck an ant-heap, some two feet high, bang in the middle, when I immediately and involuntarily vacated my seat. Yes; I left it in the same manner as a war rocket should leave its trough, and I described the same sort of a flight as one of those infernal machines very often used to do, for when I had described a parabola through the air, and had reached the full height of the trajectory, I turned a complete somersault. Then my specific gravity bringing me back to mother earth, I landed on my feet, ran a few yards so as to ease off the momentum of my flight, and came to a halt, devil a cent the worse. This was luck, and I turned round to see what had become of my companions, one or more of whom I feared must be badly hurt. Conway was all right, that was evident, as he was sitting on an ant-heap taking a pull at a bottle of whisky that had somehow escaped the debacle.

Looking round, I saw the horses still galloping, dragging the remains of the cart, smashed to flinders, behind them. They disappeared among the willows, and I could conjecture the awful mess there must be at the foot of the river's bank. I longed to go to their assistance, for

I dearly love a horse, but I first turned to our two mates, for although they were, in my opinion, far the worse brutes, still they were human brutes, and fashion makes us serve them first. Going to them as they lay amidst a debris of lamps, cushions, *karosses*, etc., I saw one of them was not only knocked silly but had broken his left arm and, by the way he breathed and looked, I diagnosed concussion of the brain. The other had broken his left leg, had acquired a beautiful gravel rash all over his face and was swearing at old Conway with much volubility.

I was rendering the poor devils first aid, and begging Conway to walk on to the hotel to get more help, when we were hailed from the road by a well-known Kimberley sawbones, who, having providentially viewed the smash-up from a cross-road, had borne down to our assistance. A mob of Dutchmen and waggon boys were also on their way from the hotel, so I was able to go and look after the horses, borrowing a Boer's rifle *en route*. On reaching the poor beasts I found them lying in a tangled heap at the bottom of a steep bank. The cart was smashed to matchwood, and I had to shoot two of the nags, while the others we extricated with great trouble, both of them being badly hurt.

This was the finale of my first joy ride with Mad Conway, and though I enjoyed many subsequent ones, none of them were so exciting as the first. I could yarn to you all night about this extraordinary critter, and on some future date may give you further reminiscences about him; but I think you will allow, from what I have told you, that he was a very queer card indeed.

CHAPTER 3

A Conversion That Failed

It has always been a source of wonder to me why so many people change their religion, for, although I have never had the time, opportunity, or perhaps the inclination, to study theology in any part of its ramifications, and have never even read the Thirty-Nine Articles which caused the fancy religionists not only to desert their church, but has now enabled them, through their co-operation with rebels, atheists, socialists and a gang of men who, so long as they can hang on to power, are ready to play any dishonourable game, to gratify their rancorous spite in looting the said church, my astonishment still remains. Yet very many people of all classes are frequently chucking up the faith of their fathers and joining another. No doubt some of these are actuated by sincere religious convictions, but I think the majority of them are prompted by the desire in some way to better themselves in this life.

For instance, to remove an obstacle that prevents them from making an advantageous marriage, to succeed to property, to advance themselves in society or to make money. Still, there are plenty of people who swap their fire insurance policy for other motives, not even so respectable as the few I have enumerated, and one sinner told me that, having been a very bad hat during early manhood, he had joined the R.C. Church as he had been assured that by doing so he had cleaned his slate of the accumulation of his past sins and had thereby choused Old Nick. This may or may not have been the case, but anyhow he was very ready to contract fresh obligations with the Old Gentleman, as before we parted he managed to swindle me out of a fiver; so that after mature consideration I came to the conclusion that he was not a brand that was likely to be snatched from the burning, thanks to his change of religion, but was still a very bad hat indeed.

Now anyone can understand, although he may not admire, a man who, prompted by greed, love or interest, changes his mode of worship. But the man who I am going to yarn to you about was not an individual of this class, and, moreover, although he was most charitably disposed, and always ready to plank down a cheque for any good purpose, yet as a rule he did not pan out on religious matters at all, and knew as much about dogma as a chimpanzee does about snowballing. But let me start the yarn from the beginning.

During the latter eighties, when I was adjutant of the D.F.H., and was located at De Toits Pan, there lived on the same diamond diggings a man who carried on the trade of baker, and whom I shall designate by his Boer name of Davy, Now Davy had begun life as a ship's baker, and having followed the sea for many years had drifted up to the diamond fields in the early times, had started in at his trade and had prospered exceedingly, so that when I knew him he was a rich man, and justly very popular with the diggers. In person he was of medium height, thick-set, with great rounded shoulders, on which was stuck, for he had not much neck to boast of, a huge round head that, owing perhaps to the effects of early piety, was as devoid of hair as a Little Englander is of patriotism. As regards manners, he was rather brusque, and until he came to know you was a bit repellent, and was totally uneducated.

But he was a white man right through, and many a score of women and children would have had to go hungry to roost, during hard times, had good old Davy cut off supplying bread, although the betting might be decidedly against his ever pouching a single *ticky* (threepenny piece) of their money. Now, this old worthy, who as a rule never attended any Gospel Mill, and was as devoid of theologic controversy as one of his loaves of bread, nevertheless, whenever he indulged in an occasional burst always developed the idiosyncrasy that he must change his religion, and would promptly set to work to do so. What faith he had been brought up in originally (if any) I know not, and I doubt if he knew himself, but he tried all there were on the diamond fields (and owing to the polyglot crowd located on the diggings there were many), with the exception of the Hebrew, from which ancient cult Davy shied, as he always affirmed there was an obstacle in the way, which required to be removed before he could become a proselyte in the Synagogue.

Well, one fine day shortly after Davy had exhausted the last available religion, De Toits Pan was invaded by a commercial traveller in a brand-new fancy faith, the name of which I forget, but it was one freshly imported from America, and was guaranteed to be something quite new, slick and up-to-date. In fact, its votaries might reckon on a first-class ticket up to heaven, without any detention at the custom-house, while, provided they subscribed liberally, they might even expect to be transmitted there in a private fiery balloon.

Now I never knew the ritual of the band of brothers, as they called themselves, but I knew it was necessary for a recruit, upon his initiation, to be soused over head and ears in water, which was meant to typify that all past sins would be washed away, although I guess it would have taken more than one ducking in cold water to have made an impression on the case-hardened iniquities of some of the converts who joined the movement. Yes, by gad! it would have required scalding water, soft soap, soda, and a wire scrubbing-brush to have shifted their moral delinquencies. Still, if the tubbing did not purify their immortal souls, it had a salutary effect on their hides, so we can pass that part of the performance as O.K.

Now, this missionary, spiritual bagman, or call him what you like, was at the first go-off of his raid very successful, doing a great business and roping in very many proselytes, so many, in fact it made the sky-pilots in the older established firms buck up, and look askance. He laboured, however, under one very great disadvantage—*viz*. there was no building in De Toits Pan procurable, large enough to contain the necessary water tank, so that until one could be built the numerous recruits had to be taken on the Sunday to the Modder River, and be ducked therein.

Well, just as the new movement was in the hey-day of its popularity, good old Davy went on one of his rare jamborees, and, *faute de mieux*, at once fell into line, signed on as a brother, and on the following day (Sunday) went to the Modder River with a number of other neophytes, male and female, to undergo their preliminary water cure. Now it chanced that, on the same Sunday evening, I happened to be chatting in the De Toits Pan club, when all of a sudden in dashed Davy in a great state of perturbation. Rushing up to the bar he demanded a double-headed whisky straight, which he swallowed like an oyster, then promptly held out his glass for another supply.

"Hullo, Davy," quoth one of those present, "you seem to be gulping down the cratur with unction. I thought you would have been nursing your new religious doctrines at this time of night."

Davy answered him not, but with a growl ordered the barman to refill his glass.

"Why, Davy, what's the matter?" queried another. "What have they been doing to you to capsize you in this fashion, and why don't you take water with your *pongello?*"

"Water, indeed," snarled Davy. "I sha'n't want no water for another month." And he made a motion to the barman to pass the bottle.

"Here, ease up, Davy," said I. "You've had enough. Leave the whisky alone, and come over here. Sit down and tell us how you got on this afternoon at the washing" fete."

"Whoi," grumbled the old fellow, whom, it seemed, the third nobbler had somewhat pacified, as he took the offered chair and proceeded to light his pipe, "I didn't get on at all, and this newfangled religion ain't worth a cuss. 'Tain't one as any man with any commonsense 'ud cotton to, and as for the sky-pilot, he's jist as hignorant as a howl."

"Well, well, tell us all about it. Did you imbibe the faith?"

"Faith, be d———d!" he growled. "I didn't imbibe nothing except a gallon or two of Modder River water." And he expectorated with disgust. However, after he had been smoothed down a bit, and had had another tot, he bucked up and related his tribulations as follows:—

"You see, boys," said he, "I went down to the Modder River this afternoon, with a large party of other converts. The shepherd, as 'e calls his blooming self, 'e comes along too, and brings two or three of the sharps as 'elps 'im. Well, when we got there we finds a couple of tents pitched: one for the ladies, and one for us men, to take off our duds in. Well, after a bit, one of the sharps, he comes to me, and sez he: 'Brother, we's going to commence along with you.' So 'e shows me into the tent, and sez he: 'Brother, remove your gaudy 'abiliments and put on this 'ere garb of simplicity.' And with that 'e 'ands me a sort of a nightgown which came to about me knees.

"As soon as I was togged out, feelin' a bit ashamed of meself rigged out like that, he leads me down to the river bank and there was the shepherd, as 'e calls hisself, long, thin, herring-gutted devil, standing up to his middle in the water. 'Enter, brother,' he sings out to me, ' and 'ave your manifold sins swabbed away.' I wades in and whin I reaches 'im the water took me up to the chin. He begins his palaver, and before I knowed where I was 'e puts his two hands on me shoulders and ducks me bloomin 'ead under. He fair took me by surprise 'e did, or I'd 'ave took an extra breath of air. As it was, I lost me footin', and 'ad to struggle to come up. Me old skull-cap comes off and I got me 'ead above water, but no sooner did 'e see me old bald pate appear than he shoved it down agin, and kep' on a-doing so until I was near drownded. Should 'ave bin, I believe, 'ad I not managed to giv' 'im a punch in the bread-basket which shut 'im hup like a pair of scissors, and then I scrambles out and runs to the tent nigh water-logged.

"Presently along 'e comes, and sez 'e to me, sez 'e: 'Brother, wherefore did you assault me while in the water?' And I sez to 'im: 'You ain't no brother of mine. What for did yer try to drown me?' 'Brother,' sez 'e, 'I knew not you was so bald, and when yer 'ead appeared above the surface of the river I laboured under the delusion it was another portion of yer hanatomy, and so as to prevent what might 'ave become an indecent hexhibition I pressed it hunder agin and continued to do so.' 'Well,' sez I, 'yer religion may be a darned foine one, and yer may be a darned foine shepherd, but whin yer don't know the difference between a conwert's bows and 'is starn-post 'tain't no religion for me, and I 'ud scorn to belong to it or own yer as a brother or shepherd, so ye and yer 'ole gang can go to h—.' And with that I left 'im and came 'ome as fast as I could git."

Now although I think that on this one occasion old Davy's plea, like himself, was a good un, and that he, under the aforementioned circumstances, was fully justified in doubting the *bona fides* of this fancy religion through the lack of acumen and also the gross ignorance on the part of the shepherd, still, as *one swallow does not make a summer,* this one legitimate case of perversion does not, in my eyes, justify the large number of people who chop or change their faith and are always thronging to hear some half-crazy tub-thumper, be he a long-haired, red-nosed revivalist, unctuous Mormon or any other hypocritical expounder of a new cult.

CHAPTER 4

Jack Ashore In 1871

Yes, I've had the honour and pleasure of serving in the same outfit as H.M. bluejackets, and I will maintain that the British sailor is second to none either as a fighting man or love-maker, the only man, in my unbiased opinion, to equal him in the above pursuits being the Irish soldier. Now Jack and Pat both keenly appreciate a bit of fun and devilment, but I think, in pursuit of diversion, Jack must be assigned the cake, as during his hours of relaxation, while at liberty, on shore, he frequently displays a bit of originality in his pranks that, in fairness I must confess, land him ahead of my dear, reckless, light-hearted countrymen.

During the New Zealand wars the Maoris called the Naval Brigade *Te Ngati Jacks*, and they insisted that they belonged to a different people from the remainder of H.M. forces; for you never could convince the old-time Maori warrior that the loose-clad, rollicking, gallant sailor was of the same blood as the tight-buttoned-up, stiff and more stolid, though equally brave, soldier. This erroneous idea was, I think, also in a great measure due to the fantastic capers Jack cut while enjoying his well-earned liberty on shore, during which treasured moments he strove to cram into twenty-four hours all the fun, and also as many of the minor vices, as he could manage to indulge in, and I am only doing him justice when I state he usually succeeded in participating in as much devilment during those few hours as would satisfy an ordinary healthy Tommy for a year.

Times, customs and manners have greatly altered since 1870, and although there can be no doubt that, changed as in many respects our fleet men are from the sailors of the past generation, still the same courage and devotion exists in our present-day, highly trained, splendid naval seamen as ever instigated the grand old hearts of oak, who boxed yards about, pulled on bits of string called halyards, braces, etc.; and, totally ignorant of electricity, cursed steam. Moreover, there has been a great change for the better in the conduct and sobriety of our ever-popular and much-loved blue-jackets when ashore on short leave.

Settlers, old identities, in colonial seaport towns, will, I am sure, endorse what I have written above, for although during the forty years I lived in the colonies I never heard of one of H.M. bluejackets committing a crime, still some of their sprees were rather alarming to nervous people, while they shocked the puritanical, hypocritical humbugs, of whom there is always a superfluity wherever the Union Jack flies. For these cattle, being able to indulge in their pet vices *sub rosa*, or else being too narrow-minded to make allowance for the festive pranks of high-spirited men, let loose for a few short hours after being cooped up on board ship for months at a stretch, where they have been subjected to the most severe discipline in the world, hold up hands in horror at poor Jack's frolics, and call the brave fellow, whose mess tins they are not worthy to swab out, a drunken, profligate sailorman, unfit to be at large in this world, and sure to be damned in the next.

Yet many of Jack's sprees were most diverting to the looker-on, as he would frequently introduce into his frolics some originality that, simple in itself, and most probably quite unpremeditated, still compelled anyone with the smallest spark of humour in his composition to thoroughly appreciate. I am now going to spin you a yarn about one bluejacket's spree that, if it does not amuse you, at all events afforded myself and some of my comrades, just down from the frontier, a hearty laugh. The scene was Wellington, New Zealand, the date somewhere about the end of 1871, when, the long war having burnt itself out, and the sharp fighting having smouldered itself away to the ordinary frontier defence work, myself and a few of my comrades had, for the first time for nearly six years, the chance of returning for a period to civilisation and enjoying such comforts and luxuries as were at that time to be obtained in the capital of New Zealand.

This we were doing with a relish only to be enjoyed by men who have for years been living, or rather enduring, a hard bush life, utterly debarred from the ordinary pleasures of society, and the refinement of ladies' companionship.

We were doing ourselves well, and going very strong, when the fun was enhanced by the arrival of a squadron of H.M. ships, with whose officers we fraternised, notwithstanding the fact that they ran us very close, if they did not quite cut us out, in the favour of the fair New Zealand ladies, for both officers and men of H.M. Royal Navy are as hard to contend against in the rosy lists of love as they are to beat in the ruddy game of war. No matter if there may have been a trifle of jealousy between us in those days it did not matter a row of pins, and we all enjoyed rattling good times.

But hold hard, I am off the trail of my yarn, and so must try back. Well, the squadron anchored, squared yards, and, after the ships had been put into apple-pie order, in due course of time, leave was given to the crews, and the starboard watches came ashore to enjoy themselves for twenty-four hours. This they did; and my word they made the town of Wellington lively, opening the eyes and elevating the hands of the unco guid in a way that, to such lost sinners as ourselves, was most exhilarating. In those days, I know not if such be the case now, every sailor had the fixed conviction that he was a perfect master of equitation, and no sooner did he get ashore than he yearned to ride a horse, or, failing to obtain one, a mule, a donkey, a cow or even a goat came not amiss.

Some four-footed beast must be obtained by hook or by crook, or, if saddle animals were quite unobtainable, then he must drive or be driven. Well, the starbowlins came ashore and painted the town a vivid red, and the streets soon became full of bluejackets, mounted on every description of animal, some of the poor beasts having to carry double, while now and again you would see some cart-horse, very long in the back, ridden by three laughing, shouting sailors, the whole of the cavalcades galloping and sidling up and down the main roads cheered to the echo by their admiring messmates, while the riders, with their bell-bottomed slacks rucked up above the knees, their elbows square with their ears, and a rein, or as Jack termed it a yoke-line, in either hand, held on like grim death to a dead nigger.

Yet numerous were the falls and collisions that took place, and it appeared to be fully understood that, should a rider be pipped, his loose horse and empty saddle should be the lawful prize of the lucky shipmate who first captured them, and sometimes you could see half-a-dozen or more Jacks trying to board the said prize from both sides and ends of the unfortunate quadruped at one and the same time. Many of the horses could and did buck a bit, but this did not seem to daunt Jack one iota; in fact, buck-jumping appeared to rather enhance the value of the mount, and I saw some wonderful and determined attempts to stick on viciously bucking animals, the rider hanging on manfully by gullet plate and cantle, yea, you might say with teeth and toe-nails, yelling, "Whoa, whoa, you!" at the top of his gamut, while his admiring comrades howled their applause, every man-jack of them anxious to try his luck the moment the temporary horseman should be grassed.

Of course it must be remembered that all of these men had been accustomed to jockey the yard-arm of a plunging ship, and as Jack is by nature and training utterly fearless, I should have bet my bottom dollar that any one of them would have unhesitatingly tried to have ridden Old Nick himself, had he chanced to have come along on four legs. Here I'm off the right spoor of my yarn again, so must circle and pick it up.

It was on the afternoon of the said day, a number of us were gathered together in the billiard-room of the club, when a tremendous cheer from the crowded street caused us to make for the verandah, to see what had caused such an uproar. And this is what we spotted. But mark time, as I must digress again for a moment.

Years before Cobb & Co. introduced into New Zealand their American coaches some speculative settler had imported one of the original London omnibuses, a vehicle of great length, on which the top passengers sat back to back, with their knees up to their chins on what was known as knife-boards, and gained these perches by crawling up perpendicular iron ladders fastened to either side of the door. A more unsuitable trap could not have been invented for New Zealand roads, so that shortly after its arrival it was stowed away and forgotten by the general public. Its owner, however, was a cute fellow, for hearing of the probable invasion of sailors, he had the old ramshackle caravan made roadworthy, horsed it, and, on the landing of Jack, promptly chartered it to a large party of them, so that it was the sudden appearance of this prehistoric tramcar, rumbling along the street, that had evoked the burst of applause which had attracted our attention.

Truly Jack had rigged and fitted out the old shandrydan handsomely, as flags, streamers and wreaths decorated it wherever it was possible to make them fast. Nor was she indifferently manned, as even musicians had been provided, for, perched along the driver's footboard, two more than half drunk fiddlers and a half-section of equally intoxicated fifers sawed and blew for all they were worth. The coachman sat on the usual raised seat in the centre of the fore cross-bench, and on either side of him lolled two huge quartermasters who, cigar in mouth and arms crossed, tried to appear quite at their ease and preterhumanly sober. The roof of the vehicle was overcrowded with brawny bluejackets all rollicking drunk, who demonstrated their good will to the passers-by and the laughing spectators in the windows by holding out to them bottles of liquor, while at the same time they exchanged badinage of a saline nature with their messmates thronging the side-walks.

The inside of the old omnibus was occupied by only two men, who ostentatiously sniffed at and frequently tasted huge bottles of make-believe medicine, while at intervals they exhibited to the on-lookers grotesque imitations of surgical instruments, and, in case it required any further explanation as to what the interior of the vehicle was intended to represent, over the windows and doors were chalked such notices as—Sick-bay, Dead-house, Boozers-locker, etc. All this was funny enough, but although the appearance of the old rattle-trap somewhat surprised us, still there was nothing, after all, extraordi-nary in its existence, nor in its festive crew, and we should merely have laughed and forgotten the circumstance had we not spotted, the moment it came abreast of us, a wondrous appendage to the vehicle itself, for at the tail-end over the door protruded two stout poles, from which was suspended a large-sized stable wheelbarrow.

Now what in the name of Comus could Jack want with a wheel-barrow? Its presence roused our curiosity, so that we at once made for the stables, where our horses were carefully locked up, mounted and followed the festive show that had taken the road towards the Hut (a small village a short distance along the sea coast from Wellington and a very pretty drive). Our journey in search of knowledge was not to take us far, for we had only just caught up to the slowly mov-ing caravan when, as it turned a sharp corner, one of the crew, rather more drunk than the others, lost his balance, tumbled off the top and landed on the road, which fortunately for him was at this spot heavy sand, with a concussion that would have killed or seriously maimed any sober landlubber.

In a moment a shout of "Man overboard" was raised and a sten-torian voice howled out: "Hard down with your helm, back the main yard, heave to," and in almost the same breath: "Pipe away the jolly-boat." Out rang a shrill pipe: "Jolly-boats away," and in a second down was lowered the wheelbarrow, down slid two men, and before even a woman could get breath for a squeal, or any of the horrified spectators could gather round the unfortunate, who lay on the road striking out with his arms and legs as if swimming, they ran the wheelbarrow up to him, dumped him in, ran him back to the door of the sick-bay, into which he was promptly hauled and administered to by the attendants. "Hook on and hoist jolly-boat" was the next order, the crew of which, disdaining the use of ladders, scrambled up the side, and the wheelbarrow was run up and made fast.

Then came the order, "Square away the main yard," the coachman whipped up his horses and away they went before the gaping populace could remember or make use of a single pious ejaculation. Now this was very funny, and we all enjoyed a hearty laugh, but Jack was far from the end of his farcical frolic, as there was, not far ahead, a house, half inn, half farm, owned by a fine, bluff old sea-dog who had himself served as bos'n in the Royal Navy, and as they were sure to halt—I beg pardon, heave to—there, thither, expecting more fun, we determined to follow them, and were not sorry we did so, as no sooner were they abreast of the house, which was situated a few feet from the roadway, than H.M.S. *Shandrydan* was again skilfully hove to, the jolly-boat was lowered and manned, and the strident voice sang out: "Pipe all hands ashore to lay in wood and water."

Then as a combined movement took place to vacate the roof: "Vast heaving, you thirsty swabs; see the sick-bay cleared first, the fiddlers and idlers, and then the rest of you take your blooming turn."

The order was carried out to the letter, each man as he got into the barrow being run up to and shot out on to the verandah, every one of them on recovering his feet touching his cap to the host, who stood beside the open door, and saluting him with the words: "Come on board, sir." We had seen enough, so cantered gaily back to the club, myself thinking how extremely useful the jolly-boat would be later on, always provided the crew of it were teetotallers, in assisting their messmates to their quarters when H.M.S. *Shandrydan* had finished her cruise and her gallant crew's back teeth were awash with their potations.

Yes, the idea of carting along the wheelbarrow was not only humorous but it demonstrated profound forethought on the part of the Jacks, and I maintain that no soldier in the world, not even my beloved countrymen, would ever have the nous to devise such a whimsical, and at the same time provident, entertainment, so I therefore declare that her late Majesty's bluejackets were the first in devilment as they ran the Irish Tommy neck and neck in war. "Here's good luck to the crowd of them!"

Chapter 5

The Conversion of Mike O'Leary

Whin a man's that cross and crabbed that his sowle's as black as paint,
An' his contrary conversation wud petrify a saint,
And he will ate mate on fast days, an scornes the praste as well,
Ould Nick will soon be after him, to escort him straight to (the guard room). Quin.

Years ago I was soldiering in South Africa, and at that time owned a few horses, my own private property and nothing to do with the government. I used to race a bit in a small way, just for the sport, and it became necessary for me to employ a groom who must be my own private servant.

Now grooms were hard to get, especially at the price I could afford to pay, and I did not want a man of the sundowner stamp. One evening my servant came to me and informed me that a man had come into camp who was looking out for a job and he thought he would do. On my asking him why he thought he would do (for Quin, though an Irishman, was, wonderful to relate, no horseman and had no knowledge of horses) replied: "The man is an Irishman, a small man, a knowledgeable man, and also a townie of my own." So I decided to see him, and Mike O'Leary was ushered in. Directly I saw him I seemed to know him, but for a time could not place him, till at last it flashed through my mind he must be Charles Lever's Corney Delaney come to life again, or at all events the creature in front of me must be a descendant of his.

Not that the dress was similar, for my man wore breeches and boots, both of which wanted renewing, but the head, the face, the cross, crabbed expression and the general appearance were exactly like the immortal Corney as depicted by Phiz in *Jack Hinton*. He was a tough, wiry little fellow, showing, as we say out in the colonies, the marks of the Whalaby.

He stood rigidly to attention, after glancing at myself and belongings with a sneering grin that would have excited the envy of Satan himself. So I opened fire with the remark: "You are an old soldier."

"I am," quoth he; "and served in the 57th, God bless them! They wor a rigimint you could be proud of, not a tearing lot of divils the likes of what you've got here. Bad scran to them! it's neither soldiers or peelers they be."

"Well, well," I said, "leave the men alone. I want a groom. Are you one?"

"It's a lot of grooms you do be wanting, judging by the look of your troop horses," he snarled.

"Leave the troop horses alone. I want a man as my own private servant. Do you want work of that sort?"

"I may take you on trial," he rejoined, "for did I not serve under your honourable father. Sir George Brown, in the Crimee."

Now Sir George Brown was not my father, nor any relation to me, but Mike O'Leary would have it so, and Sir George was trotted out of his grave and thrown in my teeth as long as Mike lived. Well, he was not a promising lot, but I was so hard up for a man, and the horses wanted so much looking after, that I took him on. As a groom he was perfect; never have I seen a man his equal. The horses took to him, and he was devoted to them. But, by the Lord Harry! he was a blister to everyone else on the station. How he had ever been enlisted in the 57th the Lord only knows, and how he had ever existed in the regiment is a mystery to me to this day. His tongue was as sharp as a double-edged sword, and as bitter as gall, but the little fiend could fight like a gamecock, and was as hard as iron, so that when his remarks were resented he was always ready to back his words up with his hands, until at last most of the troopers were only too glad to leave Mike alone.

As regards myself, he showed me neither deference nor respect, would never say Sir when addressing me, and would openly and audibly criticise my riding, my personal appearance, my drill, and my dress, and none of these to my credit. Poor Sir George was also brought to the fore every day, and the difference between us as to morals, manners, sport, or anything else that might be on the *tapis*, was pointed out and expatiated upon, and never in my favour. The little beast became quite obnoxious to me, but he did so well by the horses that I could not part with him, and came at last to look on him as a trial sent by Providence to humiliate me, and as a punishment for my sins; so I was bound to accept him as such, and put up with him.

Well, things went on like this till one day, when I came in from a long patrol, I found Quin on the sick list and that Mike O'Leary had installed himself in his place as servant. Now if I had wanted him to come and look after me, nothing on earth would have made him come, but as he knew he was the last man on the station whose presence I desired in my rooms, of course there he was and there he evidently intended to stick. In vain I told him he would be overworked looking after both myself and the horses.

"Sure, and don't I know that? "he snarled. "It's little thanks I'll get from the likes of you, who spends your money on debauchery and blaggardism, and pays your servants, who works their fingers to the bone, as little as ye can; but I knows my duty to your honourable father, God rest his sowle, and while that useless baste Quin is skulking, I'll be here to see you to bed when you come home drunk every night."

What was to be done? I though matters over, and at last determined to attack Mike on his only weak spot. Mike I knew to be a rigid R.C., but he was also saturated with superstitions. He had all those of the usual Irish peasant, and a good many more of his own.

He firmly believed in witches, ghosts and fairies, good and bad, and was convinced that the devil himself was frequently knocking around looking for someone to transport to tropical regions.

As to his religion, Mike was very devout, with one exception—he would eat meat on Fridays. "Fast, is it?" he would say. "A soldier may ate his rations."

"But you are not a soldier now, Mike."

"Well, and whose fault is that now? Did not I put my pride in my pocket and offer to join your blackguards, and did not that T.S.M. tell me I was too small? Bad luck to the lout! Was I not fighting in the Crimee with your honourable father before he was breeched? It's little the likes of him is fit to be T.S.M., but what can you expect when the captain ought to be at skule learning manners! It's little of an officer you'll ever make." Exit Mike, with a well-directed boot after him.

It was an uphill job, but I worked and worked away at him. I even persuaded the good Father de Rohan to go for him and preach abstinence to him, and even threaten him with pains and penalties if he did not put the muzzle on. But no good. Then I began to pretend that the rooms were haunted, and that rather fetched him, but yet, though he was uncomfortable, it did not quite hit the right spot.

At last Fortune played into my hands. A lieutenant who had been away on long leave rejoined and was sent up to my station. He was a very tall, thin man, very dark, with straight features, large eyebrows and moustache, and Mike had never seen him before. The first night he joined we were talking over our pipes, after dinner, when he mentioned a very swell fancy-dress ball he had been to. At once I asked him in what character he had gone. Of course he replied: "Mephistopheles." Had he brought his dress out with him? Yes, he had it in his kit. Would he do me a very great favour? Why, certainly. Then I told him about my incubus, Mike, and I earnestly requested him to put his dress on the next night and play the devil for Mike's benefit. Of course he was only too delighted to assist, and the plot was duly laid.

That night I went to my quarters. There was Mike, with his usual pleasant remarks and sneer.

I stopped short and said sternly: "You have been smoking."

"Begorra I've not," said he.

"Then you have been lighting those beastly sulphur matches."

"I've not," said he.

I walked over to the dressing-table, looked in the glass, then started back, and let out at him.

"Have done with your fooling tricks. How dare you grin over my shoulder like that?"

"I did not," he replied.

"If it was not you it must have been the devil then," I said sternly. "And I don't wonder at it, when such a cross-grained ugly beggar as you sits in my quarters alone at this time of night. Take care, Mike," I said impressively; "take care. Remember what Father de Rohan told you. If you will eat meat on Friday, and will quarrel and insult everyone, the devil will be after you in earnest.

"What's that?" I cried, looking hard past him. "Get out of this, Mike; the company you keep here when I'm out is not safe for a Christian man."

He turned very white, was evidently very uncomfortable, crossed himself over and over again, and bolted.

Next morning he brought two sticks, when he came to my room, which he crossed on the fire hearth, and when he turned up at night-time he had evidently been to the canteen, for he was pot-valiant and

THE DIVIL, BEDAD!

I could see he had a bottle with him.

"I suppose you will be afraid to stay in the rooms alone," I said, as I left for dinner.

"I will not," said he; but I saw the blue funk rising in him. It was a Friday.

"Did you eat meat today? "I asked.

"I did that," he replied, "and I will."

"Well, God help you," I said. "It's great danger you are in this night."

It was midnight when the lieutenant, fully got up in a most perfect fancy dress, and looking his part to perfection, appeared in the mess hut. In his hand he carried a few inches of time fuse, and also a huge fork, known in the service as the tormentor. The cook uses it to take the men's meat out of the boilers. We all crept up to my quarters, which consisted of a hut with two rooms in it, in the front one of which was the victim. To light the fuse and pass it under the door was the work of a moment, then to open the latter and step in took no longer. Mike, who had been absorbing courage from the bottle, had fallen asleep, but was waked up by a prod from the tormentor. He woke with a growl of rage, that changed into a yell of consternation, when he saw the terrific figure regarding him through the sulphury smoke of the fuse.

"Mike O'Leary," said a deep voice, "I've come for you."

Poor Mike, who had fallen back open-mouthed, with the sweat of fear trickling off him, whimpered: "Oh no, good Mr Devil; wait for the master."

"No," thundered the voice; "it's you I want, not your good, kind master, who's been a friend to you, and who you sneer at, insult and deride, and who, Protestant as he is, tries to stop your greedy sin of eating meat on fast days. Come on!"

And he made a pass at Mike with the tormentor, which Mike dodged by going over backwards, chair and all.

"I'll never cheek him again, by this, and by that, I won't!" yelled Mike, as he got another prod in a fleshy part, "and I'll never touch meat again, I won't." But at that he fainted. He soon came round, and was on his knees telling his beads when we entered the room, as if we were going to have a parting smoke before turning in.

"What the deuce have you been up to, Mike?" I said. "Who has been here? What is the cause of this awful smell, and what have you been making such a row about?"

196

"O holy Mary! sor," whined Mike; "he's been here."

"Who the devil has been here, you drunken blackguard?" I shouted.

"Oh, dear sor, oh, kind sor, don't spake disrespectfully of the Ould Gentleman; shure he's been here, and has just left. Oh, sor; I'll repent, I will. For God's sake send for the holy father. What will I do? What will I do?"

We got him to his quarters at last, and next morning Mike was a changed man. Although still by nature cross-grained, yet a more respectful servant or a better comrade could not be found on a month's trek, and he stayed with me till he died, two years afterwards, regretted by everyone who knew him, *R. I. P.*

CHAPTER 6

Bushed

In very many parts of the world, which on the map are painted red and collectively called the British Empire, there are huge tracts of country covered with forests of all sorts, which are known to the inhabitants of the different colonies by various names, and these have exacted a heavy toll of human life from the venturesome traveller, prospector, hunter, or others, who have entered their recesses on their own business or pleasure. If the scrub of Australia, the bush of New Zealand, the forests of Canada, and the wilds of Africa could only be examined with a microscope, the remains of thousands of men would be discovered who, having been bushed (*i.e.* lost in the forest), have died of hunger, thirst or exhaustion, and whose remains, unfound, have wasted away until only a few mouldering bones, some tattered rags, and a few fragments of rusty metal remain to tell the tale and act as a warning to others. I have on two occasions been the finder of the remains of men who have been lost.

One on the Taupo plains, who disappeared and who, although he was missed and looked for, was not found until three years after his disappearance, when I, quite by chance, stumbled on the poor chap's bones, which were identified by a glass eye. The other case was the bones of a white man I found while shooting in South Africa. Who or what he had been never transpired. That he had been a white man was evident, but when or how he had been lost I never found out. I remember well that after I had searched the vicinity for anything that could have been used as a clue to his identity, I stood over the poor bones and moralised.

This poor chap must have belonged to someone in the world who cared for him. Yet here he lay nameless, and unknown, his bones to be buried, as soon as my hunting boys with knife and tomahawk could scoop out a hole, by a man who was a perfect stranger to him, or, for all I knew to the contrary, we might have been comrades in two or three wars, or have hobnobbed together scores of times. However, there, under a tree, his bones lie, and I have no doubt that all marks of his grave, even the cross I cut out on the tree, to mark the spot, have long ago disappeared, and yet it is quite possible to this day there are people hoping and wondering if he will turn up.

In the colonies men disappear very rapidly, and they are not readily missed. So they do in this great wilderness, London, whose hidden mysteries far and away outnumber all the frontier mysteries of the British Empire put together, but yet somehow the picture of a man lost in the bush, dying, alone, of starvation, thirst and exhaustion seems, if not so pathetic, at least more romantic than the scores of hungry, ragged and homeless creatures who wander about the Embankment, or the slums of the mighty city.

Very many times during my life on the frontiers of the various colonies in which I have served I have been called on to assist in the search for a missing man; sometimes we have been successful, and have found our man alive, sometimes we have found him dead, and often we have searched in vain, the poor chap having disappeared, as if taken from earth in a chariot of fire. I could fill a book with yarns of cases of people being lost and found, and of being lost and not found, but the most wonderful case I know of is that of a young colonial, who was lost for forty days, yet was found alive, and who I believe to be still living.

In 1891 I had taken command of the De Beer's Company Expedition to Mashonaland, consisting of sixty white men, forty colonial boys (natives), and eighteen waggons. The above I was to conduct from Kimberley to Salisbury, a trek of about 1300 miles. It was no joke. Very many of my men were quite raw hands, and just after we had left Kimberley the heaviest rains ever known in South Africa came on, so that the rivers became flooded, the swamps impassable, and the roads, such as they were, so rotten that the heavily laden waggons sank to their bed plates every few minutes.

However, I at last passed Tuli, and proceeded some eighteen miles on the Umzinguani River, where I determined to halt for a fortnight, so as to rest and recuperate my worn-out oxen. In Tuli the O.C. of the B.S.A. Police had told me that some days before I reached that place a man had been lost from some waggons that had been outspanned at the Umzinguani River. Up to date he had not been heard of, so he requested me to make a careful search and try to discover any trace of the missing man. I promised to do so, and asked for all the particulars. The man was a Colonial of Dutch descent, who was acting as orderly to some Dominican nursing sisters *en route* to Salisbury. They had out-spanned across the river, in the early morning.

After breakfast the man had taken his rifle, had entered the bush on the downriver side of the road, to try and shoot a buck for fresh meat, but had never returned. The waggons had waited three days for him, and then trekked on. I also ascertained that some twelve miles farther on the road was crossed by a big creek, that ran into the river some miles below the drift. This being the case, I failed to see how a colonial man, *provided he kept his head*, could be lost, as the area in which the occurrence happened was surrounded on all sides by good landmarks. It was in fact an irregular triangle, bounded on one side by the river, on another by the creek, and on the third by the road. Provided he struck the road, he had only to turn to his left to reach the outspan. If he struck the river he would only have to follow it up and find his waggons, and if he came across the creek he would only have to fol-low it to the road or river.

This seems easy enough; but, as an old and experienced scout, I knew there were fifty sorts of trouble that might have happened to him, or he might have been guilty of a score of follies, all inexcusable but all committed frequently, even by old hands. He had gone away without his coat, that we knew; he might also have gone without matches—this was quite likely—and probably with only two or three rounds of ammunition. It was a very bad lion country: he might have tackled one and got the worst of the encounter; he might have been hurt by a wounded buck, sprained his ankle, broken his leg or other-wise hurt himself.

It is folly, a man going shooting alone in a South African bush. Any-thing may happen in a moment, and then a man by himself is helpless and unable to send for assistance. We reached the Umzinguani River at daylight, crossed the drift and outspanned. After breakfast I col-lected the men, explained my plans to them and drew them a rough map of the area over which our search was to be made. I selected seventy men, black and white, for the job, and my plan was to extend these men some ten or twelve yards apart and, keeping our right on the river's bank, to move down in line till we came to the spot where the creek ran into the river. Then, if we found no trace or spoor of him, to swing round and return to the road, taking, of course, a new line parallel to, and touching, the first one; and to enable us to do this correctly I ordered the man on the left flank to blaze the trees on his line, so that we should know we were not going over the same ground twice, nor leave a gap between the lines of search.

I had plenty of old hands among my men, both black and white, and on reaching the junction of the river and creek I was certain the work had been done thoroughly, although nothing had been found. At the junction I found a lot of Dutchmen, some twenty in number, who were outspanned there. They were trek riders, who, after delivering their loads in Salisbury, had hauled off the road and camped for the purpose of resting their oxen and shooting big game to make biltong. They had heard nothing of the lost man, but insisted on helping me to look for him. That afternoon we searched the new line of country back to the road, the right-hand man blazing the trees *en route*, but found nothing except game and lion spoor.

The next day we started from where we had left off and took a new line, the left-hand man blazing the trees, while the right-flank man worked down the line of the previous afternoon. I did not rush the men, as I had no hopes of finding the poor fellow alive, but yet I hoped to find his rifle—a lion could not eat that—or some trace of him, so I told the men to search carefully and not hurry. I had two bugles with me, and the men shouting to one another, so as to keep in touch, made plenty of noise, that the poor chap must have heard if alive. The bush was an open one, with little undergrowth, so we had a good chance of finding anything out of the common.

We kept up this search ten days, until I was convinced every bit of ground in the triangle had been prospected; but we found absolutely nothing. Then we said goodbye to the Dutchmen and continued our journey. Some weeks afterwards a post cart passed me going to Salisbury and the corporal in charge of it told me a wonderful tale. The Dutchmen had remained at their camp some time after my departure, and the day before they moved off one of them, while out shooting, had found a white man concealed in an ant-bear hole. He was stark naked, and in a dreadfully emaciated condition, the nails torn off his hands and his teeth actually worn down to his gums. He was quite mad, but the Dutchman carried him to his waggon, and trekked into Tuli; where he was taken into the hospital, and with careful nursing restored to reason and health.

He afterwards came up to Salisbury, where I was staff officer. I knew him well, and held frequent conversations with him regarding his woeful experiences. His story is a very short one. He had left the waggons after breakfast for a stroll, with his rifle, three cartridges and no matches. All at once it dawned on him he was lost, so he started running (*a fatal mistake*), and remembers no more. Up to the time he was found, quite close to the Dutchman's camp, over forty days had elapsed. How he had lived he had no idea. The state of his hands and teeth showed he must have grubbed roots and gnawed them; but he must have obtained water from either the creek or river, and, mad as he was, one of them should have guided him to safety.

Again, how did he escape my search and that of other parties who had looked for him? What became of his rifle, boots and clothes? And, above all, why did not a lion scoff him? To these and heaps of other queries I can only say that truth is stranger than fiction, that I have told the yarn as it happened, and can't answer conundrums. In the above yarn I have told you that the lost man began to run, and have noted it was a fatal mistake. Yes, it is a fatal mistake to begin to run when you discover you are lost, for I can assure you that it is not a difficult matter for even an old and experienced scout to lose himself, if he lets his mind and attention wander. But now I will spin you a yarn about one of my men who was lost on the same trek to Mashonaland.

This man was a fine, strapping fellow about thirty years of age. He was a well-educated mechanic, a good athlete and football-player, but a new chum in the bush and at frontier work. We were at the time trekking along the Limpopo River, a very bad bit of country indeed, and I had given my men warning not to leave the waggons.

I had also tried to teach the new chums some simple facts in bush-craft. The country here swarmed with feathered game: partridges, pheasants, and guinea-fowls. It was my custom to walk on before the train of waggons, on the trek, with my gun, and shoot plenty of these birds sunning themselves on the road. One evening when the men were inspanning, a very noisy job when you have eighteen waggons, I took my gun and strolled along as usual. The road was about thirty yards broad, and well-defined, the wide river running some one hundred yards on the right-hand side of it. I had progressed about two hundred yards from the outspan, but was still well within earshot and sight of it, when I saw the man I have mentioned come rushing through the trees and thorn bushes, down the slope on the left-hand side of the road.

At first I thought he had gone mad, and so, for a time, he was. He had lost his hat, his khaki clothes were torn to rags, his face worked

PUNGA (TREE FERN)

BUSHTRACK

convulsively, with his eyes bulging out of his head, while the perspiration ran down him in streams. He reached the road within a yard or two of me; but he neither saw me, the road, nor the river in front of him. I jumped forward and seized him, saying: "What's the matter with you? What are you doing here?"

He struggled for a moment, as if to try and break away; then some expression came into his face, and he gasped out: "Oh, thank God, major, you have found me. I knew you would look for me."

"Look for you?" I said. "Why, what's gone wrong with you?"

"Oh, sir," he cried—and, strong man as he was, he shook with fear—"I'm lost in the bush."

"Lost in the bush?" I said. "What do you mean? Don't you see you are on the road? Don't you see the waggons? Don't you hear the row the boys are making inspanning, or see the river in front of you?"

"I do now, sir; but I saw nothing, and heard nothing, when you caught hold of me. Oh, thank God you found me."

As he was quite unnerved, I took him back to my waggon, and gave him a tot, at the same time making inquiries as to the time he had left the camp; and I found out he had not been absent more than an hour. So much for the rapidity with which bush fear unnerves a new chum, no matter how strong he is, unless he has the will-power to fight against it. On questioning this man, subsequently, he told me he had only strolled into the bush for a few minutes, then tried to find the waggons, had failed to do so, started running, and remembered no more. Fortunately he had run in a circle that crossed the road; had he circled in the other direction, nothing could have saved him, and another case of the bush having claimed a white man's life would have been registered.

Now anyone would think that one experience of that sort would have been enough for that man, but it was not, for, some time afterwards, he again went off by himself, and again got lost. At this time we were trekking through very rough country, full of steep, high granite *kopjes*, and, notwithstanding my strict orders to the contrary, he left the waggons, and went into the bush alone. On his absence that night being reported to me, I took a party of colonial blacks with a couple of Mashonas and ascended a big *kopje*, at the foot of which we were outspanned, and from that height examined the country. It was not long before I spotted a fire, about two miles away, that was evidently a white man's fire; so I at once had an answering fire lit, and carefully took the bearings of the one I saw.

At daybreak I sent a party of men, under an experienced old hand, to bring in the straggler. They reached the place and found the remains of the fire, but he had gone. Not content with his first folly, the stupid fellow had evidently tried to find his way back to us, and lost himself again. For two days we looked for him, and on the third the late Mr Alfred Beit, who was travelling up to Mashonaland, brought him into my camp, having come across him, in a dazed condition, quite by chance, some miles back on the road. You may depend that the reception he got from me was a very warm one, and that I took most effectual precautions to prevent him leaving the waggons again.

CHAPTER 7

The Non-Com.'s Revenge, or the Curate and the Snake

I was proceeding upcountry in South Africa with a small party of troopers and led horses. The day before I was to start the bishop came to me and said: "One of my young men has to go up to headquarters. Do you mind taking him with you? He is quite new to the country and, as he is not well off, he can't afford the heavy coach fare. You are taking up led horses. He tells me he can ride a little, and you would be doing a very great kindness if you would take him."

Now the bishop and myself were rather pals in our way; for although, as a rule, I did not trouble the Church much, yet I have always had the greatest respect for the cloth, and perhaps, as this youngster might be a varsity or public school man, he would be company for me on my 500-mile ride. So I said: "All right, bishop; trot him round to the lines to-morrow morning with his traps, an hour before sunrise, and he will find us ready to start. Remember, it is a hard ride, roads bad, rivers full, horses only half broken, and warn him to be punctual."

Next morning the two light mule waggons that were to accompany us were inspanned and ready to load, the horses saddled, early coffee drank, but no curate. Now this was bad. Nothing ever goes quite right the first trek. Mules are new to their places in the span; men, with their last night's heads on them, are sulky; the officer a bit sharp, so as to knock them into shape; the half-broken horses restive; while the non-com. in charge of the waggons is anxious to pack them, and can't do so, to his satisfaction, until he has all the baggage to his hand. Consequently the curate, or, as the men profanely termed him, the bally sky-pilot, not having turned up to time, he was being growled at and cursed. At last he came, his kit consisting of paper bags, parcels and band-boxes.

How he ever expected them to stand the rough usage of the road the Lord only knows. Then he paraded in a field kit composed of a long black coat, short black trousers, low shoes and white socks. Such a get-up to ride 500 miles in I had never seen, and my men eyed him with wonder and astonishment. He came up to me and introduced himself, though he evidently did not think it worthwhile to apologise for keeping us waiting, but trusted we were going to have fine weather, that he would have a quiet horse, that the men did not swear, that we should meet no wild animals, above all, snakes. In fact he was so full of trust that I had to cut him short, and when he suggested the advisability of saying a few prayers before we started on this very dangerous journey I told him sharply to get on his horse, as smart as he could, and then he could pray there as long as he liked.

This was not perhaps quite polite; but no officer likes to be kept waiting when he is on the point of starting on a journey, and, as I said before, tempers are crisp for the first trek. I had selected for him a quiet old troop horse; and it was well I had done so, as when he started to mount he tumbled over on the other side, and when at last we got him into his saddle he gave endless trouble: first of all his stirrup leathers were too long, then too short, and he was such a noodle, unable to do anything for himself, that a man had to keep on dismounting every few minutes to render him assistance.

Now there is no class of men in the world more respectful to clergy, of any denomination, than the upcountry man, be he miner, farmer or trooper. A parson or priest is always made welcome at any camp he may choose to call at, and the best in that camp is placed at his disposal. The men, no matter how wild and godless, will listen to him with attention, so long as the time is fit and the homily straight; but the minister must have tact.

It is by no means wise for a pastor to preach a sermon against bad language when the waggon is stuck in a drift, or when the cook's mate upsets the bucket of tea into the fire; no, it is better for him, under these circumstances, to bide his time, close his ears, retire a short distance and commune with himself.

Now this Johnny had not the tact of an ostrich. He had already made a bad impression on us by being late, his wonderful get-up, and by his utter helplessness. This would have been looked over, and the men, thoroughly good-natured, would have done their best for him, and have taken all the care in the world of him, provided he would have left their souls alone, at least during the trek. Leading unbroken horses, for the first day or two, is no joke. They try to break away, and sometimes do so, when they at once head back for their old feed-grounds, have to be rounded-up and recaught; and it does not improve men's tempers when this occurs, and they drop a big D, to have a useless new chum, who, sitting like a monkey on his horse, with his trousers rucked up to his knees, raises his hands and says: "Oh, my dear, dear man, where do you expect to go if you use such horrid language? Oh, how can you say that? Please don't be so profane," etc., etc.

Likewise at the first drift, a very bad one, with a rotten bottom, a very steep pull-out, mules jibbing and waggons sticking, it is not pleasant to have an ignorant josser interfering and making himself more objectionable every minute, by praying out loud that evil should not happen to him for being in the company of such godless men. This he did, and before we reached the first outspan he had made himself decidedly unpopular; and he did not improve matters there.

I have always made it a rule, when I am trekking with a small party, to take my food in company and at the same camp fire with the men, who will never take a liberty with an officer doing this—it draws the feeling of comradeship tighter, and also only one man is required to do the cooking. Now the new chum objected to this, and that in an audible voice. He informed me he did not care to sit at the same fire as troopers, most of whom were low fellows. By the same token, most of them were gentlemen by birth, while some of them were varsity and public school men to boot, and all of them thorough good fellows. I lost my temper with the ass, and told him he could light a fire for himself, or, if he preferred it, could sit with the *Kafirs*, but if he required food he had better come and have it. This he did with a very bad grace, and noticing the old waggon non-com. (a strict Roman Catholic) cross himself before beginning his food, had the worse taste to attack the old fellow's religion and preach at him for his bad language at the drift.

The grizzled old warrior said nothing, but I could see a grin come over his face that I knew predicted danger to the new chum; and presently he began to talk about snakes and lions.

The curate opened his ears wide, taking in all that was said, and by the time we were ready to inspan for the evening trek he had become very nervous.

That afternoon he rode with two or three of the troopers, who filled him up to the chin with wonderful and awful yarns about snake bites and lion stories; so that when we halted for the night he dare not move out of the light thrown by the camp fire.

He did not object to sharing the evening meal with the men, but again made himself very offensive to the non-com., and, on the latter serving out the evening ration of rum, made most uncalled-for remarks, and preached us a sermon on temperance, and the evils of strong drink.

Well, the ration was drunk, the last pipe smoked, the sentry posted and the blankets laid down. Again he started to fuss. Where was he to sleep? He had never slept out in the open before. He could not sleep without undressing. Was there not great danger from wild animals and snakes? And he had no blankets in his kit to begin with.

The old non-com. looked after him like a mother, the men gave up blankets for his use, and at last all turned in; but as I fell off to sleep I saw the non-com. go to a thorn-tree and select, with much care, a branch. The new chum had undressed, said most voluminous prayers and, tired out by the journey, fallen asleep.

Everything was quite quiet, when suddenly we were all roused by the most piercing yells. A frontier man is awake and on the alert in a moment, and I at once demanded what the row was about.

The parson, nearly mad with terror, screamed out he had been bitten by a serpent and must die; he also held out to me his naked arm, on which I saw two small punctures with drops of blood oozing out of them.

To tie a piece of *rhimpie* round his arm above the wound, and twist it tight with a cleaning rod, jab a penknife into the punctures, and suck them, at the same time ordering the patient to hold his bally row, and the non-com. to bring a pannikin of rum, did not take long, and I at once administered a tot that would have made an old bos'n cough and splutter. Then I had him walked about and in a few minutes gave him another quartermaster's nip, which got well home on him, and he became very drunk indeed. Of course as soon as I saw him drunk I knew he was safe, and told him to stop whimpering, get into his blankets and go to sleep. He did certainly stop whimpering, but he refused to go to bed, or go to sleep. No, he declared he would not go home till morning. His holiness sloughed off him like a serpent's skin, and in a few minutes, to the huge delight of my godless troopers, he began to tell very naughty stories and to sing very ribald songs. He likewise, in his nightgown (a garment never before seen in that part of the world), began to show us some can-can steps, and at last behaved in such a manner that I was forced to tell him I would have him pegged out and gagged if he did not hold his row.

On this he consigned us all to the place it was his duty to guide us away from, got into bed, burst into tears, and sobbed himself to sleep.

I saw by the chuckling of the men, and the unholy grin of the non-com., some joke had been perpetrated; but as I could see I was not to be informed of it I gave the order "Lights out," turned over and went to sleep.

Next morning, an hour before daybreak, the rouse went, blankets were bundled up, horses were quickly rubbed over, saddled, and while they were eating their half-ration of mealies the waggons were packed and early coffee served out. But oh! the wretched new chum! He was stiff from the ride of the previous day, yet, sore as his body was from the unaccustomed saddle, his head was much worse. He groaned when he was roused up and told to turn out. Could he not be allowed to sleep longer? What had happened? Was there no soda water? Oh dear, oh dear. The non-com. proffered a pannikin of hot coffee and recommended a tot in it. The curate took the coffee but refused the tot, although the non-com. swore it was the best medicine in the world for anyone who had been on the bust the night before, and assured the poor wretch that he himself always doctored himself with one, after he had had a wet night.

Anyhow he must get up, as the waggons had to be packed, and we should move off the moment the horses and mules had finished their feed. He could not or would not, so I was called, and went to him. I saw in a moment the miserable wretch was unable to ride, so ordered the non-com. to make a place for him on one of the waggons, which was done, and, making him dress, we put him on to it. At the midday halt he was better, and at the night outspan he was so well that he began to get aggressive again. The men stood it for a bit, and then one of them repeated one of his own stories, and another started to sing one of his songs. He rushed to me and complained; but I pointed out to him that the song and story were his own, which he had favoured us with the night before, and therefore he could not crumble.

This sort of thing went on all night, and when the rum ration was served out, and he indignantly refused to share it, he was politely requested to favour the men with a discourse on the evils of drink, and bad company.

Of course the men treated him with the greatest respect in my presence, but when they could get him alone he caught it, and even at the camp fire sly shots were fired at him, such as low fellows, get drunk, shocking language, filthy songs, etc., etc., until the poor wretch was nearly driven mad with shame and contrition, and hung on to me so much that he became a perfect nuisance.

This went on for a couple of days, when at a wayside house where the mail coach stopped I had become so sick of him, and also, I must confess, sorry for him, that I paid his coach fare and persuaded him to continue his journey by it, an offer he thankfully accepted. And so I got rid of him, with equal pleasure.

It was after he had left us I was let into the joke that had so amused the men on the night of the catastrophe.

The old non-com., incensed by the new chum's tactless interference with his mules, his language and his religion, and knowing full well the course I should pursue in counteracting a case of snake bite, had taken advantage of the camp being asleep to jam into his victim's arm the thorns I had seen him go to the tree to get, and then on the alarm being given had declared he had seen a snake, so in this crafty way had gained his revenge.

The new chum proved no good upcountry, and in a few months was sent back to England, where it is to be hoped he has found a better sphere for his talents than in trying to convert members of the Lost Legion.

And now this skein is ended it is the profound hope of an old Lost Legionary that the perusal of them has not bored you, and he only wishes he had been in better form to do justice to the kind support he has received from the Press and public.

Salue!

LEONAUR

ALSO FROM LEONAUR
AVAILABLE IN SOFTCOVER OR HARDCOVER WITH DUST JACKET

IRON TIMES WITH THE GUARDS *by An O. E. (G. P. A. Fildes)*—The Experiences of an Officer of the Coldstream Guards on the Western Front During the First World War.

THE GREAT WAR IN THE MIDDLE EAST: 1 *by W. T. Massey*—The Desert Campaigns & How Jerusalem Was Won---two classic accounts in one volume.

THE GREAT WAR IN THE MIDDLE EAST: 2 *by W. T. Massey*—Allenby's Final Triumph.

SMITH-DORRIEN *by Horace Smith-Dorrien*—Isandlwhana to the Great War.

1914 *by Sir John French*—The Early Campaigns of the Great War by the British Commander.

GRENADIER *by E. R. M. Fryer*—The Recollections of an Officer of the Grenadier Guards throughout the Great War on the Western Front.

BATTLE, CAPTURE & ESCAPE *by George Pearson*—The Experiences of a Canadian Light Infantryman During the Great War.

DIGGERS AT WAR *by R. Hugh Knyvett & G. P. Cuttriss*—"Over There" With the Australians by R. Hugh Knyvett and Over the Top With the Third Australian Division by G. P. Cuttriss. Accounts of Australians During the Great War in the Middle East, at Gallipoli and on the Western Front.

HEAVY FIGHTING BEFORE US *by George Brenton Laurie*—The Letters of an Officer of the Royal Irish Rifles on the Western Front During the Great War.

THE CAMELIERS *by Oliver Hogue*—A Classic Account of the Australians of the Imperial Camel Corps During the First World War in the Middle East.

RED DUST *by Donald Black*—A Classic Account of Australian Light Horsemen in Palestine During the First World War.

THE LEAN, BROWN MEN *by Angus Buchanan*—Experiences in East Africa During the Great War with the 25th Royal Fusiliers—the Legion of Frontiersmen.

THE NIGERIAN REGIMENT IN EAST AFRICA *by W. D. Downes*—On Campaign During the Great War 1916-1918.

THE 'DIE-HARDS' IN SIBERIA *by John Ward*—With the Middlesex Regiment Against the Bolsheviks 1918-19.

ALSO FROM LEONAUR
AVAILABLE IN SOFTCOVER OR HARDCOVER WITH DUST JACKET

www.ingramcontent.com/pod-product-compliance
Lightning Source LLC
Chambersburg PA
CBHW032055080426
42733CB00006B/280